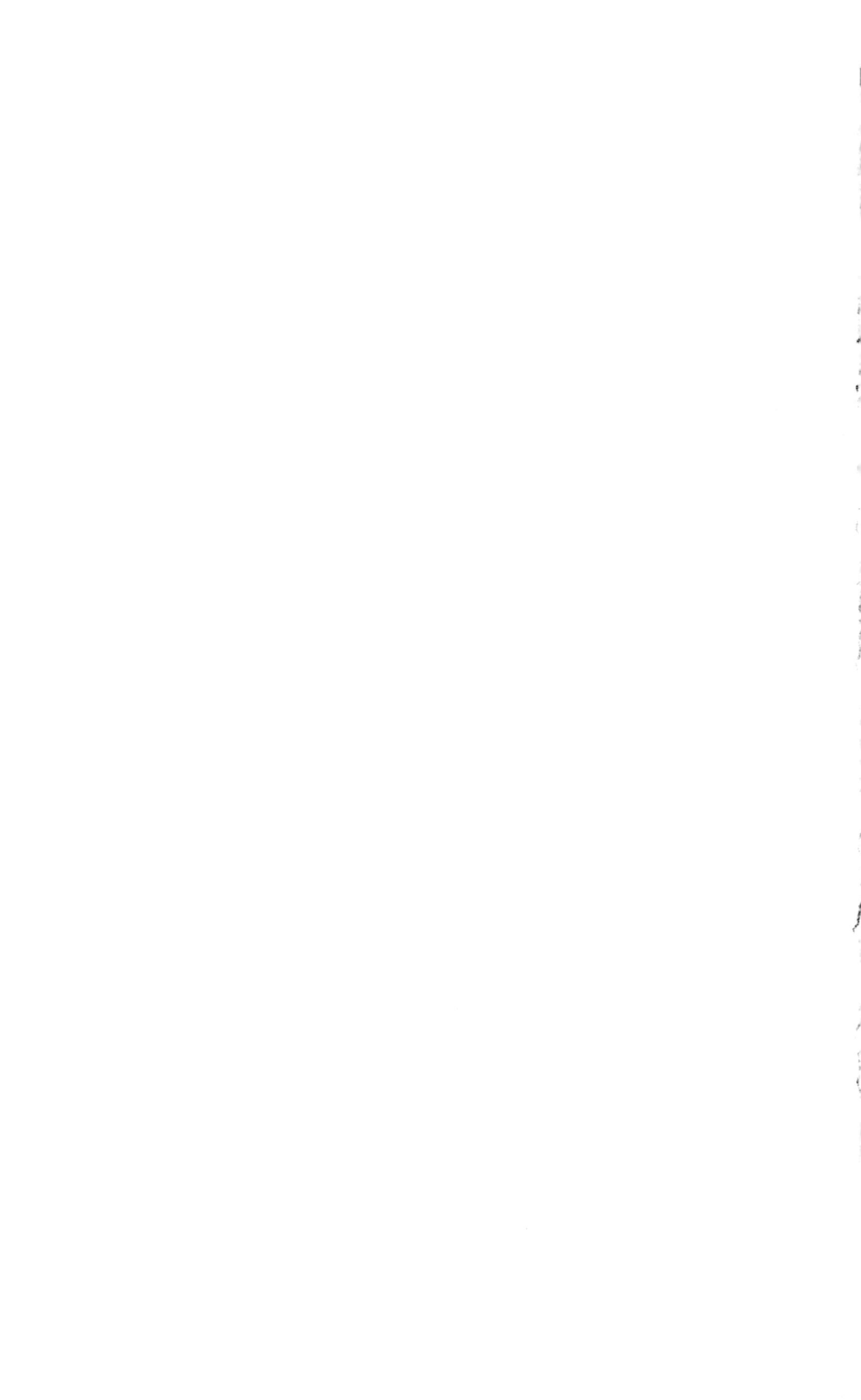

SMOKY MOUNTAIN RAILWAYS

SMOKY MOUNTAIN RAILWAYS

JACOB MORGAN PLOTT AND BOB PLOTT

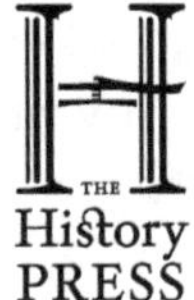

Published by The History Press
Charleston, SC
www.historypress.com

All color photos on back and front covers are by Jacob Morgan Plott (JMP Photos), and the black-and-white photo is courtesy of Thomas Plott and Ashley Swenson Hackshaw.

First published 2021

ISBN 9781540246592

Library of Congress Control Number: 2020948624

This book is dedicated to my parents—Bob and Janice Plott—who have always been there for me. And to some special friends of mine, my Smoky Mountain family: Sam and Sandra McMahan, Summer Brooke McMahan, Brayden Luke McMahan, Katie Fortner, Morgan Buchanan, Chassidy Buchanan, Dalton Buchanan, Raymond Bunn, Sandra Bunn, George Ellison, Lewis Penland, Kelly Penland, Michael Moore, Dr. David Shapiro, Dr. Tami Shearer and Ted Rowe. They all supported me while I worked on this book—and long before that too. I love you all, and I hope you share the story of Smoky Mountain Railways *with your friends and families.*

Jacob Morgan Plott, April 2020

Two people deserve dedications. First and foremost, my son, Jacob Morgan Plott, train expert extraordinaire. Love you more than you know. So proud of you buddy!

Also, George Ellison. None of my previous five books, nor this one, would have happened without you. I am eternally grateful for friendship, support and guidance. Love you, brother.

Bob Plott, April 2020

CONTENTS

ACKNOWLEDGEMENTS

Jacob Plott would like to thank his NASCAR pit crew buddies: Wesley and Samantha McPherson, Dylan and Amanda Dowell, Nate House, Keegan Martin, Beau Whitley, Jason and Mallory Postma, Kyle Power, Justin Reissmann, Kellen Mills, Lance Hanna, TJ Ford, James Houck, Greg Donlin, Adam Merrell, Ron Lemasters and Dylan Hines, as well as driver Timothy Peters and Junior Motorsports drivers Michael Annett, Justin Allgaier and Noah Gragson, for their friendship and support. You guys are true friends!

Thanks also go to Team Penske VP of operations Michael Nelson and other Team Penske associates, including PR executive Kyle Zimmerman and drivers Joey Logano, Ryan Blaney and Brad Keselowski, for their kindness and support.

Bob Plott extends his heartfelt thanks to all the above as well.

Jacob and Bob Plott both also extend their sincere thanks to our friends Dr. Tammy Shearer and her husband, Ted Rowe—we love those Cabooses!—David Brewin; Raymond and Sandra Bunn; Lewis and Kelly Penland; Charlie Brown; Sam and Sandra McMahan; Summer Brooke McMahan; Brayden McMahan; Katie Fortner; Will Jones; Michael Moore; Russell Messer; Wyatt Messer; Jeff and Anita Coggins; Gary and Pandra Mclaughlin; Chassidy Buchanan; Morgan Buchanan; Dalton Buchanan; Logan Buchanan; Cathy Owle; Christian Owle; Joel Garris and family; Julia Plott; Patty Holt, Bill Plott; Dana Ballenger, Linda Plott Chastain; Katie Talbert; Ruth Plott; Lance Holland; Rick Davis; Nate Speaks; Mike Pritchard; Lynn Moretz; Daniel Whitener; Cory Piatt; Jet Willis Piatt; Dr. David Shapiro; William Ritter; Nate Burie; and Nick Daughinatis.

Acknowledgements

Special thanks go to George Ellison, Linda Plott Chastain, Allison Lee, Wendy Meyers, Terrell Finley, Bill Gibson, William Gene Gibson, the late Dewey Sharp, the Archives and Collection Center of the GSMNP, historian extraordinaire Alex McKay, artist David Wright, Tom and Judith Plott, Ashley Swenson Hackshaw, the late Danny Shull, the late Neil Davis, Ben Cook, GSMR executive Kim Battle Albritton, Jenny McPherson and the fine folks at Hunter Library Historical Archives and Special Collections at Western Carolina University, TVA Archives, University of North Carolina Archives and Southern Railroad Archives.

Thanks as well to photographers Frank Clodfelter and Butch McDade, along with Jacob Plott and the previously noted archives, for the great photos that inspired us.

We can never thank authors and train experts Stephen Little, Gerald Ledford and Ronald Sullivan enough for their extensive research, insight and advice. Three college thesis papers written by Stephen Little, David Holcolme and William H. Abrams Jr. were invaluable to us, as were the books listed in our bibliography. Our project would never have happened without the support and input of these folks. Thanks, too, go to Kate Jenkins and the History Press staff for their continued support.

Not only have Great Smoky RR engineers Kurt Newman, Marshal Harris and Dale Spivey become heroes to Jacob Plott, but they have also become family members—as have all the above-mentioned individuals, some of whom are blood kinfolk. Their knowledge has proven invaluable as well. We love you all.

Thanks also to you the reader, especially the rail fans. Any mistakes made are our own and were honest ones. We do *not* claim to be the foremost experts in the field, and it was challenging to record more than a century of technical detail in fewer than sixty thousand words. But we did our best. However, if anyone finds an error in our work, please let us know, and if substantiated, it will be corrected.

Finally, we want to thank Mary Seidenfaden (Bob's mother and Jacob's grandmother) for being an awesome mother and grandma. We love you. And most importantly, we must thank the world's best wife and mother, Janice Brewer Plott (Bob's wife and Jacob's mom), for all she does for us both every day. Your support is appreciated more than words can convey, and none of our past projects, this book or anything else good in our lives happens without you. You have the patience of Job when it comes to almost three decades of train vacations—we love you!

INTRODUCTION

My dear friend and mentor George Ellison got me started as an author when my first book—*Strike and Stay: The Story of the Plott Hound*—was published back in 2007. He also acted as a coach and as a superb but stern editor in preparation for that first book, as well as the subsequent four titles that soon followed. George never pulled a punch with me, and I emerged a battered but better writer as a result. I am forever in his debt.

I pumped out a total of five books in less than a decade after that, and I have many more I still hope to write. George later stated—I *think* jokingly—that he felt somewhat like Doctor Frankenstein in that he had created a writing monster. I will take that as a compliment and leave it at that. Although I must add that there is now another generation to add to that monstrous literary lineage: my son, Jacob Morgan Plott. Despite Jacob's remarkable knowledge of this topic and his ability to convey the story, this book never would have happened without our literary Doctor Frankenstein, George Ellison. It all started with him.

In 2008, George wrote the foreword to my second book, *A History of Hunting in the Great Smoky Mountains*. In it, he paid me what I still consider to be one of the highest compliments I have ever received. George wrote in part:

> *"Certain people are born to write books. In retrospect, it does appear that Bob Plott, the great-great-great-grandson of (Johannes). George Plott, was destined to unveil for the first time the interrelated story of his family's*

> *history and legends in* Strike and Stay: The Story of the Plott Hound. *Plott himself is an accomplished outdoorsman and hunter with considerable knowledge of Cherokee and pioneer history. All these factors converged to transform* Strike and Stay *from a family and breed history into a regional saga of lasting significance. The same applies to Bob's other four books as well. His compilation of colorful historical sketches presented within their ongoing historical context once again transforms them into a cultural overview of lasting historical significance."*

As a child, I became obsessed at an early age with anything pertaining to mountain culture, bush craft, Cherokee history and early pioneer history, as well as with Plott hounds and their amazing story. When I wasn't reading about these topics or learning about them from friends and family members, I was spending time in the woods perfecting my skills as a woodsman and working with my own dogs.

My parents thought that I would grow out of this eventually, but I never did. I remain passionate about all these topics to this day. As a boy, my son, Jacob, was equally as passionate about his own favorite topic: trains—particularly steam trains in the Great Smokies and, more specifically, the Murphy Branch line. From the time he could walk, Jacob was consumed with learning more about trains, riding them and working on them.

I figured that Jacob would eventually outgrow this passion, just as my parents thought I would do. But like me, he never did. If anything, Jacob became even more consumed with learning everything possible about trains as he got older.

Most of our family vacations for the past two decades have revolved around visiting different railroad museums and riding steam trains across the Southeast, while doing photo shoots, research and train chasing in the process. Janice Plott—Jacob's mother and my wife—is undoubtedly the world's most patient woman, God bless her!

After seeing me write five books, Jacob decided that he wanted to write one as well. I think it is safe to say we have yet another Plott writing monster on our hands, and again we have George Ellison to thank in helping perpetuate this literary legacy.

While I may be biased (what father isn't?), I feel comfortable in extending the same compliment to Jacob that George bestowed on me in 2008. Jacob Morgan Plott was *meant* to write this book. Not only does he share my passion for our family history and our dogs, but Jacob is also even more passionate about steam trains in the Great Smoky Mountains, most specifically the building of the Murphy Branch and the steam engines used on it for more than a century.

We descend from a long line of railroad men. My grandpa worked for Southern Railroad. My uncle Cecil Plott was not only a great hunter and Plott hound advocate, but he also ran the railroad depot in Bryson City from the 1920s until his retirement in the late 1960s. Uncle Cecil's wife, Mildred—or "Aunt Pinky," as we called her—was originally a Sandlin (a renowned railroad family) and relative of William C. Sandlin, who as you will soon see was instrumental in building the Murphy Branch. And her father, Tom Sandlin, was a famous conductor on the line.

The blood from all these railroad legends runs in our veins still today. No one appreciates this history, this region and this story more than my son, Jacob Plott. Nor is anyone more qualified to tell it. It was Jacob's destiny to write this book. I have no doubt that this is the start of many more books to come, as Jacob is not only an immensely talented train historian, but he is also an equally talented photographer. More importantly, he is a fine young man who has overcome many obstacles in achieving this objective.

I am proud to assist you in this project, Jacob, and prouder still to call you my son. All aboard, Engineer Jake, let's get this train rolling!

BOB PLOTT, April 2020

IRON HORSES AND STEEL RAILS

Railroads—specifically steam-powered locomotives—revolutionized the U.S. economy following the Civil War. This economic revolution culminated with the driving of the final golden spike at Promontory Point, Utah, that connected the Transcontinental Railroad from coast to coast in 1869.

Not only did this monumental achievement provide a safe, reliable and fast form of transporting passengers and freight across the United States in almost any kind of weather, but also, just as importantly, it forced the federal government as well as local governments in all existing states to connect these railroad lines with one another, thus forming a vast national network to support the Industrial Revolution and economic renaissance that took place in the late nineteenth and early twentieth centuries.

Thanks to trains and rapidly expanding railroad lines, businesses of all kinds—including sales, retailers, manufacturers and farmers—now had the capability to ship their products almost anywhere in the United States, as well as to coastal ports, where their goods could be sold in other countries.

Furthermore, these iron horses and steel rails provided private citizens the opportunity to visit friends and family or do business in safety and comfort throughout the United States in record time. Trains also strengthened U.S. security and enhanced its power by also offering the U.S. military the ability to rapidly deploy troops, weapons, ammunition, equipment and even horses throughout the nation and into Mexico and Canada.

Yet this economic resurgence was slow in coming to North Carolina due to a variety of factors, but mostly because it seemed almost impossible to build a railroad that could penetrate the lofty Blue Ridge and Great Smoky Mountain ranges.

And of course, that is the subject of this book, sharing the story and history of how the Western North Carolina Railroad (the WNCRR) and, more specifically, the Murphy Branch was built, along with the mighty iron horse locomotives that roared across these steel rails servicing the far western reaches of the Tar Heel State.

It is a story like no other, a tale of heroism, tragedy, disaster, blood, sweat, tears and nitroglycerin that arguably saved Western North Carolina from financial ruin, or at the very least allowed the region to catch up economically with the rest of the state and, indeed, the rest of the nation.

Most of our story will be devoted to the building of the railroad, the people who made it happen and the folks that it affected. But to better understand that impact, we should first look at the evolution of the iron horses or steam engines that pulled the trains and how they work.

GSMR engineer Kurt Newman once told us, "The man who invented a steam engine was a genius. A steam engine is truly a complex precise piece of machinery, yet beautiful in its efficient simplicity. Steam trains impacted transportation history as much or more as any machine ever invented—and that includes diesel locomotives, automobile, trucks and airplanes!"

The inventor Kurt was referring to was George Stephenson, an Englishman, who in 1814 used the most advanced steam technology then available to develop the first steam locomotive. It was used initially for coal mining. By 1821, he had built a steam locomotive that pulled the world's first steam-powered passenger train, and by 1829, a Stephenson-built steam locomotive set a world speed record of thirty-six miles per hour!

The working mechanics of a steam locomotive basically consist of a boiler, a firebox, a steam cylinder, pistons and driving wheels, all working together under the supervision of the engineer and fireman to power the train. Let's examine how each part works.

Steam engines burn fuel in the firebox to create heat. A sheath of water and tubes in the boiler surrounds the firebox, where the water is boiled and converted to steam. The heat from the firebox sends heat through the tubes in the boiler—known as flues—and boils the water, thus creating the steam.

When the throttle is open, steam then travels down to the slide valve in the steam cylinders to power the pistons. The slide valve moves back and forth across the top of a reciprocating piston. This allows the high-pressure steam to push the pistons back and forth, driving the wheels.

As the wheels begin to move and gain speed, timing rods then reverse the flow in the cylinders, causing the pistons to retract and complete the cycle. Exhaust steam exits through the smokebox and mixes with exhaust from the firebox. Both shoot up the smokestack and are expelled into the outdoors.

The draft created by the smokestack pulls more air into the firebox, making the fire burn even hotter and in the process generating more steam and power. The cycle is constantly repeated faster and faster as the locomotive accelerates.

Fuel and water needed for this process are carried in a car that is semi-permanently coupled to the engine. It is known as the tender car, or just the tender. The size and capacity of specific tender cars vary, but they could hold a lot of water and fuel. For example, the tender of the oil-burning no. 1702 steam engine, now operated by the Great Smoky Mountains Railroad, holds 3,600 gallons of oil and 10,000 gallons of water.

It generally takes two people to operate a steam engine and monitor this process: the engineer and the fireman. The engineer is usually perched

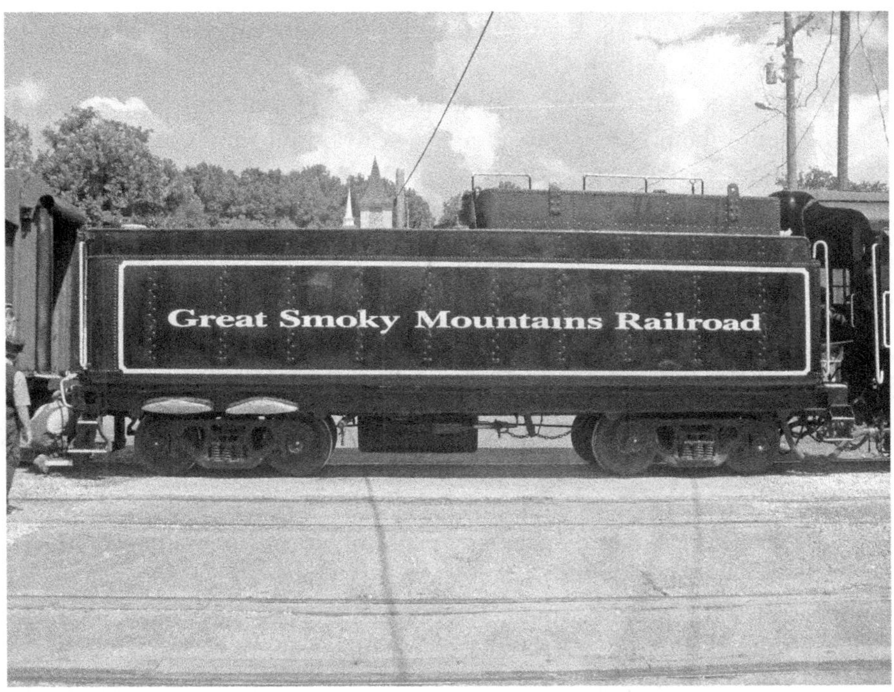

GSMR tender. *JMP Photos.*

on the right side of the engine cab, and he drives the train, while staying on lookout for obstacles or problems on the track or with the train. The engineer blows the whistle to warn folks that the train is coming and to alert upcoming crossings. In addition to driving the train, adjusting speed, ensuring safety and more, the engineer also oversees train operations and works closely with the fireman in monitoring and adjusting fuel and power needs and gauges while also staying in close contact with the brakeman and conductors on other parts of the train to remain aware of problems there.

The fireman is on the left side of the steam engine and is responsible for several things. He makes the engineer aware of any problems or obstacles on the left side of the tracks while keeping the proper amount of coal or fuel in the firebox needed to keep the fire burning correctly. He also monitors the steam pressure and adjusts it accordingly; most importantly, he makes sure that there is always an adequate amount of water in the boiler.

The fireman controls a mechanism known as the water injector, which shoots water stored in the tender to the boiler. Basically, the fireman monitors and maintains the water and steam pressure to match what the engineer requires, while also regulating how much water, coal or oil is needed to heat the boiler. He also lowers the boiler pressure when it is too hot by cooling it with cold water stored in the tender. Water flows into the boiler by gravity but is regulated by using the water injector valve.

On oil-burning engines, the fireman pulls a lever that controls the flow of oil going onto the firebox, while on coal- or wood-burning locomotives, the fireman shovels coal or wood into the firebox, taking great care to ensure that the embers are evenly spread to guarantee an even and consistent burn or temperature. Early steam engines were fueled by wood because it was easily accessible and relatively cheap and could be cut and stored along the tracks. Until 1879, all locomotives on the WNCRR were wood-burning units. They were converted to coal that same year.

Oil-, wood- and coal-burning steam engines have one thing in common: it is imperative that their boiler water level does not get too low. If it does, the boiler will explode, creating a catastrophic disaster. It's also the fireman's job to make sure that this does not happen.

To be more efficient and economical, almost all coal-burning locomotives were eventually converted to oil-burning units. The 1702 steam engine used today by the Great Smoky Mountains Railroad was one of these locomotives. Other advantages to oil include no burning cinders, which can cause injury and property fires, and no ashes left behind for removal. Oil is also easier to load and store, and by the 1900s, it was readily available.

All the steam locomotives used on the WNCRR and Murphy Branch were powered by steam using coal as their primary fuel source. We will include a breakdown and description of each engine used on the Murphy Branch shortly, along with additional railroad terminology in the glossary section. But let's get back to the history of steam engines in the United States.

Steam train technology was a bit slower in coming to the United States. The first steam-powered engine, the Dewitt Clinton, was designed and built by John Jervis and David Matthew in New York State at the West Point Foundry in 1831 for the Mohawk and Hudson Railroad. A nationwide railroad boom began shortly after that—almost everywhere except for Western North Carolina—culminating with completion of the Union Pacific Transcontinental Railroad in 1869.

Granted, our friend Kurt Newman, like us, might be a tad biased in his opinion regarding steam engines and their origins, but we think he is correct in his astute assessment. There is just something extra special about a steam train, and even more so because they were the first of their kind.

Sure, diesels and other modern-day trains and airplanes are faster and cheaper to operate, but steamers were the originals. There is something to be said for that. Plus, in their prime, a steam engine was the equivalent of a supersonic jet airliner today in terms of transportation speed and technological advances.

The initial steam engines that ran on the Murphy Branch or WNCRR from the late 1870s until Southern Railway acquired the WNCRR in 1894 (and even later during the Southern era) included 2-8-0-, 2-8-2-, 4-6-0-, 4-6-2- and 4-4-0-wheel arrangements (see the glossary section for more details on engine wheel configurations and types).

The 4-4-0 in railroad circles is generally referred to as the "American type locomotive" and was classified as being a standard-gauge rod-driven engine—also known for its horizontal cylinders, unlike the geared locomotives often used on logging lines that we will discuss in the eleventh chapter.

There were several well-known locomotive manufacturers in the late 1800s and early 1900s—most notably Baldwin Locomotive Works, Rogers Locomotive and Machine Works and the American Locomotive Company (also known as ALCO, but originally known as Schenectady).

Baldwin Locomotive Works was founded in 1831 by Mathias Baldwin in Philadelphia, Pennsylvania. At that time, Rogers Locomotive and Machine Works was considered the premier American manufacturer of steam locomotives, but by 1866, Baldwin was producing more engines than Rogers—averaging about sixty per year. Between 1831 and 1956, the Baldwin Locomotive Works built more than seventy thousand steam locomotives.

However, Rogers Locomotive and Machine Works remained a fierce rival of Baldwin's and, in fact, along with Schenectady Locomotive Works were the recognized industry leaders at the time the WNCRR would have been purchasing its initial engines prior to the Civil War.

Rogers Locomotive and Machine Works was founded by Thomas Rogers in Paterson, New Jersey, in 1832. Between 1832 and 1905, the Rogers Locomotive and Machine Works was either the nation's largest or second-largest manufacturers of steam-powered locomotives in America.

When the company started, it built mostly 4-2-0-wheel arrangements but soon diversified its product line. It began building the sturdy and reliable 4-4-0 configuration in about 1855. In 1856, the company built the first 2-6-0-wheel arrangement ever produced in the United States. But the 4-4-0-wheel arrangement was its most popular engine.

One of its biggest customers was the Union Pacific Railroad, which used these 4-4-0s on the legendary Transcontinental Railroad, and it was a Rogers 4-4-0 engine that first ran across Promontory Point, Utah, when

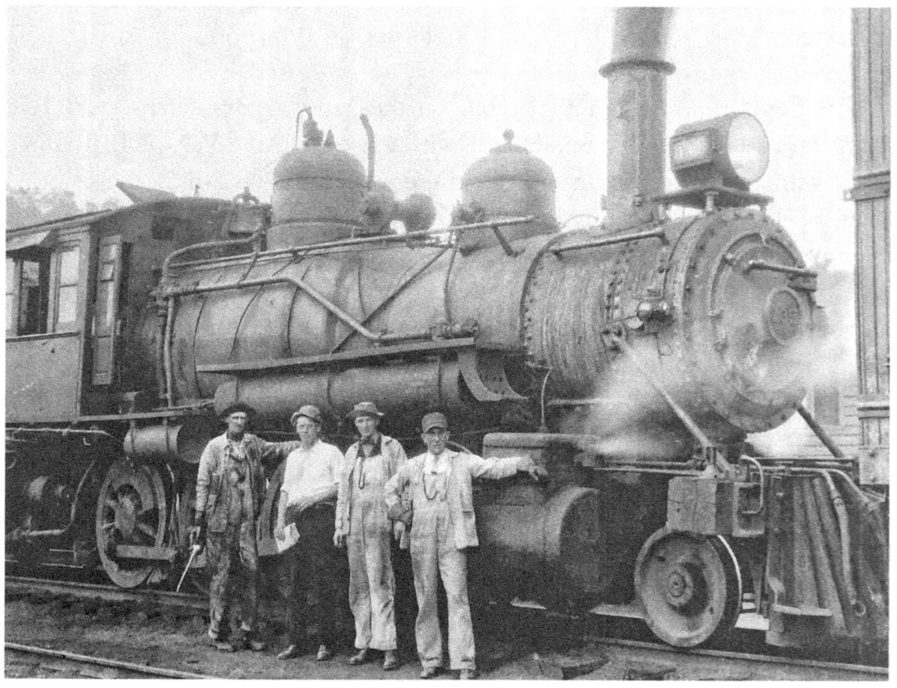

Engine no. 135, a 2-8-0 Schenectady, and crew. The 135 was one of the early Murphy Branch engines. *Thanks to Thomas Plott and Ashley Swenson Hackshaw.*

the iconic last Golden Spike was driven—thus connecting U.S. train service from coast to coast in 1869.

The other engine at Promontory Point—a Central Pacific 4-4-0, known as the Jupiter—was built by the third major player in the engine building industry: Schenectady Locomotive Works. It was founded by the Norris brothers in Schenectady, New York, in 1848. It was an industry leader for the last half of the nineteenth century. In 1901, it merged with seven other manufacturers, becoming the American Locomotive Company (ALCO).

Most of the steam engines that ran regularly on the Murphy Branch before 1894 and during the Southern Railway steam era between 1894 and 1952 can be documented, and some still are operational or in existence today. They included engines built by the Baldwin Locomotive Works and the American Locomotive Company, based in Schenectady, New York, which by 1905 had surpassed Rogers for the number-two sales slot behind Baldwin.

One of the earliest engines on the Murphy Branch was no. 135, an ancient 2-8-0 built in 1885 by Schenectady (ALCO) and later sold to Virginia Central RR in 1926.

Here is a partial list of the Southern Railway Murphy Branch engines that we were able to find, largely with the assistance of Gerald Ledford:

- Southern Railway K Class Consolidation locomotives used on the Murphy Branch: nos. 573, 586, 599, 630, 651, 685, 695, 698, 711, 712, 722, 735, 848, 857, 862, 857 and 871. The GSMR owns the 722 and hopes to restore it in the future.
- 573, 586, 651, 695, 698, 711 and 735 were all built as K Class but were later changed to Ks-2. 599 and 630 were built and stayed Ks-1 models. 685, 712,719, 722, 848, 857 and 871 were all built as a K but were later converted to Ks-1.

Documentation is sparse regarding the exact dates these engines first arrived on the Murphy Branch, but certainly between 1904 and 1910 and continuing into the 1930s. All the K, Ks and Ks-1 engines were built by ALCO Richmond and ALCO Pittsburgh between 1903 and 1910. They include the 630 and 722—both primarily used to pull freight trains.

- G Class 2-8-0 Consolidation no. 154 was built by Schenectady Locomotive Works in 1890. All the G Class Consolidation engines built between 1885 and 1890 were first operated for

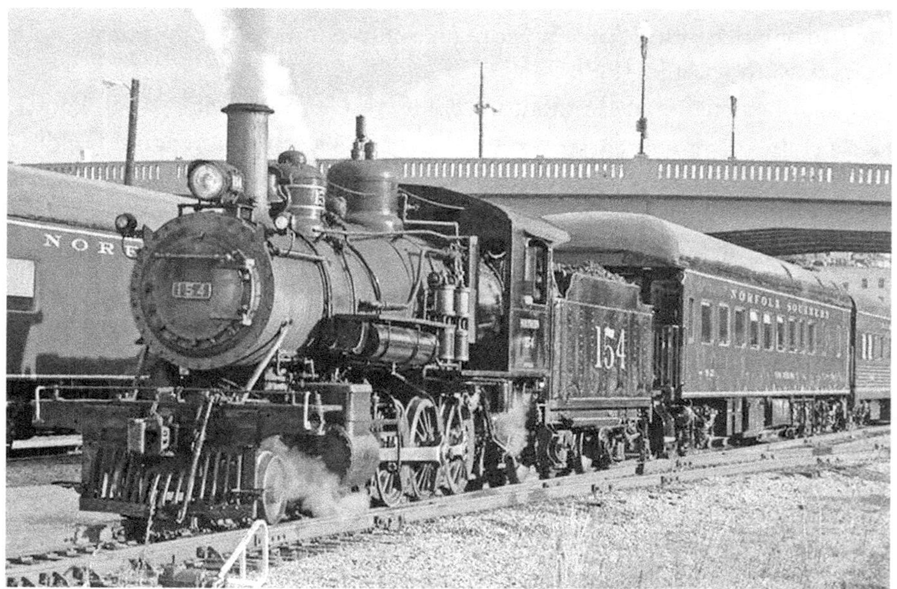

Engine no. 154 at Three Rivers Rambler Museum in Knoxville, Tennessee. *Three Rivers Rambler Museum.*

the East Tennessee and Georgia Railway until it merged with the Richmond and Danville (which owned the WNCRR) to become a part of Southern Railway in 1894. The purchase of all these engines occurred when the original respective lines were consolidated with Southern Railway, hence the name "Consolidation." The G Class engines were primarily used to pull freight trains. Some experts say that the no. 154 never ran on the line, while others believe it did. Southern 154 remains operational today at a tourist railroad known as the Three Rivers Rambler in Knoxville, Tennessee.

- F Class 4-6-0 ten-wheelers were built by either Baldwin, Rogers or Pittsburgh Locomotive and Car Works between 1889 and 1895. Pittsburgh was acquired by ALCO in 1901.

The 2-8-0 630 is operational today at the Tennessee Valley RR Museum in Chattanooga, Tennessee, while the 722 is owned by the Great Smoky Mountains Railroad, which hopes to eventually restore and operate it again on the Murphy Branch.

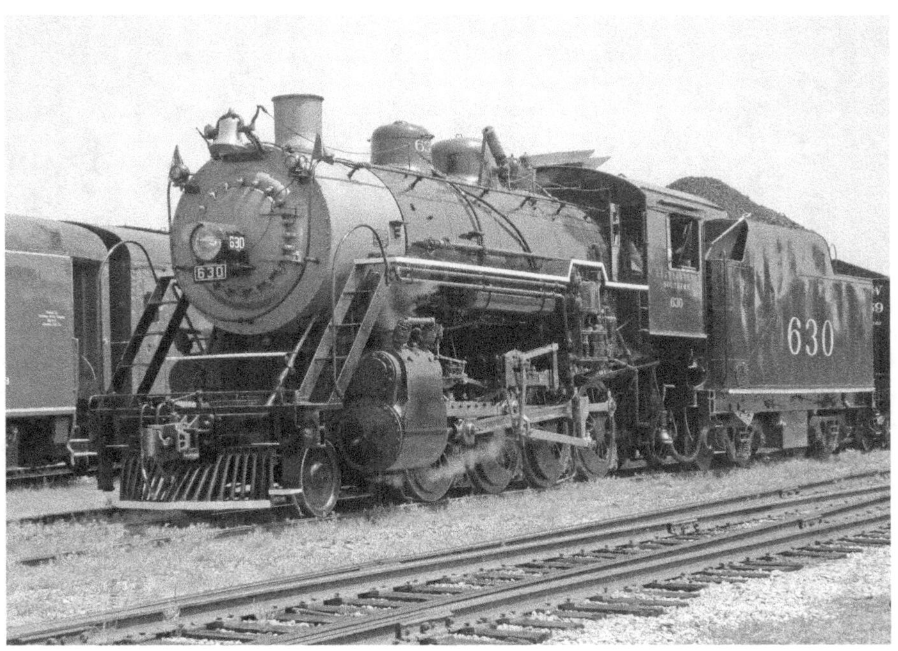

Front shot of no. 630. *JMP Photos.*

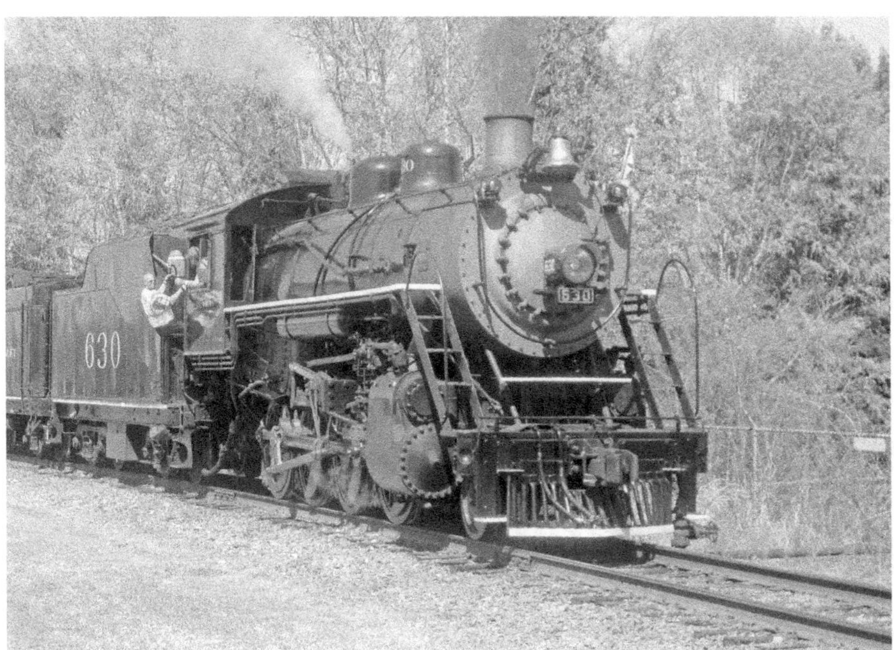

No. 630 and tender. *JMP Photos.*

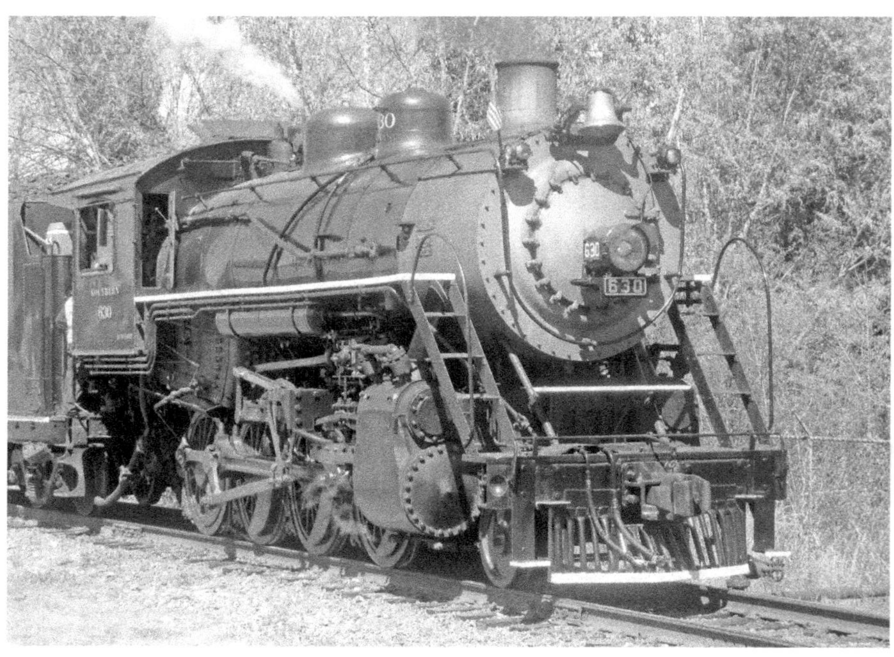

Front and side shot of engine no. 630. *JMP Photos.*

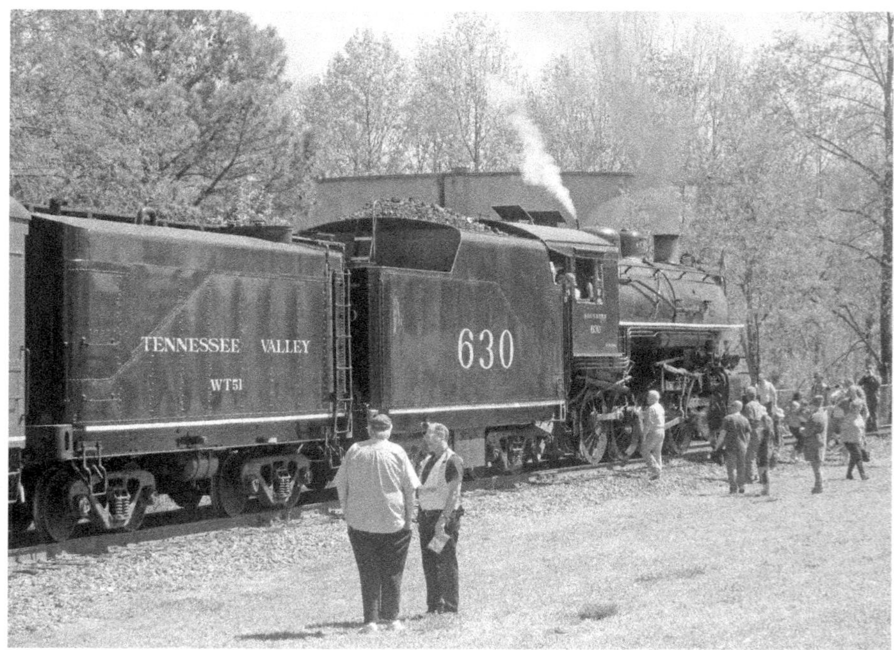

Back angle of no. 630 showing Tennessee Valley logo. *JMP Photos.*

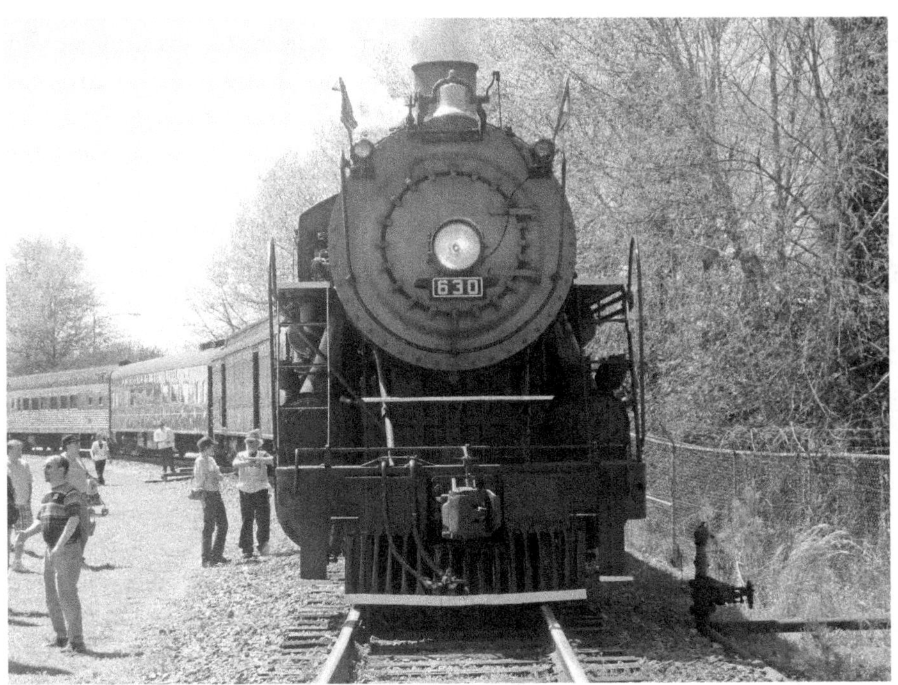

Head-on shot of no. 630. *JMP Photos.*

- The very light P Class and PS-2 Class 4-6-2 Pacific steamers were built by Baldwin and ALCO Richmond between 1912 and 1914. These engines typically pulled passenger trains. Their roster included nos. 1252, 1256, 1260, 1267, 1278, 1281, 1288, 1290, 1297, 1298 and 1302. They arrived at various dates during the early 1900s. No. 1278 was involved in a wreck that killed the engineer and fireman in Rhodo in 1941.

The PS-2s included nos. 1252, 1256, 1260, 1267 and 1302. Their arrival date was 1947.

- Although 2-8-0 Consolidation no. 1702 never originally ran on the Murphy Branch until it was purchased by the GSMR in 1991, and began service there in 1992, we have included it on our roster because it played a major part in the resurgence of steam on the Murphy Branch, which we will discuss in later chapters.

Plus, the 1702, which was built by Baldwin in 1942, proudly served our country as a military train stationed at Fort Bragg, North Carolina, until 1946, further entrenching its roots in the Tar Heel State. The 1702 was sold to an Arkansas freight operation in 1946 before later becoming a tourist train in both Arkansas and Nebraska. In 1992, the 1702 returned steam to the Smokies on the GSMR and today is the star of its steam operation.

GSMR engineer Kurt Newman was right. Steam engines are amazing machines that were invented by a true genius. It is doubtful that any machinery has done more for our great nation than steam locomotives. Nor does any have a more colorful history.

As special as they were, and still are, even the greatest steam locomotive is useless without steel rails, which allow the engine to run at full speed and capacity. For iron horses to run efficiently, safely and at reasonable speeds, routes had to first be surveyed that avoided steep inclines. Then land had to be cleared and graded for laying tracks.

Once these difficult tasks were completed, trees were cut and sent to sawmills for crossties. These crossties—also called sleepers—supported the steel rails and kept them level. They were further supplemented by gravel ballast beds that allowed for slight flexibility for the rails and aided in drainage.

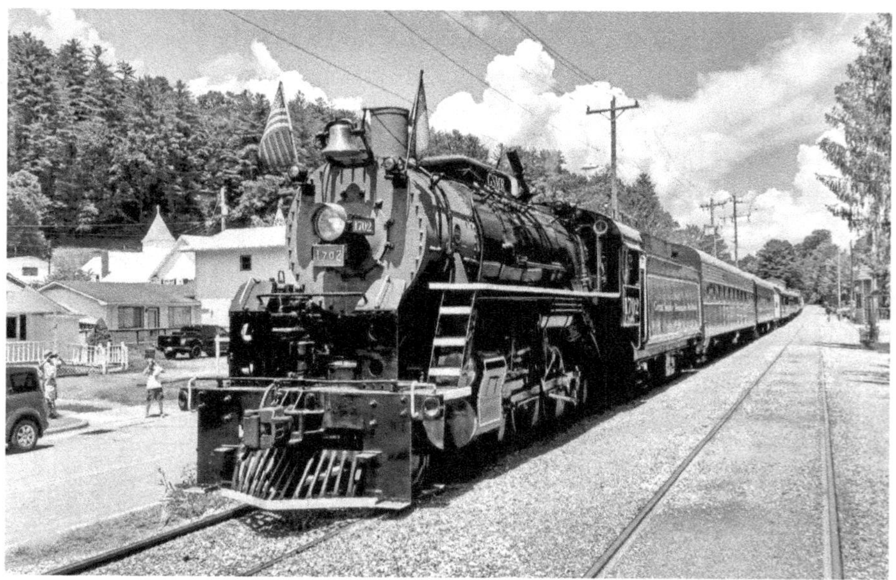

Front and side view of no. 1702 in Dillsboro. *JMP Photos.*

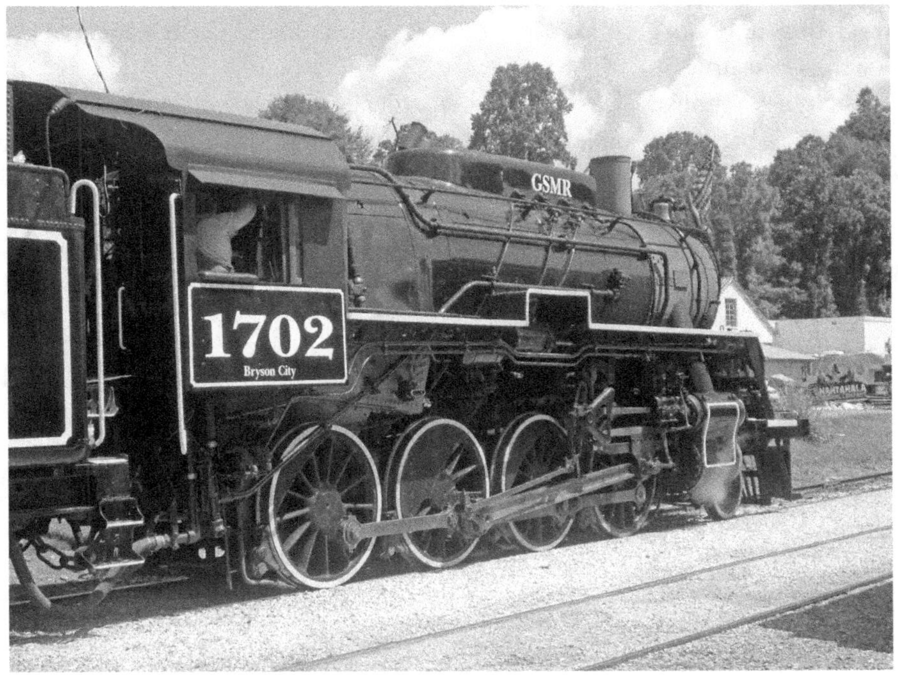

No. 1702 eastbound in Bryson City. *JMP Photos.*

And finally, rails were laid across the sleepers and hammered in—by hand on the WNCRR and later the Murphy Branch—with long spikes to hold them in place. The early European railroads were built with wooden rails before 1845—before their conversion to metal. The WNCRR and Murphy Branch were built first with iron rails and then later steel rails. The iron rails weighed fifty-six to sixty pounds in five-foot broad gauge. Railroad rail is classed by the weight per yard. Thirty-nine feet was the standard length at that time.

Keep in mind, too, that there are at least three different gauges or track widths used in building railroads. They are narrow, standard and broad—narrow being the smallest and broad the biggest or widest at five feet. All the WNCRR and Murphy Branch was originally laid as a broad-gauge line, but in 1886, it was converted to a standard-gauge line—except for some logging spur lines that were narrow gauge.

Of course, this brief explanation of laying track is not even taking into consideration the need for building bridges, trestles and tunnels, which were common on the Western North Carolina Railroad and Murphy Branch, nor does it factor in the then unheard-of difficulty of grading the track beds and moving thousands of tons of soil to keep them level enough for the trains to run.

Building a railway was a brutal, physically taxing job in the best of conditions, preferably on level ground. And nowhere was it more difficult to lay these steel rails than in the "Land of Blue Smoke."

THE LAND OF BLUE SMOKE

To best comprehend the massive economic and personal impact that steam engines and the Murphy Branch railroad line had on Western North Carolina—and, indeed, on the entire state—one must first go back in time to the days of the ancient Cherokees and to the arrival of the first European settlers to the Great Smoky Mountains. Still later, the lack of economic development in North Carolina during the early nineteenth century through the devastation of the Civil War and Reconstruction eras and the difficulty of getting the railroad built even as far as Asheville, North Carolina, must also be taken into consideration.

One must first examine the modes of transportation needed for survival and commerce in the Tar Heel State during these eras, while also appreciating the unique geographical aspects of this remote and rugged region of Western North Carolina that made these modes of transportation nearly impossible. Where better to start than the mystical Land of Blue Smoke?

Shaconage ("the Land of Blue Smoke") is the Cherokee term for the Great Smoky Mountains. The lofty peaks towering above the lush river bottoms and isolated coves of the area are often framed by a bluish, smoky haze of cloud-like mist that give this magnificent mountain range a spooky, ethereal look depending on the time of day and weather conditions.

It was first home for Native Americans and later European explorers, traders, farmers, businessmen and even runaways, all of whom were drawn to the region seeking opportunity, solace and sanctuary. Long before cars, factories or even steam engines, this majestic mountain range appeared as haven of hope, deep blue from a distance and almost always shrouded by a

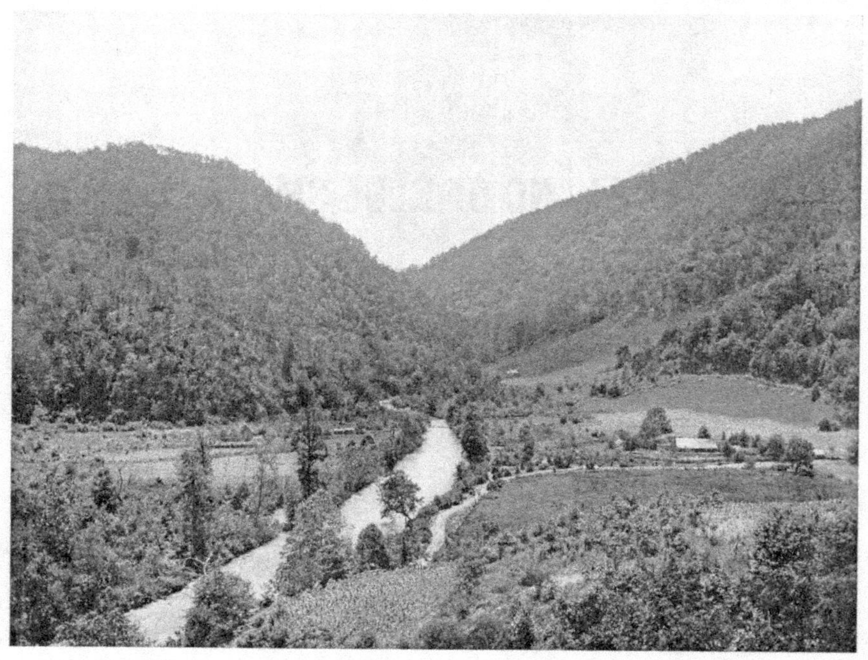

THE NANTAHALA RIVER AND GAP, "LAND OF THE SKY."

Southwest from Asheville, some two-score miles away, lies the gorge of the Nantahala River, through which the Murphy branch of the Southern Railway passes for more than a dozen miles (see opposite page). By many this gorge is believed to be the most picturesque and beautiful in Western North Carolina, where

"The mountains that shield from the rude northern blast — mute monitors, they, of the ages long past —
Like sentinels watch o'er the valley below where the swift crystal streams unceasingly flow.
The pure, healthful breeze, the life-giving air, the beauteous landscape, oft new, ever fair,
Are gifts that have come from the Father on high; to Him be all praise for 'The Land of the Sky.'"

In some sentimental verse the Indian, in passing off the earth, is made to say to his white brother: "Our name is on your waters, you cannot wash it out." Nowhere is this more true than in North Carolina, where one finds the Tuckaseegee, Savannah, Tennessee, Elijay, Cartoogajay, Tuskeegee, Oconaluftee, Stekoah, Tusquitta, Nantahala and kindred others.

An 1800s photo of the Nantahala River and Gap. *Hunter Library Archives at Western Carolina University (WCU).*

distinctive crown of clouds and haze. A haven of hope that proved almost impossible to access aside from rough foot paths.

The first inhabitants of the region, the Cherokees, traveled by foot on hunting trails formed by buffalo or other wild game. They also used dugout and birch-bark canoes to more speedily traverse the mighty rivers that dissected the region. Water travel was faster and easier, but the tribe was limited to the number of navigable waterways and their access to them.

Foot travel was far more common among the Cherokees. They possessed the athleticism and stamina of world-class endurance athletes, as they could commonly cover twenty-five miles or more per day on foot—as could some of the European fur traders, farmers and hunters who would later settle in the region.

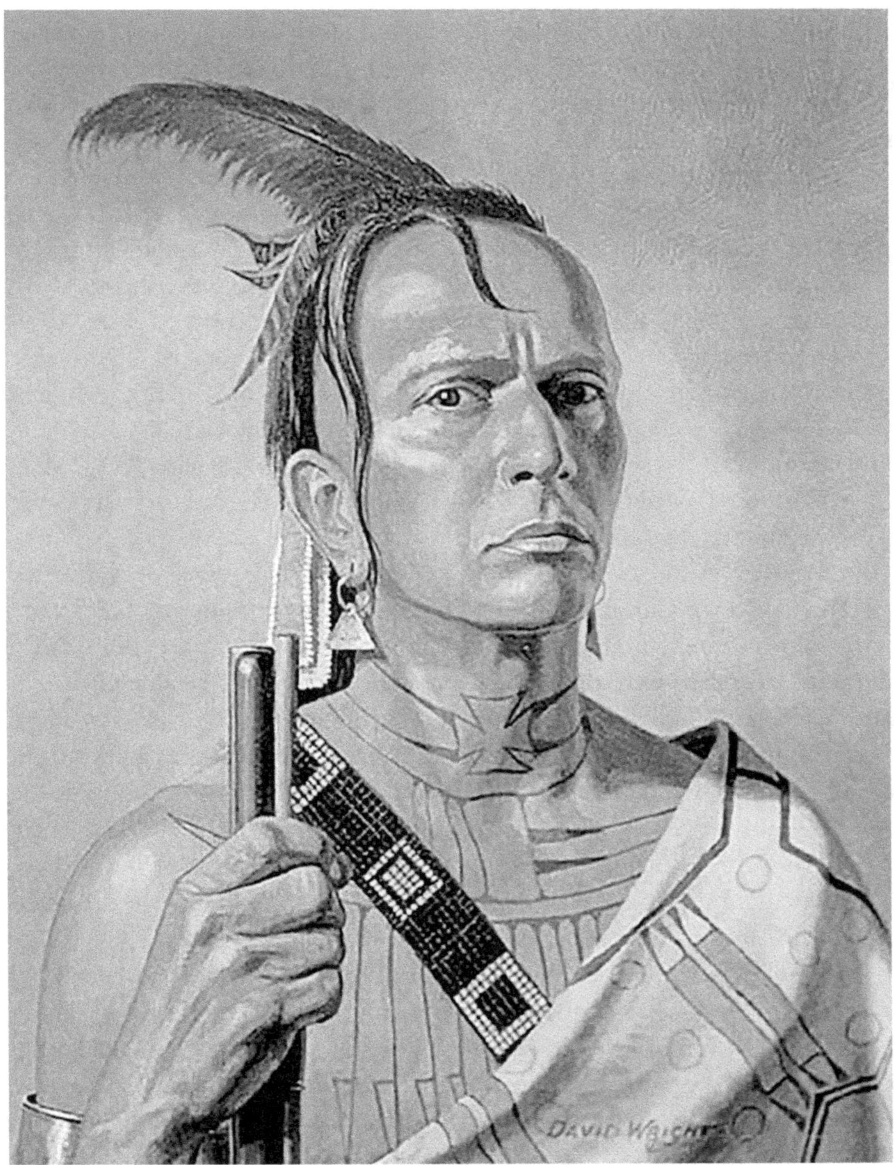

Cherokee warrior. *David Wright.*

Horses—brought to the region by Spanish conquistadors in 1540—revolutionized travel and commerce to the southern mountains. However, it was not until 1700 before any significant number of horses could be found in North or South Carolina, as fur traders were enticed to the region to trade with the Cherokees. Horses not only offered a reliable and easier form of travel, as they could cover up to fifty miles or more daily, but they were also invaluable to commerce, as they could be loaded down with more than two hundred pounds of furs or trade goods.

These traders traveled on foot and horseback and transported their trade goods, as well as the furs they took to market, on packhorses—or, if passable paths could be found, by horse-drawn wagons. In some cases, the Cherokees transported their own furs to trading posts in places like Salisbury, North Carolina, but they usually preferred having the traders come to them.

The tribe (and later merchants, white hunters and traders) used a vast network of primary and secondary trails that connected multiple Indian villages to one another and to trading posts in the North Carolina Piedmont and coastal plain, as well as locations in Upstate South Carolina, to conduct their business. This network of trails was commonly referred to as the Great Trading Path or the Occaneechi Path.

Between 1700 and 1773, the fur trade was the leading source of commerce in Western North Carolina and the Piedmont. Vast amounts of hides were harvested and sold in Piedmont and coastal markets. More than thirty thousand deerskins were traded and exported from Salisbury alone in 1753, and between 1755 and 1772, more than 2.5 million pounds of deer hides were shipped from the port of Savannah, Georgia—although Charlestown, South Carolina (today known as Charleston), was the undisputed hub of the southern fur trade.

Horses were the primary means of shipment navigating these back roads. The only thing as important as a horse in these days would have been a good rifle or fine hunting dog.

Many of these wagon roads, game trails and war paths were later used in building the first railroads to the region, or as former engineer Frank Clodfelter told author Michael George, "The railroad was constructed hastily along ancient cow paths and Indian trails." Indeed, history clearly shows that almost all the Murphy Branch was originally a wagon road or a hunting trail.

Following the path of many of these old trails, the first primary road in Western North Carolina—the Buncombe Turnpike—was completed in 1828. It ran north and west, starting in Greenville, South Carolina, traveling through Asheville, North Carolina, to Greenville, Tennessee. Another road, known as the Western Turnpike, was built in the 1850s.

These two roads were the primary connection to commerce of any kind in Western North Carolina with the eastern part of the Tar Heel State, as well as north to Tennessee and south to South Carolina. It resulted in the first

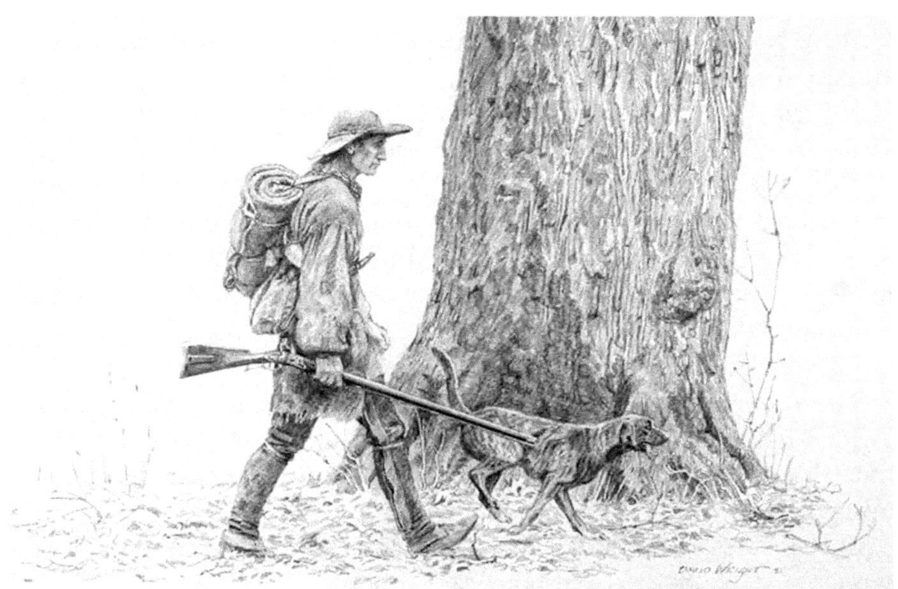

Frontier hunter on foot with dog. *David Wright.*

tourists—wealthy Lowcountry planters—being introduced to the region. However, even with the two turnpikes, highway travel remained treacherous in any sort of bad weather. The main sources of commerce in the Land of Blue Smoke were self-sustaining farms, small-scale manufacturing operations and retailers.

During the first three decades of the nineteenth century, North Carolina was often referred to as the "Rip Van Winkle state" because the state's economy was sleeping while nearby states up and down the eastern seaboard were enjoying an industrial and economic renaissance.

Economically and geographically, Western North Carolina seemed frozen in time. To better illustrate this point, coast-to-coast rail service was completed across the entire length of the United States in 1869 when the Central Pacific Railroad and Union Pacific Railroad connected at Promontory Point, Utah. For the first time in American history, freight and/or passengers could travel by train from major cities on the East Coast of the United States all the way to California. This was a landmark economic achievement.

Neighboring states South Carolina and Virginia were busy building their own networks of railroad lines and aiding their own rapid economic growth. No fewer than eight eastern and southeastern states built and operated railroad lines between 1827 and 1831.

Yet in North Carolina, railways remained nonexistent even in the relatively flat Piedmont and coastal plain until 1833. And it would be almost sixty years later—and more than two decades after train tracks traversed the entire United States—before trains could travel the length of the Old North State.

To be fair, the Piedmont and coastal plain regions of North Carolina did enjoy a brief economic recovery in the late 1830s. This was due to high demand for cotton and tobacco crops, both of which flourished in these regions. The newfound ability to transport those crops on a network of railroad lines ranging from the foothills and the Piedmont to the coastal market ports of Wilmington and Morehead City further encouraged this resurgence.

The Wilmington and Raleigh Railroad—later called the Wilmington and Weldon RR—was founded in 1833 and by 1840 had completed a 161-mile route that began on the coast in Wilmington and ended in the Hanover County town of Weldon. At the time, it was the longest railroad line in the world.

In 1849, the North Carolina Assembly chartered the North Carolina RR. It ran from Charlotte to Goldsboro via Salisbury and Raleigh and connected to the Wilmington and Weldon RR in Goldsboro in 1856. For the first time, planters in the North Carolina Piedmont and coastal plain had reliable routes to take their crops to market in any direction from Salisbury to the ports on the coast.

Like the war trails used a century before to transport furs to market, now railroad lines were built along many of these same pathways to transport the new cash crops—cotton and tobacco. Cotton alone generated more than $140 million in sales in the southern cotton belt in 1860. Tragically, it was mostly slave labor that was used to both harvest these cash crops and build the desperately needed railroad lines, and it was the rich planters and slave owners who usually profited.

Despite a terrible human toll, the result was a reliable, safe and fast network of transportation throughout the Eastern Seaboard and from the Piedmont to the coast. North Carolina towns across the Piedmont such as High Point and Thomasville sprang up in the 1850s and were built around their dependence on railroad commerce, thus revitalizing the region economically.

Realizing the need to ultimately connect Asheville, North Carolina, with these Piedmont boomtowns and railroad lines in central and eastern Tar Heel counties, as well as to jump-start the floundering economy in Western North Carolina, the North Carolina legislature approved funding in 1855 for two major extensions of the North Carolina railroad system. A route from Goldsboro to Beaufort was completed in 1858. The second route, from Salisbury through Statesville to Morganton, known initially as the Western

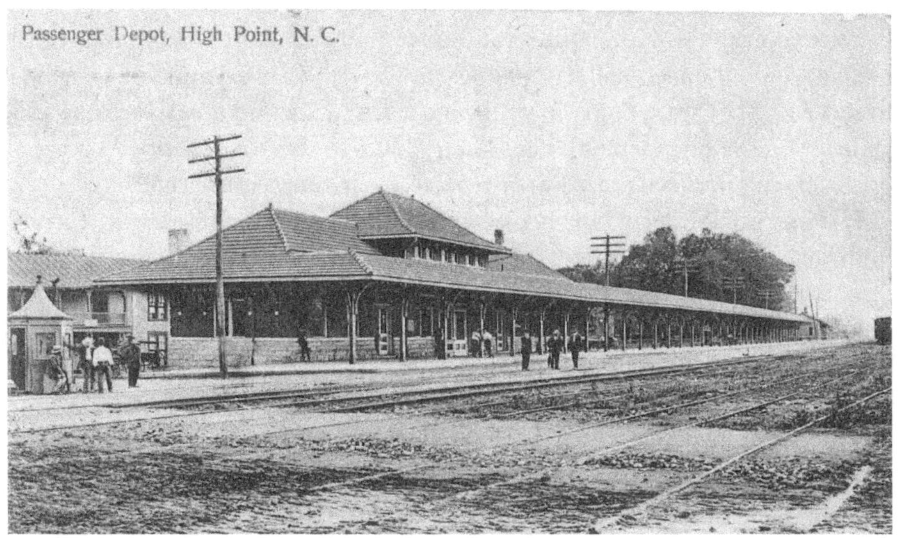

Late 1800s photo of High Point, North Carolina depot. *UNC Archives.*

North Carolina Railroad, (WNCRR), proved to be much more difficult and expensive. The Civil War (1861–65) brought the already troubled project to an abrupt halt.

When the war ended, the WNCRR extended only as far west as about six miles east of Morganton, North Carolina. The region remained in an economic funk, made worse by the war. There wasn't much difference economically in Asheville, North Carolina, when it was formed in 1793 than it was in 1866 more than seven decades later—and this was the largest city in the mountain empire, with a population of about 1,200.

The commercial and transportation gains that had taken place in the remainder of the state between 1833 and the start of the Civil War were lost as a result of the conflict. But as bad as things were throughout the state, it was even worse in the mountains.

Mountain farmers still had to herd their livestock to market—a risky endeavor at best. No major cash crops could be grown or sold, as there was not a reliable means of transporting perishable goods to major markets in a timely manner. Massive crop failures and a subsequent famine in 1845 illustrated the urgent need for mountain residents to more efficiently connect with outside commercial resources. After the famine, the price of corn in Western North Carolina tripled from $0.50 cents per bushel to $1.50 in 1846. Yet in Eastern North Carolina, corn remained cheap and abundant—often left to rot in the field—while mountain folks struggled to survive.

Even after the war, even after railroads connected the United States coast to coast, mountaineers still had to make or grow most everything they needed to survive. They were incredibly intelligent and possessed a resilient and self-sufficient sense of independence. Their ability to survive depended on these qualities. But it often limited their options to do much more than that.

Having no Western North Carolina railroads and virtually no formal highway systems prevented any influx of industry and major trading opportunities with the bustling outside world. Between 1869 and 1876, only one run-down train ran daily from Salisbury, North Carolina, to Old Fort, North Carolina. It consisted of an ancient wood-burning steam engine pulling five to six freight cars and one ancient passenger car that was partitioned in two parts—one for first-class passengers and the other side for second class. First-class customers paid one cent more per mile than their second-class counterparts, although there was little difference between the two sections.

Turntables were situated in Salisbury and Old Fort, allowing the engines to turn in the opposite direction for either their eastern or western route. One train left Salisbury heading west daily at 7:00 a.m., making stops in Statesville at 8:15 a.m., Hickory (then Hickory Tavern) at 11:50 a.m. and Morganton at 1:11 p.m., finally arriving at Old Fort at 3:35 p.m. It was an 8.5-hour trip one way. The eastbound train was equally as slow and left Old Fort around 4:00 p.m., making the same stops in reverse and arriving in Salisbury around midnight.

Any passenger wishing to travel to Asheville did so by horseback, buggy or stagecoach. The Great Western Stage Line, owned by Edward T. Clemmons from 1851 to 1888, monopolized the Asheville market. After the Civil War, it became the only daily form of commercial transportation and mail delivery to and from Old Fort and Asheville.

The stage picked up passengers where existing RR lines ended and transported them to other locations—usually another river port, railway hub or station. For example, passengers wishing to travel to Asheville rode the train to the Henry Station RR depot (two miles west of Old Fort) and then rode the stage across the Swannanoa Gap to Asheville, where Clemmons also owned a hotel.

The stagecoach lines, hotels and stations helped to slightly revive the dormant economy by reintroducing cash payments (as opposed to bartering) as a viable means of doing business and encouraged other similar business opportunities for like-minded entrepreneurs.

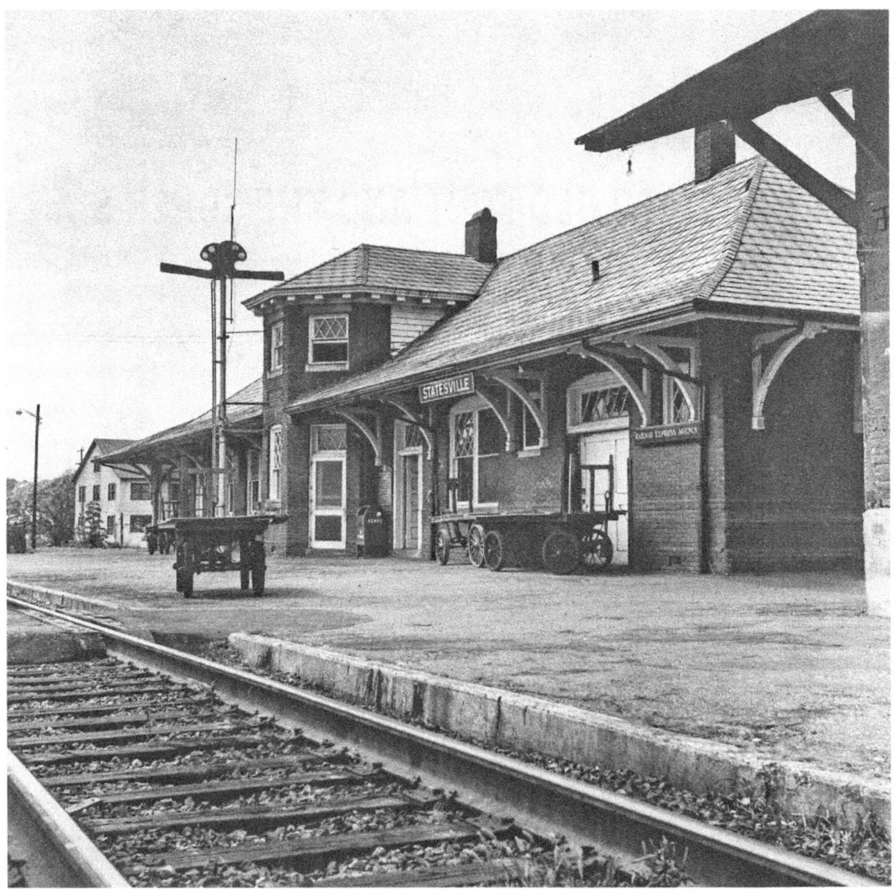

Late 1800s photo of Statesville, North Carolina depot. *UNC Archives.*

Yet the mountains remained in an economic slumber—a remote, geographically isolated island in the sky abundant in natural resources but with few ways to market them and with limited sources of income. Folks looking for work or better lives for their children were often forced to migrate to the western states in search of opportunity or move to the Piedmont to find jobs there.

For those who stayed in the Land of Blue Smoke, the future seemed bleak. But men like Colonel A.B. Andrews, Major James W. Wilson, Colonel Thad Coleman, Governor Zebulon Vance and William C. Sandlin—among others—would soon turn that despair into hope.

THE ROAD TO OLD FORT AND THE SUPER SIX

In 1866, with the Civil War over and the state embroiled in the tumultuous Reconstruction era, the WNCRR was hopelessly stalled near Morganton, North Carolina. It seemed impossible that anyone could achieve the task of connecting the Land of Blue Smoke with the rest of the Tar Heel state—much less other parts of the nation. Western North Carolina appeared destined to remain mired in an economic depression.

There was no funding or labor available for a project of this magnitude, but more than that, who could imagine, much less design, a viable method of climbing the almost vertical Eastern Continental Divide, which loomed over the existing terminus of the railway? An engineering plan on this scale, over this type of terrain, was unheard of.

Further complicating the situation, the Civil War had left railroads throughout the state in shambles. Tracks and bridges had been destroyed and poorly maintained. In 1866, the entire inventory of WNCRR rolling stock consisted of five steam engines, three passenger coaches, two mail cars, twelve flat cars and five box cars.

Five former Confederate army officers—Colonel Zeb Vance, Colonel William Thomas, Colonel A.B Andrews, Major James Wilson and Colonel Thad Coleman—took the lead in the resurrection of North Carolina railroading—more specifically, in connecting railroad service to the mountains from the east.

Still later, a young man who was not even born until *after* the Civil War, William C. Sandlin, better known as simply Will Sandlin, would join the illustrious ranks of what we like to call the "Big Five" of the WNCRR and the Murphy Branch. We will profile Sandlin and discuss his amazing accomplishments later in upcoming chapters. But without the incredible men who make up the roster of the "Super Six," it is entirely possible that the WNCRR would never have been built—or at least not until many years after its actual completion. And the Western North Carolina economic renaissance that later occurred in the late 1880s—due to the WNCRR—certainly would not have occurred until deep into the twentieth century.

The Super Six are not the only people responsible for this stunning achievement. There were many others, but few could argue that anyone else was more important to the project than these five supremely talented men who shared many of the same attributes. Before continuing our story, we want to briefly examine them and their relationship to the WNCRR.

Five of the six were battle-hardened Civil War officers and proven combat leaders. All six were native North Carolinians, proud sons of the Tar Heel State, fiercely dedicated to making life better for its residents. For five of these men, the job was intensely personal, as they were born and raised in the mountains.

Three were graduates of the University of North Carolina, two of them lawyers, while the others had little formal education. Yet each member of the Super Six was highly intelligent with a tenacious work ethic; all shared the mindset that anything they could envision could be made reality. There was no quit in them. *Impossible* was not a word in their vocabulary. Three of the Super Six were elected to public office and were masterful politicians, but all were born leaders, stellar businessmen, successful negotiators and superb deal makers.

Let's start with Will Thomas. Western North Carolina native Colonel William H. Thomas, a fascinating and complex multi-talented character, was one of the strongest early advocates of the WNCRR, as was former North Carolina governor John Motley Morehead, who along with Thomas was instrumental in getting the western RR extension started in 1855.

Colonel Thomas commanded the Thomas Cherokee Legion during the Civil War. He was an adopted son of the great Cherokee chief Yonaguska and was the first and only white chief of the eastern Cherokee tribe. Thomas was largely responsible for the formation of the Qualla Boundary. Under his skilled leadership in legally securing land for the boundary and using his talents as an attorney, Colonel Thomas saved many members of the Eastern Band of the Cherokee from being forcibly removed to Oklahoma in 1838.

Colonel Thomas and his Confederate Legion hold another unique position in American history, as they are believed to have fired the last shots of the Civil War east of the Mississippi River before surrendering what is now the town of Waynesville to Union forces in the spring of 1865.

However, for twelve years prior to the conflict, as well as shortly after the war (before becoming disabled), Thomas was a champion of building the railroad to his mountain homeland while serving in the North Carolina Senate from 1848 to 1860.

Sadly, Thomas was unable to continue his efforts for long after the Civil War as he was stricken with mental illness issues in 1867. The condition left him basically incapacitated for long periods the reminder of his life, much of which was spent in insane asylums until his death in 1893.

Nevertheless, thanks in part to his leadership and encouragement, momentum was gained to resume work on the WNCRR after the Civil War. The track was completed into the town of Morganton in 1866, although construction ended there due to lack of funding at that time. The railroad remained stranded due to a bond scandal, first engineered by Milton Littlefield and George Swepson in the late 1860s, that had bankrupted the project by 1871.

Littlefield and Swepson's scheme literally and figuratively derailed the project, as the state lost $4 million due to the issuance of fraudulent railroad bonds by the two culprits. This proved devastating to the slowly recovering North Carolina economy and government, but it was a death blow to the WNCRR project. The state government stepped in to salvage the situation, and under the leadership of Republican governor Curtis H. Brogden, the WNCRR was purchased by the State of North Carolina in 1875.

Political alliances and party affiliations played a big part in determining management positions in projects of this nature. And partisan politics would continue to plague the WNCRR and the Murphy Branch until it was completed in 1891. Governor Brogden immediately named a three-person board of directors or commissioners to manage the newly acquired WNCRR. Like Brogden, the commissioners were all Republicans, but to their credit, they all seemed united in their desires to put party alliances and differences aside in the best interests of the much-needed railroad.

Governor Brogden named William W. Rollins as president and superintendent of the WNCRR, and W.R. Cannaday—the mayor of Wilmington, North Carolina—served as vice-president. Both Brogden and Cannaday deserve credit for their leadership that likely saved the WNCRR—or, at the very least, jump-started it back to life.

Governor Brogden was the first to suggest the use of convict labor for the WNCRR and was supported in this decision by the director of the North Carolina State Penitentiary System, Henry M. Miller, who complained that the state's prisons were terribly overcrowded and underbudgeted. The next governor, Zebulon B. Vance, not only agreed with this controversial decision but also later fully implemented it in 1877 with assistance from the state legislature. However, it should be noted that by late October 1875, the first convicts had already arrived in Old Fort and had begun working there. Governor Brogden deserves a large part of the credit—right or wrong—for that decision.

In many circles, the purchase of the railroad by the state was questioned as being a waste of taxpayer money, especially after the Littlefield and Swepson debacle. But the majority of North Carolinians realized the urgent need to resolve the situation and supported the purchase.

Nevertheless, as usual, politics again came into play, and in 1876, Democrats led by newly elected state assemblyman and Super Six member Major James Wilson demanded that all Republican leadership be removed from the WNCRR. Wilson and his supporters felt that an investigation was needed due to mismanagement of the project, primarily related to the supervision (or lack thereof) of the newly acquired convict labor force.

An investigation was conducted, and it was determined that there were indeed management problems, particularly with inmate supervision on the WNCRR. Public outcry from the investigation results, combined with other factors, resulted in the election of a Democratic governor—Super Six member Zeb Vance—in 1876, as well as a third term in 1877.

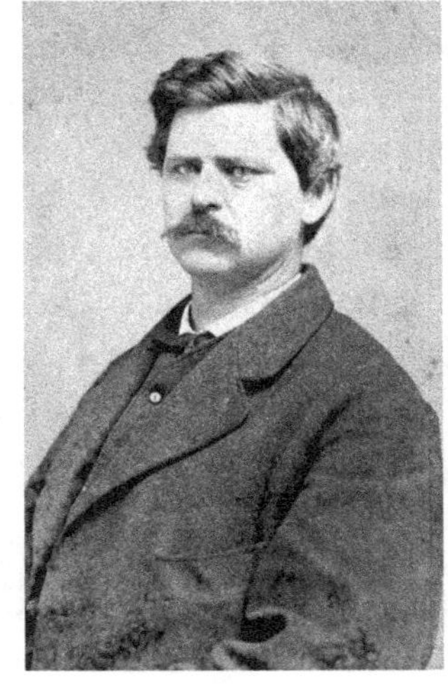

Governor Zebulon B. Vance. *UNC Archives.*

The WNCRR, yet again in trouble, seemed bound for oblivion until Zebulon Baird Vance, a native mountaineer born in Buncombe County, North Carolina, came to the rescue. Vance, one of the most beloved politicians in North Carolina history and probably the most popular and well-known member of the Super Six, led an interesting life. After obtaining his license to study law from UNC, Vance embarked on a legal career in 1858 before serving as a U.S. congressman from 1858 through 1861.

Although he did not support state secession and was opposed to the war, the battle at Fort

Sumter and Lincoln's call for troops in 1861 resulted in Vance enlisting in the Confederate army that same year.

Vance quickly earned the rank of captain and was later promoted to colonel, commanding the Twenty-Sixth North Carolina Regiment. Colonel Vance was commended for his bravery and leadership at the Battle of New Bern and the brutal Seven Days Battles near Richmond—both Confederate victories.

Vance resigned as an officer and was elected as governor of North Carolina for the first time in 1862, and he would eventually be elected as governor three different times before his death in 1894. As the war ground to an end, Governor Vance was arrested by Union forces on May 13, 1865, and imprisoned—for no reason—until July 6 in Washington, D.C. Vance was granted amnesty by President Andrew Johnson in 1867 but was not allowed to hold political office again until 1876.

Between 1867 and 1876, Vance resumed his career as an attorney. He represented Tom Dula (the inspiration of the famous folk song "Hang Down Your Head Tom Dooley"), who was charged with the murder of Laura Foster in 1868.

Despite Vance's regional popularity and skills as a barrister, Dula was convicted of murder and hanged in Statesville, North Carolina, on May 1, 1868. Vance nevertheless continued to practice law, but his passion was politics and he became a fierce advocate for the WNCRR, public education and veterans' rights. He was elected to a second term of governor in 1876 and a third term in 1877; he would later enjoy a long, distinguished career as a state senator from 1878 until his death.

One of Vance's first orders of business as governor in 1876 was to secure additional funding for the bankrupt WNCRR and clean up the mess left from the Swepson and Littlefield fraud scandal. The recent investigation regarding poor supervision of convict labor and overall mismanagement of the WNCRR by his Republican opponents also had to be addressed. Vance hoped to get the railroad partially running and use those funds to further supplement his pitiful budget.

In the meantime, Vance managed to scrape enough money together to resume the dormant railroad project but soon realized that the project remained badly underfunded and lacked an adequate labor force. Governor Vance arrived at two astute conclusions—one of which proved to be extremely controversial—that arguably saved the railroad.

An engineering plan was needed to devise a way to scale the steep grade that rose 1,100 feet in less than three miles from outside Old Fort, North

Carolina, across the Eastern Continental Divide to Ridgecrest. Vance had just the man for the job: Major James William Wilson, a fellow Civil War veteran and the third member of the Super Six.

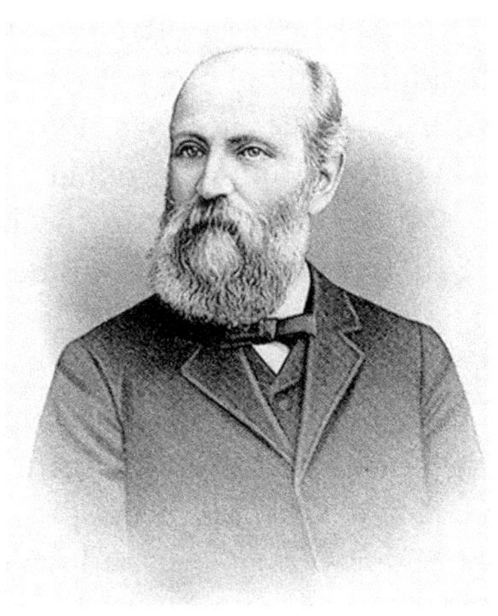
James Wilson. *UNC Archives.*

Governor Vance named Major Wilson president, chief engineer and general superintendent of the WNCRR Mountain Division project in 1877. Wilson was a wise choice, as he was already serving as Democratic state representative at that time and was a highly respected private contractor for the railroad.

Major James Wilson was native of Granville County, North Carolina, and graduated from UNC in 1852. Wilson began his illustrious railroading career as a civil engineer. He was first a rod man on the survey crew laying out the earliest route for the WNCRR and later was promoted to assistant engineer while working in Morganton, North Carolina, in 1856.

Wilson was on the fast track to railroading success when the Civil War began in 1861. Like many Tar Heel men his age, Wilson joined the Confederate army, eventually being promoted to captain in Company F of the Sixth North Carolina Regiment. Wilson was likely the most battle-hardened veteran of the Super Six team and certainly the most highly skilled engineer—no small feat among this esteemed group.

Wilson served with valor and saw heavy combat with the unit between 1862 and 1864 in major battles such as Cedar Creek, Chickamauga and the Seven Days. Despite being considered a Confederate victory, more than twenty thousand of Wilson's comrades, were killed, wounded, captured or went missing in action during the weeklong Battle of Seven Days in 1862. Wilson witnessed more than two thousand of his troops perish at yet another Confederate victory, Chickamauga, in 1863—a memory that haunted him the remainder of his life.

While serving his first term as governor of North Carolina in 1864, Governor Vance named Major Wilson—a fellow veteran and Democrat ally—as the superintendent of the WNCRR. Major Wilson was removed from the job by the Union government during the Reconstruction era but had remained working as a private contractor for the railroad through some of its darkest times after the war.

In his role as a private contractor, Major Wilson secured contracts for building some of the tunnels already planned for connecting the WNCRR with Asheville and was doing quite well as an independent businessman while also running for public office.

Wilson was elected to the North Carolina House of Representatives in 1876, further reinforcing his ties to the soon-to-be-reelected Governor Vance. The governor appreciated the skills of his talented friend and promoted him to head of the WNCRR project, which became known as "the Mountain Division" and would later connect with the still-to-be-built Murphy Branch.

Vance asked Major Wilson to refine the plans to cross the Swannanoa Gap and to manage the project. Vance's faith in Wilson was confirmed, as Major Wilson designed what is still considered a miracle of engineering today. He designed and built six tunnels and the infamous Loops while overseeing arguably the largest land-moving project in American history.

However, that miraculous plan would not have been completed without the assistance of Colonel Thaddeus Coleman, the fourth member of the Super Six. Governor Vance promoted Colonel Coleman to the position of Wilson's chief assistant on the WNCRR in 1877. It was yet another superb choice by Vance, as Wilson and Coleman proved to be a dynamic railroad building duo, and Coleman was undoubtedly Wilson's most valued associate and confidant.

Like Vance and Wilson, Colonel Coleman was a staunch Democrat and graduate of UNC. And like Vance, Coleman was a native of mountainous Buncombe County, North Carolina. Coleman also shared an impressive combat record with his fellow Super Six associates while serving as a Confederate officer in the Civil War. However, Coleman's greatest claim to fame was his assistance to Wilson in designing the railroad engineering marvel now known as "the Loops" and in the construction of six tunnels, numerous cuts and several trestles.

But even the best of plans are worthless without the money and manpower to execute them, and the state had neither. Vance realized that even with the recently secured additional funding, the project's budget remained woefully inadequate, and there was also not enough cheap labor available to do the job.

The project was precariously teetering toward yet another bankruptcy when Vance once again turned the tide by managing to secure more funding. Nevertheless, it still was not enough to pay for the project and solve the insufficient labor force.

Vance intensified his efforts to save the railroad, desperately searching for a way to supplement the already established convict cheap labor program.

Shortly after his third election as governor and after he promoted Major Wilson to WNCRR superintendent, Governor Vance made an impassioned plea to the North Carolina legislature requesting that the "entire available force of the penitentiary" system be delegated to work on the railroad for the "heartbroken Western people."

In other words, Vance planned to use a huge workforce consisting of almost entirely convicts to complete this dangerous project. He would empty the prison system if needed—"leaving only the feeble"—to secure the manpower needed to finish the job. The North Carolina legislature immediately approved Governor Vance's request for additional convict labor in 1877, and convict labor for railroad and highway projects would be common for years to come throughout the state.

Despite the controversy of using almost entirely inmate labor, the railroad would likely have never been completed had Vance not made this decision. And no one can question the wisdom of his hiring of the engineering genius Major James Wilson, who was also placed in charge of directing the new convict workforce eventually consisting of more than seven hundred inmates.

Thanks in large part to Vance's leadership and his promotion of Wilson, combined later with the incredible leadership skills of yet another Confederate

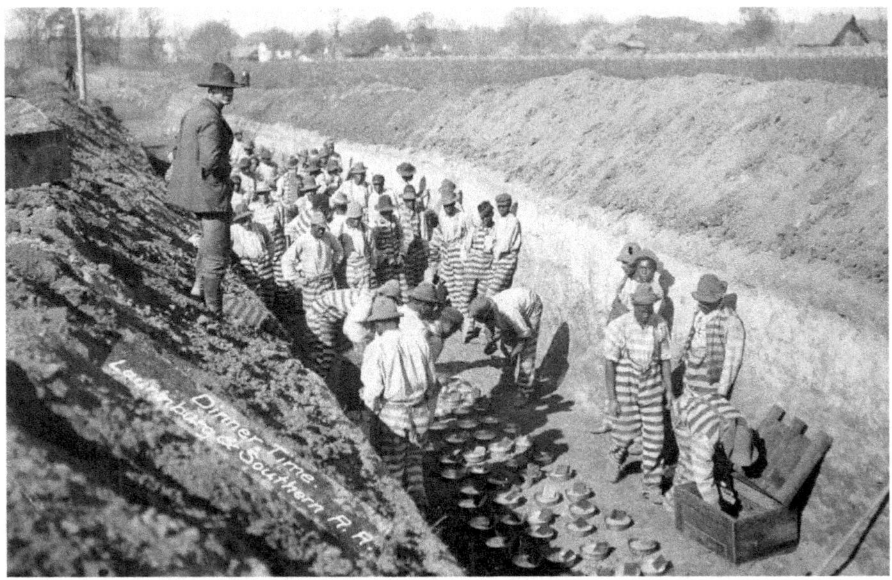

Convicts on lunch break working on railroad in Laurinburg, North Carolina. *UNC Archives.*

veteran, Colonel W.B. Andrews, the WNCRR project emerged from the ashes.

Many historians feel that Colonel Andrews was the most valuable member of the Super Six. However, it must be noted that the contributions of Colonel Andrews did not take place until *after* the railroad finally made it to Asheville. He had nothing to do with the Mountain Division project from Morganton to Ridgecrest. But regardless of his ranking, and despite some later political and business problems, few can deny Andrews's major contributions to Western North Carolina railroading.

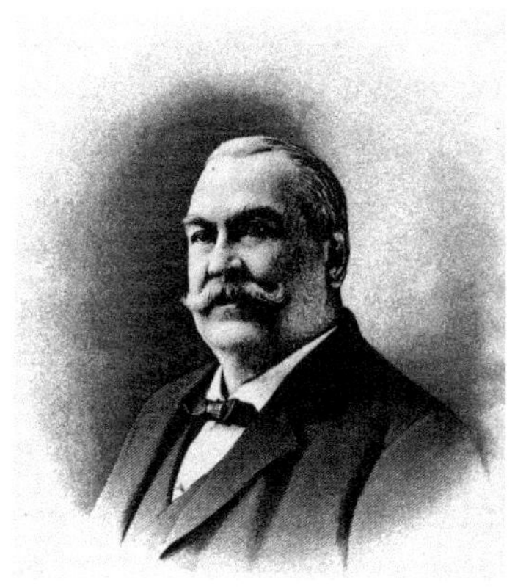

Colonel A.B. Andrews. *UNC Archives.*

Colonel Andrews—the fifth member of the Super Six—was born in Eastern North Carolina in 1841. At age seventeen, he was tragically orphaned and left school to work for his uncle, Philemon B. Hawkins, on the construction of the Blue Ridge Railroad near Pendleton, South Carolina.

It turned out to be a fortuitous move for the youngster, as Andrews was a natural railroader and possessed an incredible work ethic and keen intellect. He exceled in numerous jobs, eventually being promoted to general superintendent of the project shortly before the Civil War began in 1861. Andrews quit the job to enlist in Company E of the First North Carolina Cavalry in the Confederate army.

Andrew's courage and skills as a leader were apparent, and he was promoted to captain in 1862. Andrews saw extensive action in major conflicts during the war before being severely wounded—shot through his left lung—in the 1863 Battle of Jack's Shop, one of the bloodiest battles of the war. Andrews's commanding officer later said, "There is no braver or better man than the gallant Captain Andrews." Andrews required a long recovery period from his wound, a d this forced his retirement from the army in 1864.

Andrews returned home penniless after the war and borrowed $100 to start a successful ferry business in Weldon, North Carolina. This job eventually led him back to his true passion: railroading. Between 1866 and 1877, Andrews, a lifelong Democrat, worked in a variety of high-level railroad jobs, drawing the admiration and respect of Governor Vance.

The two powerful men made a formidable team that proved mutually beneficial to them both between 1877 and 1881; more importantly, it resurrected the railroad project. Unfortunately, they later became enemies, but not before partnering in the completion of a project that economically revolutionized life in Western North Carolina and indeed the entire state.

Despite his differences with Governor Vance, Andrews was later instrumental in the completion of the line not only to Asheville and Paint Rock, Tennessee, but also all the way to the town of Murphy—the namesake of the Murphy Branch. Under the masterful management of Andrews, the railroad later fully repaid the State of North Carolina more than $600,000 spent on the project.

However, none of these things would have happened were it not for the engineering miracle we now refer to simply as "the Loops." Even today, almost 150 years later, the story of the building of "the Loops"—the six tunnels and the tracks from Old Fort to Ridgecrest—is told with awe and respect. And it likely never would have happened were it not for the efforts of three of the six members of the Super Six: Governor Vance, Major Wilson and Colonel Coleman.

Nor would the remainder of the Murphy Branch ever have been completed were it not for the contributions of the youngest member of the Super Six, Will Sandlin, who we will discuss in detail later, along with Colonel Andrews. But first, let's look at how "the Loops" were built—the latest major obstacle in the completion of the WNCRR and the Murphy Branch.

THE LOOPS AND LIGHT AT THE TUNNEL'S END

John "Jack" Pence tightly reined in his six-horse team, attempting to slow them down while adding heavy pressure on the stagecoach brake lever as he began the precarious journey down the mountain from Ridgecrest to Henry Station. It was late 1878, and Pence, the senior drover and star employee of Clemmons Great Western Stage line, had been running this precipitous route since 1859. But it never got easier for him.

Although he had never experienced an accident in his long, illustrious career, Pence lived in constant fear of his massive Concord stagecoach, pulled by his team of six white horses, and its passengers and mail careening off a cliff to their deaths in the valley below.

The coach carried nine passengers inside and had the capability of that many or more riding on top along with the mail bags. Pence made the trip daily from Henry Station to Ridgecrest—where they changed out their horses—and then on to Asheville and Wolf Creek, Tennessee, the head of the Cumberland Gap and S&O Railroad. Another stage departed Asheville daily for the return trip to Henry Station, located west of Old Fort.

Pence routinely drove both routes. On a good day, the six-mile journey to Ridgecrest took more than three hours, with the even scarier return trip taking that long or longer. Pence preferred making the return trip at night so his passengers could not see that they were often less than a foot away from certain death most of the way back to Henry Station.

Navigating the dangerous road daily, Pence, more than most, surely understood the folly of attempting to build a railroad over and through this mountain range. It just did not seem possible. After all, more than six years after the completion of the Transcontinental Railroad, the WNCRR remained stalled—as it had been for decades in the North Carolina foothills.

Being illiterate, Pence probably knew nothing about the newspaper reports of the Western North Carolina railroad's progress and tragedies. Yet he likely had heard stories about it. Nevertheless, Jack Pence almost certainly felt secure in his job, even though he could see the fires and lanterns twinkling from numerous convict work camps in the valley below. These convicts were in the process of building the railroad from Henry Station to Asheville and beyond.

The first convict workers arrived at Henry Station on October 19, 1875. The initial group of 35 inmates immediately began to build a stockade and living quarters for themselves, as well as chopping wood for heat and cooking. Over the next twelve months, 265 male inmates and 16 female prisoners joined them, bringing their total number to 316 by November 16, 1876. The female inmates served mostly as cooks, maids and seamstresses and operated a laundry.

Clothed in the distinctive and standard black-and-yellow-striped convict attire, the inmate work crews were hard to miss. So, too, was their skin color,

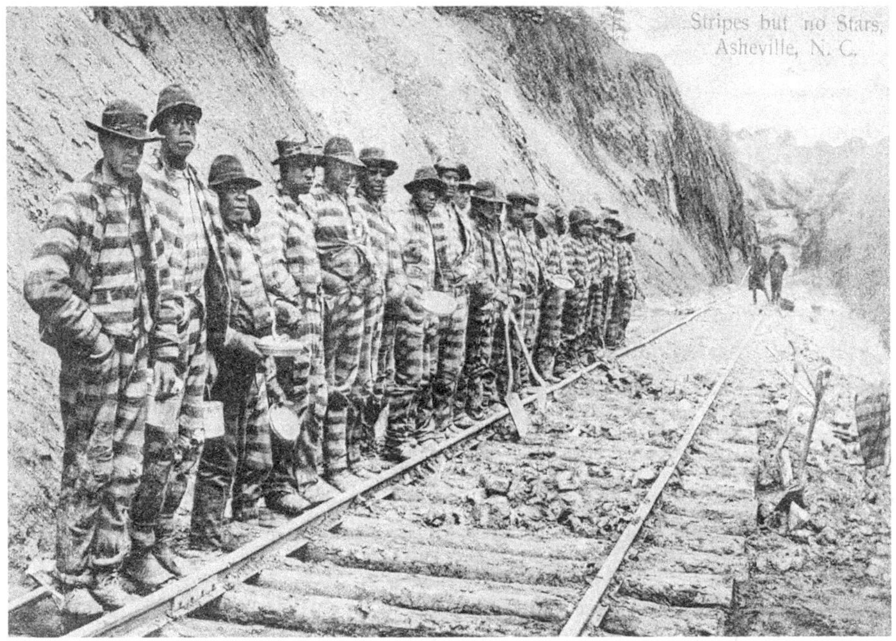

An 1880s photo of convicts and guards near Asheville. *UNC Archives.*

as most of them were Black men from Eastern North Carolina, involuntarily working in an area where few Black folks resided.

A casual review of the inmate records—particularly those of convicts later killed in various accidents such as the Swannanoa incident on the Mountain Division and the Cowee Tunnel tragedy on the Murphy Branch—clearly indicates that many of them were likely only guilty of minor crimes such as loitering or vagrancy. At least some of them were arrested for nothing more than the color of their skin or for being poor men in the wrong place at the wrong time. But to be fair, there were more than few hardened criminals among their ranks as well, although they were likely in the minority. Even so, it does not excuse the harsh treatment they all endured, nor the reasons some were incarcerated.

In many ways, this inmate workforce was legalized slavery. But regardless of how it is categorized, the brutal treatment of these inmates and the inhumane working conditions in which they were forced to live and work is unimaginably horrible. Even in this turbulent post–Civil War era, people were understandably critical of this decision—but not enough to stop it.

These initial groups of convicts were dispatched by Governor Curtis Brogden. The decision, which was controversial from the start, further intensified with claims of Republican mismanagement of the project by their Democratic opponents.

The ensuing investigation later verified some of these mismanagement claims, and Governor Vance's third term as a Democratic governor in 1877 allowed him the opportunity to take full control of the WNCRR project while further increasing the volume of inmate labor.

The convicts were referred to as "creatures" in an 1876 report and were considered to be expendable inhuman tools. Vance added that the cost of jailing prisoners was much higher than working them in the mountains. The governor promised to empty the prisons, if need be, to complete the railroad and vowed to keep a minimum of five hundred convicts working on the project until it was completed.

Vance proved true to his word. After Governor Brogden ordered the first convict camp built west of Henry Station at Round Knob in 1875, the newly elected Vance ordered four more camps built at different locations as the railroad progressed up the mountain in 1876 and 1877.

The first three camps—Round Knob Stockade, Lick Log Stockade and Top of Mountain Stockade—all housed 125 convicts or more. Two more camps—the Long Branch Stockade and the Tomahawk Stockade—were subsequently added, each housing close to 100 prisoners each.

In 1875 alone, twenty-six inmates died working on the WNCRR. Four were killed in accidents or shot trying to escape, while the other twenty-two convicts succumbed to disease, injury or exposure. And that number would do nothing but increase over the next fifteen years.

By 1878, there were 766 inmates working in the Mountain Division of the WNCRR, more than 90 percent of them Black men, the majority being from Eastern North Carolina. The work crews were usually segmented into two categories: tree gangs and diggers.

The tree gangs built their own camps and worked full time cutting wood for fires, crossties, bridge supports and other construction-related needs for the duration of the project. Just as their name implied, the focus of the digger crews was to move and excavate dirt as they worked on achieving the proper grade, digging tunnels and cuts and laying track.

The convict totals varied on the Murphy Branch and Mountain Division depending on the year and number of inmates rotated in as replacements, as did the camp locations or sleeping arrangements, but the work was the same in all locations, although the terrain varied.

The inmate workforce had earlier been split into two large crews. Crew Number One's objective was to get the railroad finally connected from Old Fort to Asheville while working at it from both ends—from Asheville toward Swannanoa Gap and from Old Fort to Swannanoa Gap. Crew Number Two focused on connecting the WNCRR from Asheville to Paint Rock, where it could connect with the Cumberland Gap and S&O RR in Wolf Creek, Tennessee. The second crew had a much less difficult job, as its route followed the river valley northwest through Marshall and Hot Springs and on to the Tennessee border, but it was far from easy.

Henry M. Miller oversaw all convict labor. Overall work management for both crews and planning for same was handled by crew supervisors or managers, also known as "walking bosses." They, in turn, had assistants, referred to as "captains." The walking bosses and their captains reported directly to Mr. Miller, although Major Wilson and Colonel Coleman instructed them daily as to their expectations. Each captain was responsible for about twelve men, and each of these crews was usually assigned an additional guard, armed, to oversee the work.

Work crews—diggers or tree gangs—were supervised by guards at the same ratio of twelve inmates per guard, meaning there were usually about sixty-five guards working full time. They were authorized to shoot to kill any attempted escapees, and disciplinary action for any sort of infraction—real or imagined—was brutal and swift.

For lesser infractions, convicts were "black marked," meaning that time was added to their prison sentences as punishment. More serious offenses warranted physical retribution. Inmates were often beaten with fists or whipped with a leather strap at the discretion of the guards.

Guards on the WNCRR were paid thirteen dollars per month, while a guard working at the prison in Raleigh made almost twice that amount at twenty-five dollars per month. To the railroad and the government, it was a matter of simple economics. Inmate and guard labor were far cheaper than public labor, and it was much more expensive to feed and house convicts in prison than on the WNCRR.

Furthermore, the WNCRR still paid the state about one dollar per day per inmate, ultimately resulting in a substantial source of income to the state. And the contract carefully stipulated that the WNCRR was in no way liable for inmate deaths, injuries or mistreatment. It was indeed legalized slavery.

No matter how you classify it and regardless of their job description or who was in charge, guards and inmates started working before dawn daily and never stopped until after dark—except for Saturday, when work ended around 4:00 p.m. Guard staff also worked at night to oversee the sleeping inmates and prevent escapes. If required, convicts worked seven days, but usually they were given Sunday off to recover and prepare as needed for the upcoming workweek.

Weather had a minimal impact on their schedule. It took a two-foot snowstorm to cancel work, and even then, management was still upset. Accidents such as cave-ins or landslides were a constant threat to inmates' health. Under the best of circumstances, with no injuries or deaths, the landslides resulted in extra cleanup work for the crews. It was a grueling, often terrifying job that never seemed to end. One writer described the working conditions as "wretched."

Inmates were fed twice daily. On good days, their total rations consisted of eight ounces of bacon, twenty-two ounces of ground meal and either one pound of potatoes or half a pound of peas, washed down with cheap coffee made from coffee beans, rye and molasses. At least, this was what was budgeted. Costs were often cut to provide the prisoners with nothing more than navy beans and cornbread for their daily sustenance. Black strap molasses was considered a special treat or reward.

An 1878 budget report indicated that the total labor cost of supporting Mountain Division inmates was barely thirty cents per inmate per day. Seven cents went to food, ten cents for guard pay and about thirteen cents for miscellaneous costs such as clothing, medical attention and so on. (If you add in tools, machine and parts costs to this total, you get about another seventy cents per inmate, bringing the grand total daily operating cost per convict to ninety-eight cents. And these costs remained constant for the most part on the Murphy Branch until its completion.)

Aside from being allowed to work outdoors—usually more than twelve hours daily—most convicts likely would have preferred to stay in prison. They were forced to work in any weather and regardless of how they felt. Only seriously ill inmates were given doctor-approved rest. The primary convict physician, Dr. W.A. Collett, reported that the physical condition of the inmates was "comparatively very good."

His replacement, Dr. H.F. Burgin, stated in 1879 that the convict housing was "suitable" and that it was "cleaned and limed daily." Dr. Burgin added that the primary ailments of inmates were due to exposure and that 7 percent were on the sick list daily. Punishment for refusing to work was severe. However, some inmates routinely chose punishment over work, yet another indicator of the brutal nature of the job.

Under the best of conditions, building this railroad would have been a major achievement. But considering the harsh conditions that this involuntary workforce was subjected to for almost two decades, their accomplishments are miraculous.

By 1879, the WNCRR was employing 1,455 men—588 of them convicts, along with 16 female prisoners and 464 paid contract workers, including guards, foremen and engineers, as well as 403 teenage boys used for miscellaneous lighter work or errands. The workforce was supported by 560 carts, 50 wagons, 780 horses and 44 oxen.

Let's briefly outline what the WNCRR workforce achieved from 1875 until late 1880 in the Mountain Division, and in later chapters, we will discuss their accomplishments—led in part by Will Sandlin—on the Murphy Branch until 1891.

Earlier, we discussed the relatively simple but physically demanding process of laying railroad tracks. But even the best-laid railroad tracks won't work if the grade is not properly calculated. To fully appreciate the difficulty building the WNCRR and the Murphy Branch, we must first understand what the term *grade* really means and how it applies to efficient railroad operations.

In layman's terms, grade refers to the steepness of the railroad (or any kind of road) bed. A 4 percent grade indicates that rails climb four feet vertically for every one hundred feet of horizontal travel. Grade percentage greatly affects the pulling power of a steam (or diesel) locomotive. A 1 percent grade requires three times the normal pulling power it takes to pull that same load on level ground. Curvature of tracks also affects grade and is expressed in degrees as well. Even the slightest of engineering grade miscalculations can be catastrophic at worst—at best, it can make the railroad inoperable and require work being redone.

Not only do these mathematical and structural engineering calculations have to be considered in railroad planning, but geological knowledge is required as well. A soil evaluation must be done to determine soil types, how the dirt drains and how much weight it can handle on the rails and how the ground will react to this sort of pressure.

Soil composition must also be taken into consideration. Solid rock was a severe challenge that could be addressed with chisels or explosives. But an even worse geological obstacle was soil known locally as "white mud." As the name implies, white mud was light-colored wet clay and kaolin with the consistency of jelly or thick mud. In limited amounts, wooden or stone barriers could be constructed by the inmates to stabilize it or hold it back from adversely affecting level and stable railway grades.

In larger amounts, it had to be hauled away in massive loads until it was gone. Rail beds mistakenly built on white mud had been known to raise or lower as much as ten feet or more over night, unacceptable for any sort of construction requiring a firm foundation. White mud was often prevalent on narrow, steep ridges that were too thin to tunnel through. In these cases, the soil had to be removed in massive amounts by hand, literally removing as much soil as necessary to meet grade requirements. These excavations, done by cutting huge gashes into the mountainside, were called "cuts." The steep cuts were notoriously unstable even with good soil composition but were especially tricky when consisting of white mud. (These problems persist today with the same issues on state roads and interstate highways—landslides often result in road closings in the Nantahala Gorge and Pigeon River Gorge.)

It's doubtful that Super Six members Major James Wilson and Colonel Thad Coleman had much of a geological background, but they knew railroad construction inside and out and they were geniuses when it came to engineering. That knowledge, combined with an unlimited disposable workforce, proved to be incredibly effective in getting an impossible job done.

With inmates housed and operating as the railroad construction advanced, the next step in this process was always clearing additional land to lay more tracks and making grading adjustments as needed, following the plan and survey laid out by Wilson and Coleman. Different types of grading and road preparation were needed depending on the location, which varied greatly geographically and was almost constantly rising in elevation. But the process was always basically the same throughout the construction of the WNCRR and the Murphy Branch and would ultimately include two of the steepest railroad grades in eastern America.

Depending on the plan and location, this could mean inmate work crews had to dig through a cut by hand, using only pickaxes and shovels, adding or eliminating fill dirt for elevation. Building bridges over streams and ravines were common; they not only had to build the bridge, but they also had to cut the lumber needed to construct it. Having to chisel or blast through solid rock to build a tunnel or clear a cut was unimaginably difficult, but at least rock, unlike white mud, was relatively stable—dangerous, but stable. Working with white mud was more unpredictable. And the dust inmates inhaled from grinding rocks often resulted in serious lung disease years later.

One especially treacherous area notorious for white mud was on the eastern slope of Swannanoa Mountain. It was known as Mud Cut and had to be redone at least three times before 1879. Sometimes drainage systems, ingeniously designed by Major Wilson, were utilized to divert existing stream flow, sluicing away unstable ground or mud and thus adding even more work for the convicts—and setting the project even further behind schedule, raising the ire of politicians and their constituents, who as North Carolina citizens technically owned the railroad.

Many experts now believe that this removal of more than 80,000 cubic yards of soil, followed by another 110,000 cubic yards removed after three subsequent avalanches, was the largest land-moving project in the United States. That is debatable, but it almost certainly was the largest earthmoving project ever done up until that time. And don't forget that in that relatively short span of less than fifteen miles, it was almost all done by hand.

The route from Henry Station west to the Round Knob Stockade was mostly flat and straight. But that changed quickly where the Loops began near what is now Andrews Geyser—west of present-day Old Fort. In order to keep the track grade level enough for train operation, the Loops had to be very winding and curvy. Most of the engineering marvel now called the Loops is within a five-mile section just east of where the six tunnels were later built.

The track—all graded and built by inmates—begins to rise just above Andrews Geyser and starts to curl or loop like a snake as it climbs the mountain. The track was built with an amazing curvature of 2,776.4 degrees—the equivalent of *eight* complete circles! It winds so much that the

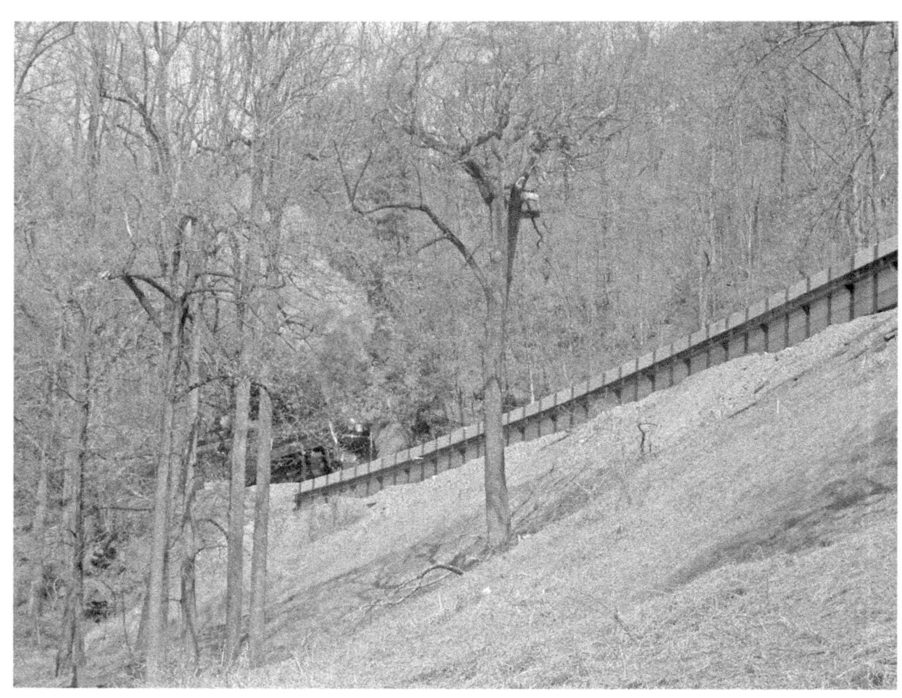

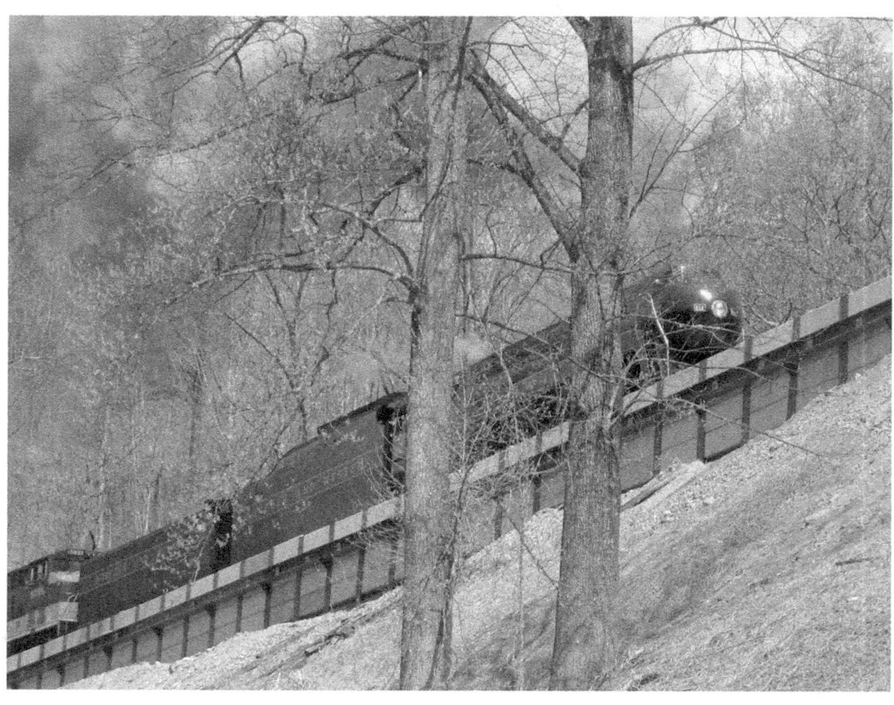

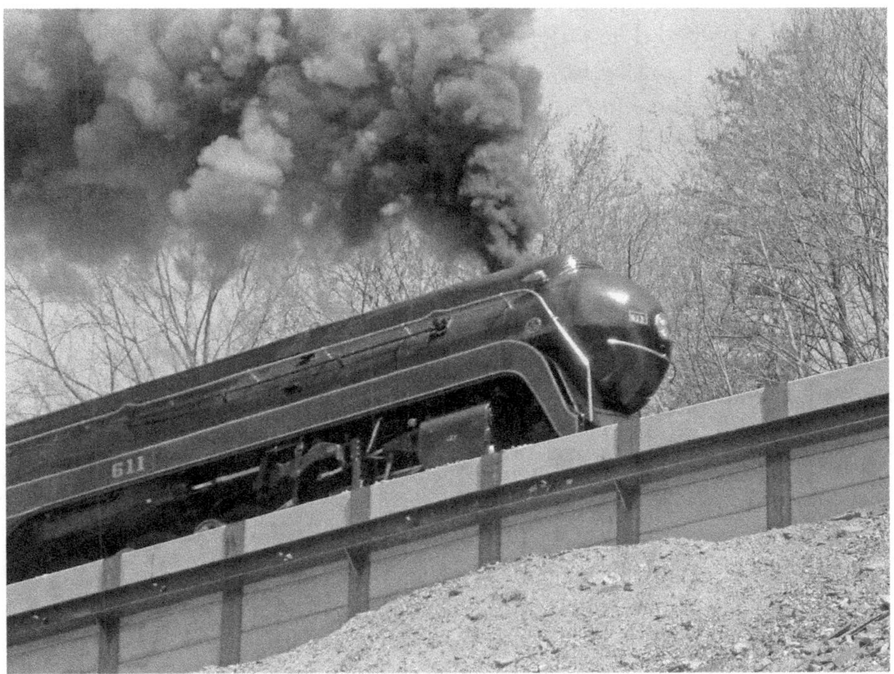

This page and opposite: No. 611 on the Loops west of Old Fort. *JMP Photos.*

valley below can be seen in five different places—the exact *same* location on *different* opposite sides of the track!

Bad weather—heavy rain, hailstorms, snow and sleet—in addition to white mud caused repeated landslides and slowed work down drastically. And even in good conditions, progress was slow, yet Major Wilson, Colonel Coleman and their inmate brigade fought their way up the mountain, ready to tackle even more difficult obstacles: the building of six tunnels.

Construction of the western portals of several tunnels had begun as early as 1868, with work done by private contractors, including Major Wilson's own company before he returned to work with the WNCRR. But the bulk of work and completion of the tunnels was the result of the inmate Mountain Division.

By 1876, work had begun in earnest on the following six tunnels. Jarrett's, first called Long Branch, is 125 feet long. Lick Log, named for a nearby cattle salt lick housed in a log, is 562 feet in length. The shortest of the six tunnels, McElroy, is 89 feet long. The High Ridge Tunnel, so named for the ridge it penetrated, is 494 feet long. Climbing closer to the Gap is the Burgin

Tunnel at 252 feet. The largest of the six, the Swannanoa Tunnel, 1,800 feet, is located at the mouth of the Swannanoa Gap, which is technically considered to be the end of the storied Mountain Division.

All six of the tunnels had to be at least 15 feet in height, in order to accommodate the tall smokestacks on the steam engines, and at least 12 feet wide. That comes out to a total of 3,322 feet of solid rock that had to be dug and blasted out of the mountains creating tunnels big enough to safely accommodate a train. How did they do it? The work began with pickaxes, powered by blood, sweat and tears. When explosives were required, they first used the hot/cold blasting method and eventually became the very first operation to utilize nitroglycerin in the Land of Blue Smoke.

Dynamite—originally called Nobel's Blasting Powder after its inventor, Swedish chemist Alfred Nobel—was not invented until 1867. Nobel continued the work of Italian inventor Ascanio Sobneno—who invented nitroglycerin in 1847—to develop dynamite, as well as an improved version of nitroglycerin. (As a historical side note, Nobel later became so distraught over the use of his inventions for war and destruction that he created the prestigious Nobel Peace Prize to promote world peace.)

Dynamite and nitroglycerin were more powerful and easier to manage than black powder, but both were expensive. Therefore, the Mountain Division initially preferred using a more primitive, but cheaper, method of excavating rock known as hot-cold blasting. It required no explosives—only fire, water and a lot of muscle. It was a method supposedly first used by the Cherokee tribe, who shared their knowledge with the earliest white settlers.

When a rock or tunnel was found that was too big to move or too difficult to chisel through, the inmates built huge fires fueled by pine logs that burned hot and fast on the rock surface and/or walls. Once the stone became almost molten, the rock was doused with buckets of cold water by the convicts, causing the boulders to crack.

The inmates then removed the cracked rock by chiseling it out and carrying it outside by hand. Larger stone masses often required multiple fires to break, and breaking or excavating the stone was only the first part of the process.

All the debris then had to be carried out to clear the grade or tunnel. And that work was done by hand as well, as inmates loaded wagons with rock, while another eight to ten inmates—who were deemed by management to be the equivalent of one mule—pulled them away. Stone-laden wheelbarrows, also powered by men, were used for earth removal. It was backbreaking and dangerous work, and aside from daylight, the only illumination in the dark, dusty tunnels was provided by candles made by the inmates.

It soon became clear that a more effective and faster method of stone removal was necessary—especially in the tunnels. In these cases, inmates would drill narrow, round holes two feet deep into the stone and then carefully pack the holes with nitroglycerin mash—also known as Nitro Mash.

Raw nitroglycerin is a liquid explosive and is extremely powerful and volatile even in small amounts. It had been banned for railroad transport in 1866 after an explosion blew up a Wells Fargo office and killed fifteen people during construction of the Transcontinental Railroad.

To make it a bit easier and safer to use—and, just as importantly, to get more economical use out of smaller amounts—Major Wilson instructed the inmates to mix their own Nitro Mash. It was made with small, carefully measured amounts of nitroglycerin and mixed with equal parts of sawdust and cornmeal, producing a pliable mash like plastic explosives used by the U.S. military today.

A shed was constructed a safe distance from the Round Knob Stockade specifically for this purpose. Under the supervision of engineer James Cambar, inmate work crews eventually produced about eighteen thousand pounds of Nitro Mash in the building starting in 1877.

As work on the WNCRR continued, explosive shacks were a constant presence near most convict camps on the Murphy Branch. In the event of an accident, the shacks were always built far enough from camp to ensure only those working in the shack would be injured or killed. And in accordance with the law passed after the 1866 Wells Fargo tragedy, explosives were transported from the shack to the work site only by a wagon driven by an inmate, with a guard riding behind for safety to minimize losses in the event of an accidental explosion. Future Super Six member Will Sandlin lived nearby at Henry Station. As a child, Sandlin began his education in both railroading and explosives at the Round Knob Stockade's explosive shed. But let's get back to the explosive process used to build tunnels.

Once the holes were drilled in the base of the rocks and filled with Nitro Mash, a crude detonating fuse was improvised by the inmates. They carefully cleared a narrow path filled with tinder (dried leaves, pine needles or twigs) directly to the rock hole and filled the rest of the hole with tinder too. They lit the tinder with a torch and ran for cover before a good portion of the mountainside exploded.

Between 1876 and 1879, thirty-eight inmates died or were killed—some of natural causes but most of them work related—while working on the

Loops, cuts, railroad and tunnels. Countless others were injured to varying degrees. Forty-two managed to escape, while almost one hundred others were pardoned or discharged.

Official reports vary pertaining to the number of convicts killed in work-related incidents by the time the WNCRR eventually reached Murphy—ranging from actual accidents and disease to prisoners being shot. Unofficial reports indicate that the death total was at least 461. No one will ever know for sure, as prison records were notoriously inaccurate and the dead were casually cast aside to rest for eternity in unmarked graves. And keep in mind that these casualties are just for this project. Convict works crews for public works were common well into the early twentieth century.

While these casualty numbers are tragic, considering the difficulty and magnitude of the job, it is amazing that they were not higher. And even more so when you consider the incredible task the inmates accomplished in the summer of 1877 to speed up completion of the massive Swannanoa Tunnel.

After completing the construction of five tunnels, Major Wilson was frustrated by the difficulty of removing debris from the tunnels by inmate power. Under fire by politicians in Raleigh, he decided that there was a more efficient method available. Wilson ordered the one wood-burning steam engine owned by the WNCRR, known as the Salisbury, to be moved to the western portal of the sixth and largest tunnel, the Swannanoa Tunnel.

It had been under construction since 1868 and was the last major obstacle for the WNCRR Mountain Division. There was, however, one major problem: there was no way to move the engine up to the western portal except by utilizing manpower and draft animals.

The massive locomotive had to literally be pushed and pulled ten miles overland across the summit of Swannanoa Gap to the western slope of Swannanoa Mountain in the Valley of Eagle Rock. Using nothing more than inmate muscle, combined with a few mules, block and tackle and several yokes of oxen to assist them, the convicts somehow managed to lift the Salisbury from its permanent tracks onto some hastily constructed temporary tracks that they had spiked directly to the ground.

Once the engine was placed on the temporary track, the inmates then embarked on the impossible task of pushing and pulling the bulky two-hundred-ton locomotive up the mountain, partially following the stage road driven daily by Jack Pence from Henry Station to Ridgecrest at the top of the mountain.

As they pushed and pulled their way up the old stage road, another group of inmates removed the temporary track behind the train and moved it to the front to advance the engine farther up the mountain. This process was continually replicated until their destination was reached. Pulling the engine up the grade was terribly difficult, but it was equally as hard trying to carefully control the locomotive on downhill stretches as well. There was no break in this tedious and dangerous process.

Track was already in place at the western portal of the Swannanoa Tunnel, so when the Salisbury arrived in the summer of 1877, it was placed in position to pull cars filled with debris out of the western portal, as well as transport supplies from the Swannanoa Valley to the tunnel. Meanwhile, work continued in the eastern portal as well, excavating and moving soil and rock by hand or by explosives. The plan was for the two crews to eventually meet in the middle.

Even with the assistance of the Salisbury, it took almost two years for the two crews to finally connect on March 11, 1879. It was an accomplishment—not just the tunnel, but the entire project—that few believed would ever happen aside from Major Wilson and Colonel Coleman. But it was not without great human loss.

With the tunnel nearly completed on March 11, 1879, engineer Jack Edwards carefully backed the Salisbury into the western portal of the Swannanoa Tunnel with plans to remove the remaining debris from the tunnel to clear the tracks. He had just pulled the Salisbury outside the tunnel when the roof caved in on the remainder of the train, killing a guard named Ellison along with twenty unnamed inmates trapped inside.

Edwards and the steam locomotive were unharmed, and work crews immediately removed the debris and dead bodies from the tunnel. The guard's body was sent home to his family for burial, while the dead convicts were quickly interred in unmarked graves—cast aside like garbage with little thought given to their next of kin. The crew finished the job of clearing the tracks and tunnel of debris with minimal fanfare.

Little was written about the terrible accident; as always, completing the job was priority number one with the WNCRR, no matter the human toll. The Salisbury would later be used as one of the first steam engines working on WNCRR and Murphy Branch upon its completion in 1891.

After the tracks were cleared and the bodies disposed of, Major Wilson sent Governor Vance an understated telegram notifying him of the momentous tunnel completion on March 11, 1879. The telegram reads in part: "Daylight entered Buncombe County today through the Swannanoa

Tunnel. Grade and Centers meet exactly." Wilson made no mention of the tragedy that took place that same day—either before or after the telegram was sent. Depending on which report is believed, some say the cave-in occurred prior to the telegram being sent, while another report indicates that the accident took place after. But either way, no mention was made of the loss. Finishing the tunnel was all that mattered.

After almost eleven years of work—from the time the first tracks were laid at the base of Swannanoa Mountain to the top at Ridgecrest—and a quarter of century since its inception, the hardest part of the WNCRR project was finally done.

The next stop was Asheville, and their arrival on October 3, 1880, was met with tremendous public accolades. But it came at a terrific price personally and economically. At least 125 inmates and 1 guard had died building the WNCRR from Old Fort to Asheville. And countless others had been maimed for life in ways that left them permanently handicapped, along with hundreds more who likely later died of job-related lung disease.

Even with the cheap convict labor, it was estimated that a little more than $2 million was spent on the project—a tremendous amount of money at any time, but an astronomical amount for the late 1800s and the equivalent of $50 million today. Nevertheless, it would have cost twice that much, maybe more, had the job been done without inmate labor.

There was no time for the WNCRR to rest on its laurels or despair over lives lost. As usual, it was behind schedule and over budget. Little did it know that an entirely new set of political and geographical challenges awaited beyond Asheville on the 121-mile line that would be known simply as the Murphy Branch.

COLONEL ANDREWS TO THE RESCUE

Governor Vance had moved on to the U.S. Senate after resigning as governor in 1879 but remained a staunch advocate of the WNCRR in his new political role. Thomas Jarvis had served as lieutenant governor under Vance and replaced Vance as governor in 1879. Like Vance, Jarvis was Democrat, and like his former boss, he was constantly under fire from Republican opponents for a variety of issues—most notably mismanagement of the railroad's inmate workforce, for which he and Major Wilson were investigated and acquitted.

The fact that the WNCRR was a state-owned operation only made these allegations worse—an operation that even with cheap convict labor was constantly behind schedule and over budget and had been for almost a quarter of a century. Taxpayer patience was wearing thin, and politicians from both parties—depending on what party was in charge at the time—feverishly fanned the flames in opposition of the WNCRR, or at least in how it was operated.

Once again, even with the recent success in finally reaching Asheville, the situation looked dire for the WNCRR until Super Six member Colonel Alexander Boyd Andrews came to the rescue. Andrews had resumed his railroading career after the Civil War and had served as superintendent of two major railroad operations—the Raleigh and Gaston Railroad and the Richmond and Danville Railroad—for several years following the war.

While successfully managing these operations, Andrews carefully cultivated and built a powerful network of business and political allies, including

Governor Vance and Lieutenant Governor Thomas Jarvis. Andrews served in Vance's cabinet in several leadership positions, as well as on the state railroad commission.

With the WNCRR project being under more political and public duress than ever, Governor Jarvis had turned to Colonel Andrews for help in 1879 and placed him in charge of the business. It should be noted, however, that Andrews and Jarvis were both smart enough to keep Major Wilson and Colonel Coleman in their operations management roles as chief engineer and assistant chief engineer, respectively.

It is not clear if Major Wilson and Colonel Andrews were friends prior to their employment on the WNCRR. But the two were lifelong friends from that point forward. Wilson quickly became one of Andrews's most trusted confidants. Colonel Andrews wisely allowed his friend to oversee RR operations, while Andrews focused on the business side of things.

Despite the endless political turmoil, Major Wilson and Colonel Coleman celebrated the WNCRR arrival in Asheville on October 3, 1880. It was a momentous occasion for Western North Carolina. The railroad not only connected the North Carolina coast to Asheville but also would soon connect it to the Midwest and beyond. It was also the first time the Land of Blue Smoke had a legitimate platform with which to conduct business and pleasure in other parts of the state.

Whereas the Clemmons Stagecoach could only bring the mail and about eighteen passengers daily to Asheville, steam trains could now bring one hundred or more passengers and tons of freight to the mountain city daily. And they achieved these results in a much faster and much safer fashion.

Plus, with the capability to run daily freight and passenger trains to Asheville, the WNCRR for the first time could be run like a business and, ideally, turn a profit. This would be huge in not only growing the business but also repaying debt to the state. We will discuss the massive economic impact the WNCRR and Murphy Branch had on the region in upcoming chapters.

Understanding the positive impact the project had on the region as we do today, it is hard to imagine how close the WNCRR came to stopping in Asheville due to public outcry and political infighting. But to be fair, the operation had dragged on for decades with no end in sight and was seen by many as an inhumane operation and a bottomless money pit funded at the expense of the citizens of North Carolina. Many of these same citizens no longer sympathized with the plight of their mountain brethren or, even if they did, were no longer willing to fund it.

With Colonel Andrews now at the helm and the dynamic duo of Major Wilson and Colonel Coleman planning and managing the actual work, the pieces were finally in place to resolve this dilemma, but not before additional political strife ensued.

Colonel Andrews recognized that the best way to get the public support back on their side was to sell the railroad to private investors, thus eliminating all state involvement and costs. Senator Vance and Governor Jarvis agreed and gave Andrews permission to pursue investors within his large network of business associates. But the politicians remained insistent that the state loan of more than $500,000 be repaid in a timely manner as part of the deal.

William J. Best, a wealthy New Yorker and friend of Colonel Andrews's, agreed to the terms to buy majority stock of the WNCRR while enlisting a host of other investors to assist him. The North Carolina General Assembly approved the purchase on March 20, 1880, with one major additional stipulation: Best had to complete the WNCRR route to Ducktown, Tennessee, by January 1, 1885, or forfeit the purchase, and he still had to repay the massive state loan.

With Major Wilson and Colonel Coleman at the helm, the WNCRR convict crews focused on completing the Northern Branch of the WNCRR toward Paint Rock and Wolf Creek, Tennessee. With no need for tunnel construction and few issues with switchbacks or steep grades, the project moved at a faster pace. Nevertheless, the work was difficult, and the job remained behind schedule and overbudget.

Investors concerned with the possibility of not meeting the construction deadline and financial terms of the agreement began to bail out on Mr. Best and Colonel Andrews. Just when it seemed bankruptcy and/or forfeiture of the deal was a certainty, Colonel Andrews negotiated a deal with his former employer, the Richmond and Danville RR, to loan Mr. Best the money he needed to survive.

But there was one caveat: failure to repay the loan on time resulted in the Richmond and Danville RR (R&D RR) taking full ownership of the WNCRR. Best was also named president of the WNCRR as part of the agreement. Best remained optimistic that he could make the deal work but further compounded problems when he became embroiled in a feud with North Carolina politician Captain Rufus Walker.

Captain Walker owned a huge farm in Valley Town—now known as Andrews, North Carolina, and named for Colonel Andrews. The WNCRR was originally planned to cross right through the middle of it. If completed,

Walker's property would become a commercial hub for the WNCRR, and Walker stood to get rich from it.

Walker, however, raised the ire of Mr. Best and Andrews when he introduced a bill in the North Carolina General Assembly that would require contractors who hired convict labor (like the WNCRR) to pay an extra $1.50 per convict per day to the state in addition to the typical $125 dollars per convict paid annually to the state. It was an unexpected additional cost that would bankrupt the project.

Best was furious, and to repay Captain Walker for his betrayal, he ordered WNCRR surveyors and planners to reroute the railroad to avoid Walker's farm entirely. The vengeful decision would require additional tunnel building, along with a very steep grade to access the tunnel. The change in plans not only raised costs greatly but also slowed the project to a crawl. And as we will later see, the WNCRR ended up crossing near there anyway.

As a result, Best was unable to pay off the loan, and the R&D RR acquired full ownership of the WNCRR in late 1880. The R&D RR then named Andrews as president. Arguably, this was the best thing that could have happened for the WNCRR. Vance was nonetheless infuriated and demanded an investigation accusing his former friend of a conflict of interest and corruption.

Nothing came of the charges aside from the former allies—Vance and Andrews—becoming lifelong enemies. Suddenly the State of North Carolina was without influence, ownership or control over the WNCRR. Having gained full responsibility for WNCRR operations and having funding to finance them, Andrews then turned his full attention to doing what he did best: running the WNCRR, which became a division of the R&D RR.

Andrews wanted to speed up the building projects and did so by increasing his work details. By 1881, he had added six hundred convicts to his total workforce, supplemented by an additional five hundred hired laborers. Scurvy, injuries and frigid, inclement weather continued to batter both work columns, drastically impeding their progress.

Colonel Andrews then asked the State of North Carolina for additional financial support while also requesting an extension on the payoff date that the R&D RR still owed the state. He blamed their past problems on mismanagement issues by Senator Vance and Governor Jarvis. Andrews further escalated the feud by accusing Vance of cruelty to his convict workers.

While Vance was certainly no saint regarding his usage and treatment of convict labor, Colonel Andrews was no better. Despite his perhaps legitimate later remorse as an advocate for better treatment of prisoners, the truth is that the treatment of convict labor was as bad—if not worse—under the management of Colonel Andrews. It remained nothing more than legalized slavery, and it was getting worse, not better, under his leadership.

Prisoners continued to receive meager daily rations at minimal costs. In fact, Andrews eventually spent less money per convict than Vance did. Working conditions remained brutal, with convicts operating in all sorts of weather and in an exceptionally dangerous workplace. Guards routinely beat the inmates and whipped them for the smallest of disciplinary infractions. One convict, George Caldwell, attempted to escape and was shot and killed. The *Morganton Herald* newspaper reported that a guard had shot an inmate on the Murphy Branch for insubordination but noted that the inmate's wounds "were painful but not serious."

Vance was outraged with Andrews, and their feud continued at a fever pitch. With his request for a loan extension payoff and additional state funding at a stalemate, Colonel Andrews used his political connections to bypass Senator Vance's influences. He finally gained approval from the state railroad commission for financial assistance and a loan extension and resumed his full-time efforts in completing the WNCRR project in late 1881.

The Northern Branch to Paint Rock, Tennessee, was completed in December 1881. Praise for this achievement rang across the Old North State as North Carolina finally had railroad access from the coast, through Asheville and Madison County into Tennessee and on to the Ohio Valley and beyond. It was now possible to reach Louisville, Kentucky, by train from Asheville in only twenty-one hours.

As the Northern Branch was being completed, a separate work crew concurrently began to extend the Murphy Branch west of Asheville. However, the obstacles of the Pigeon River Gorge, along with a continual series of flash floods, repeatedly brought the project to a halt. Further complicating matters, repeated crossings of the serpentine Hominy Creek, east of the Ford of the Pigeon, required the construction of five bridges within a seven-mile span. As usual, inmates cut the timber for the bridges and built them by hand.

It took more than a year to complete the eighteen-mile route from Asheville to the Ford of the Pigeon. Battered and bruised, the Murphy Branch inmate workforce rolled into the Ford of the Pigeon—now known as Canton, North Carolina—on January 28, 1882.

The WNCRR reached Clyde, North Carolina, seven months later in August 1882. Harsh weather, tough terrain, sickness and injuries continued to impede progress of the convict crews. Despite all the difficulties, the

WNCRR was finally making steady progress, but more obstacles lay ahead as the railroad moved toward Jackson County, North Carolina.

More than one hundred miles of track still had to be laid from Waynesville to Murphy. An even bigger concern was the steep and perilous Plott Balsam Range, which loomed above them. A decision had to be made regarding whether to build tunnels through the mountain or attempt to design and build a track layout that could navigate the steep grade over the Balsam Gap.

No matter the decision, the work would remain hazardous and hard as the WNCRR unknowingly inched toward yet another terrible disaster, arguably the worst one of them all: the Cowee Tunnel tragedy of 1882.

THE COWEE TUNNEL TRAGEDY

When it came to the construction of a successful railroad, Super Six members Colonel Andrews, Major Wilson and Colonel Coleman subscribed to the adage that if isn't broken, there is no need to fix it. After all, their recipe of using cheap convict labor, excellent but harsh field supervision and superb engineering, technical planning and shrewd behind-the-scenes business dealings was getting the job done *and* the WNCRR was finally making money. Why should they change a thing?

As usual, while work on the WNCRR was progressing steadily westward, advance tree crews worked ahead, clearing land and building camps or stockades to house staff and inmates—mostly staff—as the railroad construction continued. Four inmate camps were constructed in Haywood County in the early 1880s as the WNCRR plunged deeper into the area.

Each camp housed about 125 prisoners in each location. Alfred Fortunate supervised the camp at Saunooke. It was here that for the first and only time during construction of the Murphy Branch, temporary supplemental local labor (non-convicts) was hired and paid one dollar per day to speed up completion of two miles of railroad. A second camp was located near the high trestle east of Canton. It was operated by John McMurry. The third and fourth camps were located east of Clyde and near Lake Junaluska—both were managed by Arnold Jones.

Despite the additional camps, reports indicate that inmates usually slept stacked like firewood locked inside poorly ventilated railroad box cars or wagons, while the off-duty guards and paid labor slept in the barracks built by prisoners. Journalist Rebecca Harding Davis reported in the August 1880 edition of *Harper's Magazine* that inmates "were tightly boxed for the night in locked train cars on the WNCRR with no chance for air or light."

Clearly the treatment of convict labor was not improving. Nor was Governor Thomas Jarvis concerned enough to make any operational changes in inmate labor usage or treatment. In an apparent show of solidarity for the management of the WNCRR, the December 23, 1882 edition of the *Raleigh News and Observer* reported that Governor Jarvis had recently inspected the local MB convict camps and found them to be satisfactory.

In fairness to him, perhaps WNCRR managers provided a false impression for the governor's visit, or maybe, like most officials of the era, he simply did not care and viewed the inmates as nothing more than disposable tools. But regardless, it is particularly ironic that the governor's approval was given on the eve of what the *Raleigh News and Observer* later described as "the most awful accident that has happened in any of the public works of the state."

While the governor was conducting his interviews and applauding the safety and working conditions on the WNCRR, secondary crews were also working farther down the line on other projects such as bridges and tunnels, including what is likely the most famous tunnel on the Murphy Branch, the Cowee Tunnel. After survey and engineering work was done, crews typically worked on each end of the tunnel portals, planning to meet in the middle. The 836-foot Cowee Tunnel was no different in this regard.

A major bend in the Tuckasegee River west of Dillsboro resulted in the need for the Cowee Tunnel—so called because the tunnel was bored through the walls of Cowee Mountain. A convict stockade was built on the east side of the river, and inmates were dispatched from the camp to work daily at the eastern and western portals of the tunnel.

In late December 1882, prisoners had already been working on the tunnel for several months. Their workday that began at dawn on Saturday, December 30, 1882, surely seemed no different than any other day, as they were loaded into boats at a primitive ferry built just for this reason.

The inmate crews, locked in heavy leg irons or shackles, were transported across the river every morning in flat-bottom boats to work on the tunnel on the west side of the river. They made the same return trip nightly at sundown under close supervision of the guards and trusties.

There are many versions as to exactly what transpired next on this icy December morning, but award-winning Jackson County author and playwright Gary Carden, along with renowned historians and authors John

Parris, Dave Waldrop, Matt Bumgarner and Homer Carson III, offer what we believe is the most accurate portrayal of the tragedy.

The boats could hold up to fifty passengers in ideal conditions, but the conditions on that day were far from ideal. Heavy rains the night before had raised the water level and increased the already swift river currents. Also, your passengers typically would not be weighed down with heavy shackles and chains. To further complicate matters, about two inches of water had frozen in the bottom of the boat from the night before, and as the inmates were loaded into the boat, their weight and chains broke up the ice. The water sloshed across the bottom of the vessel, adversely impacting the balance of the boat. It was a recipe for disaster.

A strong steel cable secured on each side of the stream aided in navigation; some of the chained inmates utilized the cable for stability, using muscle to assist in pulling the craft across. Others on board used long poles to push against the bottom of the tributary. The convicts were supervised by two guards and an unchained prisoner trustee.

One of these guards was William J. "Fleet" Foster, and the trustee was a young Black man—all the prisoners were Black—by the name of Anderson Drake. As the prisoners pulled and poled their way across the river, the melted icy water and slush drastically shifted the weight to the stern of the craft.

The inmates panicked, thinking that the boat was taking on water, and rushed toward the front of the vessel as the guards shouted for them to stop, reassuring them that the boat was not sinking. With the weight of the boat shifting dramatically, the craft suddenly capsized, tossing all the passengers into the swift and frigid currents. Already burdened by their chains and frantically trying to stay afloat, nineteen of the prisoners plunged to the bottom of the river as they became tangled together and quickly drowned.

Twelve other convicts and one guard were swept down the stream and somehow managed to survive thanks to inmates and guards on shore who came to their rescue. There were several acts of heroism reported on this tragic day, but none more notable than the actions of Anderson Drake. Some reports indicate that Drake was a trustee on the capsized vessel, while others say he watched from shore and acted from there. Either way, the result was the same. Anderson Drake heroically risked his own life to save the life of one of his guards, William "Fleet" Foster. That much is certain.

Multiple witnesses later verified this fact and sang the praises of the young inmate. One would think that heroism of this nature would result in some sort of significant reward—perhaps even freedom, or at least a reduction in the prisoner's sentence. But that was not the case. When the guard Foster recovered, he realized that his wallet and the thirty dollars inside it were missing. At first, the guard thought he might have simply lost the wallet and its contents. However, a search after the incident revealed the wallet and money to be in possession of Anderson Drake, the trustee who had just saved the guard's life.

While thirty dollars was indeed a lot of money in 1882—more than two months' salary for the typical WNCRR guard of that era—it would still be logical to assume that the guard might show some mercy to the man he owed his life to, regardless of the theft. Mercy was an uncommon quality on the WNCRR. Instead of a reward or a release from prison, the inmate hero was savagely whipped as punishment, and some reports say that an additional thirty years were added to his already long sentence—one extra year for every dollar he had stolen. Governor Jarvis ordered an investigation into the matter, as after all, he had just praised the operation and conditions there a few days prior to the tragedy in several newspaper reports.

Perhaps attempting to do damage control, the investigation determined that Anderson Drake was guilty of theft and deserved his punishment yet was allotted a "small reward" from the governor in appreciation of heroism. A second inmate, Sam Pickett, was lauded for his heroics in saving several men from drowning and was given a full pardon by the governor, along with $100 in cash to restart his civilian life.

But there was only one problem: Pickett did not save anyone from drowning, much less several men. By the state's own admission in official documents, only one man had been saved from death in the frigid Tuckasegee on that terrible day, and it was the guard William "Fleet" Foster. And it was Anderson Drake who rescued the guard yet still paid a terrible price despite his compassionate act.

Newspapers throughout the Southeast reported the tragedy, although few had their facts correct. Some claimed that there were twenty victims and others eighteen (there were nineteen prisoners killed). And accounts varied on the dates the bodies were found and buried as well. A few indicated that they were located and buried the same day, while others stated that it took several days after the incident for all the bodies to be accounted for and interred.

But most accounts were consistent in one alleged fact: all nineteen of the dead were buried together in a mass grave above the tunnel by January 1, 1883. Railroad historian and writer Matt Bumgarner has recorded all their names, ages and hometowns. Following are some interesting facts pertaining to the deceased inmates.

They hailed from seventeen different counties in North Carolina—two were from the same county, Hertford—and one was from South Carolina. The youngest was only fifteen years old and the oldest fifty-five. Their average age was twenty-eight; all the victims were Black males, and all had been charged with the same crime, larceny. As noted, these men were legalized slaves, and they certainly were not hardened criminals. It was a tragedy of epic proportions on multiple levels.

Like most tragic incidents in the southern mountains, folklorists quickly added their own layers to the story. Legend has it that Anderson Drake placed a curse on Foster and the WNCRR to avenge his horrid treatment. Foster allegedly was fired from his job soon after the incident and became terribly sick, never recovering from the mystery illness that eventually killed him.

The story also is told that the water that drips incessantly in the Cowee Tunnel still today are the tears of the nineteen dead inmates who are buried nearby. The actual site of their burial is a mystery that was recently solved by Jackson County historians Gary Carden and Dave Waldrop and residents Dennis Wilkey and Ellen Sutton. For more than a century, the victims were thought to be buried in one mass grave overlooking the tunnel. However, Ms. Sutton and Mr. Wilkey argued that the inmates lie in three mass graves near what is now the Jackson County Green Energy Park outside Sylva, North Carolina. Additional research by Carden and Waldrop, assisted by Tom Stewart, proved that their assertion was true.

Since then, Carden has championed the cause to formally recognize the burial site and build a monument to the inmates while also writing and producing an award-winning play called *Tuckaseegee Rising* that documents in the incident. We wish them success in these endeavors, which are long overdue, but would add that perhaps a monument should be dedicated to all the workers who lost their lives while building the WNCRR—well over four hundred.

There were at least two other incidents where nineteen or more lives were lost on the project, and all of them were tragic. But the Cowee Tunnel incident stands out for two reasons. One, unlike other deaths that resulted from cave-ins, exposure or other accidents that were often seen as a part of the job for both inmates and paid workers, the Cowee Tunnel deaths could have been avoided by using some common sense and compassion regarding the river crossing. And second, the terrible treatment of the inmates who risked their own lives to save both guards and fellow convicts was unimaginably cruel and inconceivable given the facts we now know.

No matter the magnitude of the tragedy—and arguably none was worse on the WNCRR than the Cowee Tunnel incident—nothing slowed the WNCRR down or stopped construction. They kept working regardless. Convict labor, despite some negative publicity, was considered easily disposable and easily replaced by adding more legal slaves as needed.

While work continued simultaneously in numerous locations, inmates based in three primary camps between Waynesville and the Cowee Tunnel site frantically continued their construction efforts. The Cowee stockade was on the east bank of the Tuckasegee River near the western portal of the tunnel. The Balsam Camp, near Balsam Gap, housed 160 inmates, and the camp at Addie and Cowee Tunnel held 425 prisoners.

The Addie Camp, according to one story, was named after the pregnant wife (Adeline) of a crew supervisor. Another version holds that the hamlet was named after Adeline Calhoun, the daughter of the first postmaster. Her father, John, opened the first post office there in about 1885. Either way, the camp, and later the post office, stood at the bottom of the western slope of the still-to-be-built Balsam Grade along the banks of Scott's Creek.

Seven months after departing the village of Clyde, the WNCRR arrived in Waynesville in April 1883, almost three decades after the railroad's inception in 1855. Relatively unbothered by the 1882 Cowee Tunnel tragedy, which had occurred only a few months before, the crews left Waynesville that same month and began working steadily toward Jackson County.

At about this same time, the Cowee Tunnel was nearing completion. The May 3, 1883 edition of the *Raleigh News and Observer* reported that Major Wilson was confident that the tunnel would be completed by no later than May 20. Wilson made no mention of the tragedy and stated that inmate works crews were working from both portals of the tunnel and could hear each other's drills clearly through the rock.

True to his word, the Cowee Tunnel was soon completed. Seventy-five of the convicts working on the tunnel were transported to the west side of the Nantahala in Cherokee County to begin grading work up the Valley River Mountain near Murphy.

Meanwhile, Captain A.E. Ward, one of the superb construction captains or field supervisors reporting to Wilson and Coleman, led the charge out of Waynesville toward Balsam Gap. The Plott Balsam Range stood ominously above them at 3,351 feet. Initial plans were for the crews to attempt tunneling through the range in order to avoid the exceedingly steep grades on both the eastern and western slopes of mountain. It was originally estimated that as many as fourteen tunnels would be required to cut through the Plott Balsams.

After their experience with tunneling on Swannanoa Mountain, WNCRR management was confident in its abilities to get the job done regardless of the difficulties or dangers, but test results of the mountain soil showed it to be unstable and virtually impossible to tunnel through. The only other option was to build the line over the gap—not through it.

Engineers designed the plan over the mountain, ending up with a 4.3 percent grade—incredibly steep. To better illustrate this point, consider that the infamous Saluda Grade near Tryon, North Carolina, is considered the steepest railroad grade ever built east of the Mississippi, and it is rated at 4.7 percent. The Red Marble Grade near Topton on the Murphy Branch is supposedly 4.2 percent. (We will discuss it shortly.) If so, this would make the Balsam Grade the second-steepest railroad grade in eastern America.

It should be noted that this grade percentage is hotly debated among railroad experts. All agree that Saluda is the steepest at 4.7 percent. But some say that Red Marble is the second steepest at 4.4 percent and argue that the Balsam Grade is "only" 4.0 percent. Regardless, one thing is for certain: the two steepest railroad grades in eastern America were built by the WNCRR on the Murphy Branch, and at worst, the Balsam grade is the third-steepest grade and possibly the second. Either way, both are remarkable achievements.

The steep grade was only part of the problem—albeit a big one. Multiple switchbacks were required to make the grade accessible, as numerous ravines had to be either crossed with a man-made bridge or else filled in with dirt. It was yet another massive excavation project, as soil was constantly having to be removed to create a cut or moved to other locations to fill in ravines and gullies. And once the summit was reached, the problems were just beginning, as the elevation dropped drastically—more than seven hundred feet in just four miles descending the western slope.

Despite these obstacles, Wilson was up for the challenge. But he would achieve this accomplishment alone, as his right-hand man, Colonel Thad Coleman, had been reassigned to work as chief engineer of the Spartanburg and Asheville line. Captain A.E. Ward proved to be a more than able replacement.

While Captain Ward and his crew worked hard on the Balsam Grade, Major Wilson had separate crews clearing land and doing preliminary grading and tunnel preparation as far west as Wesser, North Carolina. Meanwhile, other crews worked in the area near Andrews. The idea being, of course, that the separate crews would eventually connect and complete the Murphy Branch while all working in different locations at the same time. It was the same formula used in working on the Northern Branch to Paint Rock and continued throughout the construction of the Murphy Branch.

By the middle of 1883, the Balsam Grade had been conquered, and a railroad depot was eventually built there by 1885. It was originally and incorrectly believed to be the highest depot in eastern America at 3,351 feet. (Later, it was proven that White Top Mountain Depot in Southwestern Virginia was higher at 3,577 feet.)

Trains arrived with passengers, mail and freight six times per day, further increasing the profitability of WNCRR. The same type of services were then occurring at all points east of the Balsam Gap, all the way back to the Piedmont. The WNCRR, still years from completion, was already having positive impact on the economy of North Carolina. The WNCRR was finally making money, and there was much more to come.

The completion of the Balsam Grade was another miraculous achievement in the annals of WNCRR history; the Balsam Gap is the highest point east of the Rocky Mountains crossed by a standard-gauge rail line. With the Balsam Grade in its rear-view mirror, the Murphy Branch connected with crews already working in Willits, Addie, Beta, Sylva and Dillsboro in 1883, all of which would be future sites of train stations.

The construction of the Cowee Tunnel was no small feat either and should be celebrated as well were it not for the tragedy that occurred there. It was an accomplishment that came at terrible price that still haunts us to this day, and it did not end there.

Between 1881 and 1883, an average of 483 inmates were working at any given time somewhere on the Murphy Branch. During that period, a total of 243 convicts were lost—149 escaped; 74 died of disease, exposure or injury; and 20 were killed in accidents or shot while trying to escape.

As a result of this continuous tragic cycle, Edward R. Stamps, the state superintendent of convicts, ordered and personally supervised an investigation into inmate mistreatment, focusing specifically on the Cowee Tunnel incident. The result? Stamps found no proof of mistreatment, misconduct or any other sort of violation by either the WNCRR or its employees.

Then as now, money and big business often trump the truth and make tragedy easy to ignore or hide. Collateral damage is irrelevant, even at the loss of human life and inhumane treatment of workers. High profit margins and a better quality of life for the masses often makes it easy to see only the good and ignore the bad. Many folks likely recognized the wrongs but were not directly affected by them, so they were easily forgotten. Nowhere was this more apparent than on the construction of the WNCRR and indeed in the rest of the state as well—wherever convict labor was utilized.

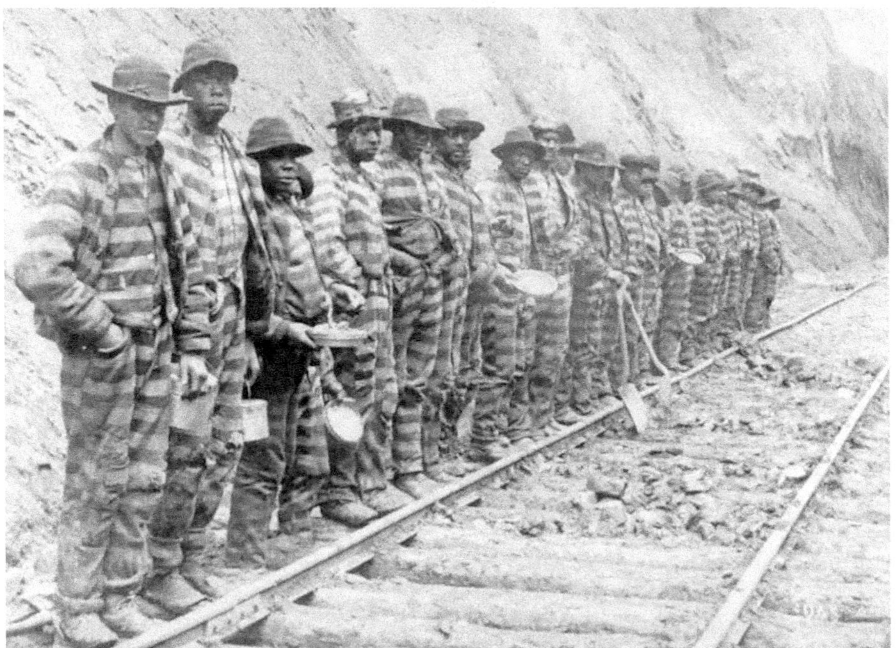

Prisoners working on WNCRR. *UNC Archives.*

With the WNCRR finally making money, and thanks to deft business management by Colonel Andrews, early in 1884 the WNCRR paid off its agreement with the North Carolina State Treasury. The hefty payment of $600,000 not only paid off the WNCRR's debt to the state, but it also allowed politicians to exempt all North Carolina citizens from paying a state railroad tax. This was an incredible amount of money in 1884—the equivalent of more than $15 million today—and raised the already high level of popularity of Colonel Andrews to stellar heights with the citizens of the Tar Heel State.

And nowhere was that immense popularity more apparent than with the folks in Western North Carolina. A huge gala was held in Waynesville, North Carolina, on April 4, 1884, celebrating the arrival of the WNCRR to Waynesville and loan repayment to the state. (Authors note: The train arrived in 1883, but the party was held in 1884.) A reporter from the *Raleigh News and Observer* wrote that "no people in North Carolina love the name of and appreciate the good work that Colonel Andrews had done for them, more than the people of Haywood County."

Colonel Andrews, Major Wilson and Colonel Coleman had done the impossible. They had extended the WNCRR to Jackson County, paid off

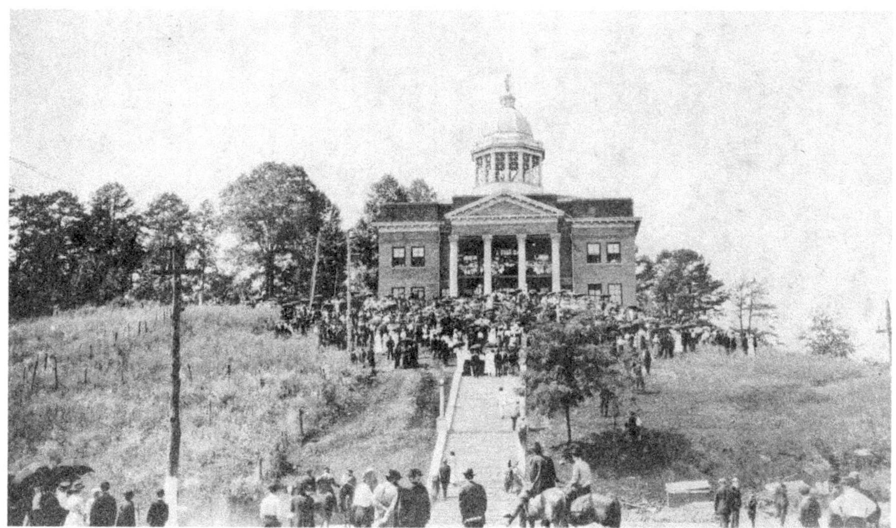

Celebration at Sylva Courthouse, late 1800s. *Hunter Library Archives at Western Carolina University (WCU).*

a massive debt and made the WNCRR profitable. The WNCRR was now celebrated, not despised, by citizens throughout the state. Sadly, the tragedy of the Cowee Tunnel—one of several horrific incidents—was nothing more than afterthought, if that, to the majority of North Carolinians.

Life moved on, as did the WNCRR and the Murphy Branch.

NITRO, BRAINS AND MORE BLOOD, SWEAT AND TEARS

With the Cowee Tunnel completed, the convict work crews had no other choice but to try to put the tragedy behind them. They made good progress as the Murphy Branch proceeded steadily westward in 1883 and 1884.

The WNCRR line clung tightly to the banks of the Tuckasegee River as it moved through the lush valley communities of Barkers Creek and Wilmot. Soon the railway entered Thomas Valley, the home of Super Six member Colonel Will Thomas, who owned a large farm along the tracks in the valley named for him.

Colonel Thomas was still alive then, though in bad health both mentally and physically. But according to reports, he had periods of lucidity and hopefully took great solace in seeing the railroad he had first championed in 1855 becoming a reality.

His rock house still stands along the left side of the westbound tracks today—just before the WNCRR enters the Qualla Boundary, the fifty-six-thousand-acre home of the Eastern Band of the Cherokee, the sanctuary that Colonel Thomas had helped secure for his people while serving as their only white chief.

Always moving west, the tracks divided the site of the sacred mother town of the Cherokees, Kituwah, which was then known as Ferguson Fields. It was then the home of a large dairy farm owned by the Ferguson family, said to have once been the largest dairy operation in Western North Carolina. Gola Ferguson, a member of this storied clan, was once the sheriff of Swain

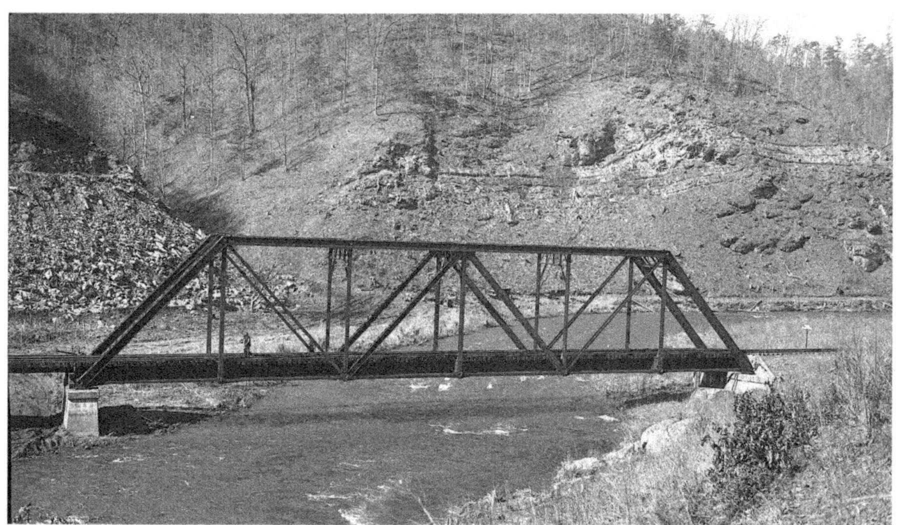

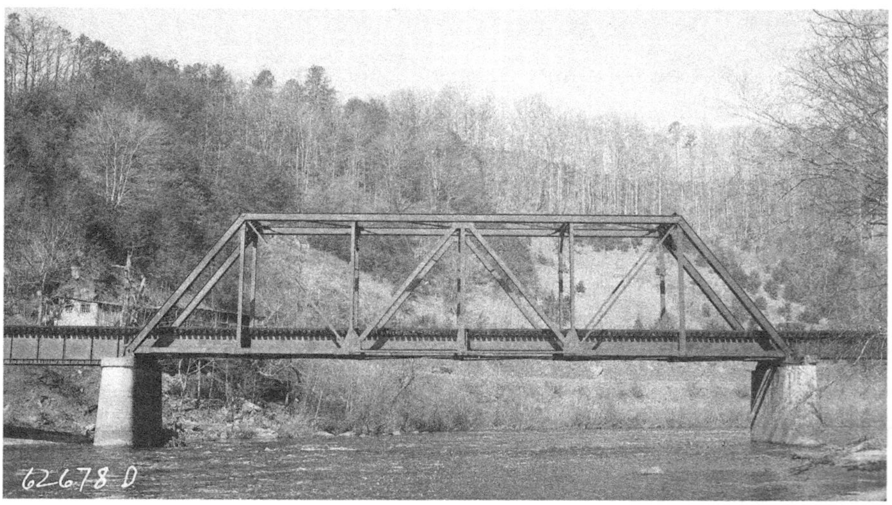

This page and opposite: Different shots from start to finish of railroad bridge construction on Murphy Branch. *UNC Archives.*

County and an iconic figure in Plott hound breed history. The Murphy Branch was truly entering what writer Horace Kephart would later describe as "the back of beyond."

The WNCRR rolled into the county seat of Swain County—then known as Charleston but now Bryson City—in 1884. It was another victory and memorable day of celebration for local citizens, who were finally provided with reliable access and services to the remainder of the state and indeed the

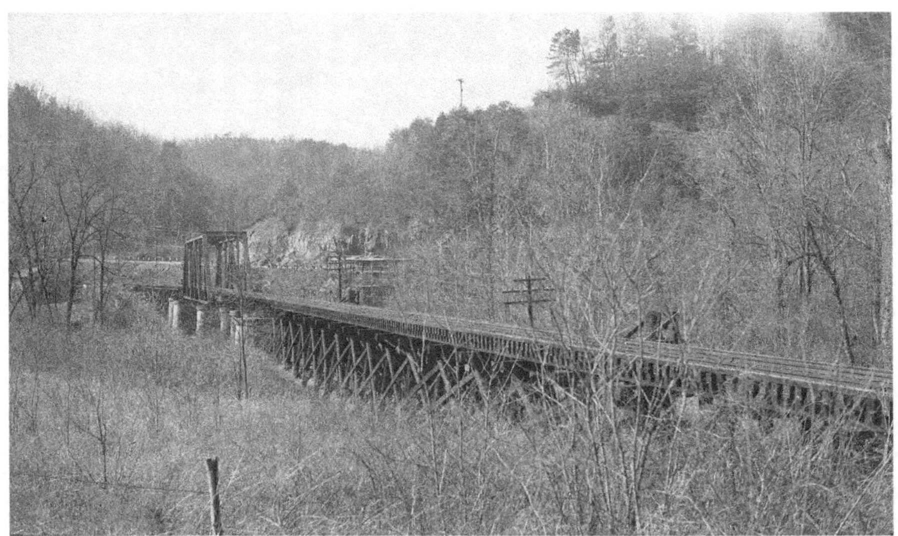

entire nation. For the first time in recorded history, Swain County farmers were able to reliably ship and sell their produce, wares and livestock outside their home county. It was a life-changing moment for the Western North Carolina economy.

Despite its elation and progress, there was no time for the WNCRR to celebrate. As usual, it remained behind schedule, quickly losing hope that it would beat the Marietta and North Georgia Railway to Ducktown, Tennessee, in order to tap into the lucrative freight business for the copper mines located there. (The Ducktown dream was dashed when Marietta and North Georgia Railway eventually won the race and secured the copper business in 1885.)

Still following the north bank of the Tuckasegee River as it flowed southwest of Bryson City, the Murphy Branch was originally 8.5 miles longer than it is today. Inmates worked at a feverish pace as they raced to reach the community of Bushnell, where the Tuckasegee River emptied into the Little Tennessee River.

The WNCRR followed the tributary for three miles downstream, where 1,900-foot Indian Ridge blocked its path. The inmates bored a 621-foot tunnel through the solid rock of Indian Ridge and entered a gorgeous, mostly flat and fertile valley filled with lush farms.

The Indian Ridge Tunnel and many of the communities that the WNCRR passed through on this original route are now under the waters of Fontana Lake. (More on the rerouting of these original eight miles and logging boomtowns shortly.)

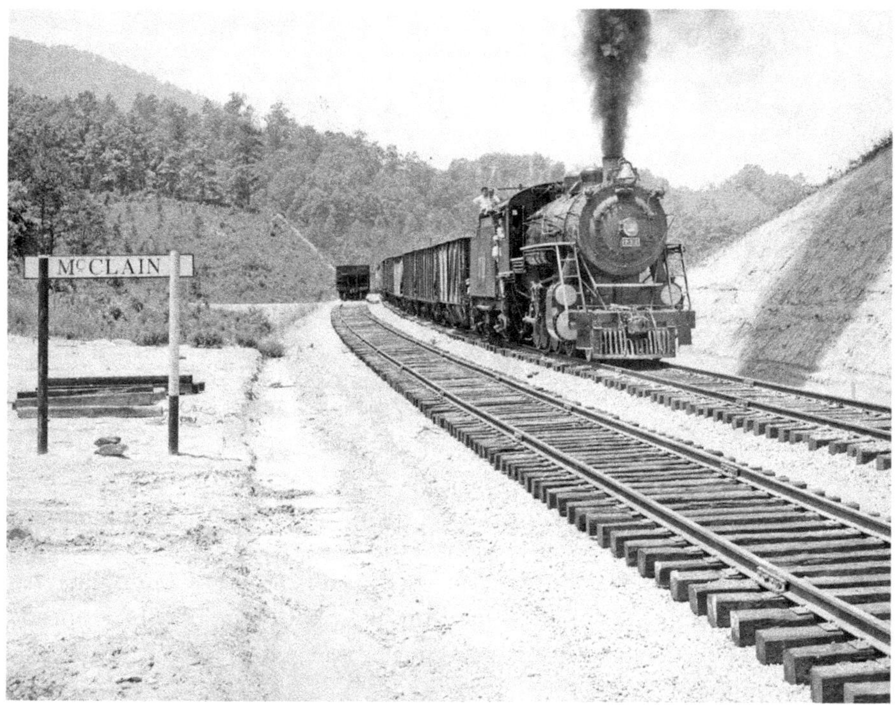

McClain Siding, Milepost 75.3, west of Bryson City. The siding was removed by 1954. *Thanks to Ashely Swenson Hawkins and Tom Plott.*

It had taken almost a year for the WNCRR to extend its tentacles about fifteen miles from Bryson City in early 1884 toward the Nantahala Gorge. And it would take a total of eleven years, from 1880 to 1891, to complete the tortuous journey from Asheville to Murphy. The railway snaked along the rivers—the Tuckasegee, the Little Tennessee and the Nantahala—through the communities of Bushnell, Whiting, Almond, Wesser and Hewitt before arriving in late 1884 to what became known as the Nantahala Station. It was located near the base of the legendary Red Marble Grade.

All these communities, soon to have their own depots and way stations, were remote farming hamlets until the coming of the WNCRR. And like the hunting trails and wagon roads before them, the railroad was usually not far from one of the regional rivers. Thanks to the Murphy Branch, most of these valley villages and stations would become booming centers of commerce by the early 1900s.

Before we complete our documentation of the remainder of this story, it is time to introduce you to the youngest and last member of the Super Six of the WNCRR: William C. Sandlin. During his illustrious career, Will Sandlin would be personally responsible for building more than three hundred miles of railroad tracks on the Murphy Branch, as well as multiple logging spur railways, along with numerous bridges and at least one highway—some of which are still considered as engineering wonders today.

The timing of our introduction is especially appropriate, as it was Sandlin who was instrumental in the completion of the Murphy Branch between Bryson City and Murphy, and it was Sandlin who helped conquer the infamous Red Marble Grade.

It was 1882 when fifteen-year-old Will Sandlin first became an employee of the WNCRR. But he had already been around the railroad business since birth. If there was ever a man destined to be a railroader, it was Will Sandlin. To better appreciate the inquisitive nature, courage and intelligence of Sandlin, let's flash back briefly to his childhood in Old Fort, North Carolina.

Will was born there on July 14, 1867. George Sandlin, his father, was among the first managers working on supervising the building of the WNCRR up through the Swannanoa Gap with the Mountain Division, as well as later along the Murphy Branch.

Young Will's dad had first served as a rodman on the survey crew of Super Six member Thad Coleman, who was Major James Wilson's chief assistant. George Sandlin quickly rose through the ranks to a crew management position in the WNCRR and was a hero to his beloved sons, Will and Madison. Will was two years older than Madison.

The Sandlin family lived about five miles east of the Round Knob inmate camp. As a boy of about eight, Will was already captivated by the railroad and the swirl of activity that constantly surrounded it. He often visited with the inmate workers, some of whom were barely ten years older than him, and through them he first learned the vices of smoking and chewing tobacco. Unbeknownst to his parents, Will soon began indulging in both.

In order to secretly procure tobacco for his newfound bad habits, Will and Madison started a side business where they gathered trade goods, especially chestnuts, which were still prevalent in the southern mountains back then and a valued commodity. The boys traded chestnuts and apples to the inmates for tobacco. It didn't take long for the youngsters' desire for tobacco to surpass their fruit and nut inventory. They needed to generate larger quantities of apples and chestnuts faster for increased trade. Picking them off the ground or climbing trees to reach them was difficult and took too long.

According to authors Mead Parce, Bob Terrell and John Parris, Will's father was working on the grade near the High Ridge Tunnel at that time.

Mr. Sandlin had recently hired an explosives expert, named James Cambar, to produce an explosive blend of nitroglycerine, sawdust and cornmeal. The pliable but potent mixture became a thick paste like modern-day plastic explosives used for blasting tunnels. It was known as Nitro Mash and produced in the remote explosive shacks built apart from each of the convict camps along the line, for safety reasons.

Mr. Cambar took a liking to young Will and, with George Sandlin's permission, taught the boy how to mix his own explosive mash. Little did Cambar know what he had just unleashed. It didn't take long for Will to figure that the use of Nitro Mash was a much quicker way to secure larger quantities of both apples and chestnuts for trade.

Soon Will convinced his brother to assist him in blowing up apple and chestnut trees, thinking that it was faster to destroy the big trees and reap the fruits and nuts, versus having to climb one or, worse yet, cut it down. Madison agreed that it seemed a logical approach to securing more trade goods and in record time. He was all in.

Will was convinced that Mr. Cambar wouldn't miss a small amount of the explosive recipe and blasting cap from his operation. After all, the boy had watched as Cambar produced more than eighteen thousand pounds of the potent explosives. The next day, the lads headed to the explosive shack carrying a five-gallon bucket to obtain the ingredients needed to execute their plan.

The Sandlin brothers had already located a monster chestnut tree—too big for them to climb or cut—and they targeted it for their initial takedown. Will instructed Madison to find shelter behind another large tree about seventy-five yards away while he dug a hole at the base of the huge trunk and filled it with Nitro Mash. Satisfied with his efforts, the eight-year-old child set the charge to detonate using a line of dry tinder for ignition just as he had seen his inmate mentors do many times.

Will had learned his lessons well except for one important point: he had vastly underestimated the power of the Nitro Mash and had used far more than needed for the job. Ever the inquisitive boy, Will made sure that his brother was safe but could not resist the chance to stand up and admire his explosive handiwork himself.

With Madison safely concealed behind him, Will eagerly awaited the blast, and it did not disappoint. An ear-piercing roar, followed by what felt like an earthquake, rocked the ground around him and catapulted the child into the air. As he slammed back to earth, Will was enveloped by a tornado of chestnuts, along with a dense cloud of soil, pebbles and tree fragments.

Somehow, the youngster had miraculously escaped injury but found himself buried up to his neck in dirt clods and tree debris. As the dust cleared, Will shouted for help and attempted to survey the landscape around him. Sandlin later said that the monster tree was completely obliterated along with a significant part of the forest surrounding it. And where the timber had once stood, there was a huge hole deep enough to conceal a six-room house.

Between the gaping orifice in the ground and the earth-shaking explosion, there wasn't much chance of hiding what happened. And despite their best efforts to deny it, it didn't take long for George Sandlin to figure things out. According to the renowned writer John Parris, both Will and his younger brother received their punishment that night in the form of a razor strop administered by their father. As harsh as that may seem to some today, it cured the boys of their need to blow up any more trees. But it only further ignited Will Sandlin's desire to be a railroader.

This also did not curb the boy's creativity. As Will and Madison grew up, they worked and lived right beside their father as the WNCRR continually progressed west. After it reached Asheville in 1880 and continued westward, Will enjoyed seeing trains regularly on the same rails his father built. Trains then ran daily from Salisbury, North Carolina, to Asheville and eventually to Canton by January 1882.

Still short on quality equipment, the WNCRR's passenger cars were famous for their rough, bone-bruising ride. Most of them were built before the Civil War and had no springs under the seats to absorb shock. They badly needed to be replaced. But they made do.

In order to make the ride a bit more comfortable, the WNCRR took thick pieces of rubber, cut them into three-inch-thick and twelve-inch-wide squares and jammed them under the seats to act as crude shock absorbers. It's doubtful they were very effective, but they were better than nothing. Occasionally, more rubber would be added, and the old absorbers were discarded along the track—there was no concern for littering back then. Will Sandlin, always looking for an advantage, took the used pieces and crafted them into baseballs. He sold them or traded them to friends—keeping some for himself and his brother to play with too.

Playing baseball and crafting his own equipment was far from enough to contain Will Sandlin's curiosity and high level of energy. At the tender age of fifteen, he was already an explosives expert and had personally witnessed more miraculous railroad construction secrets and learned more engineering skills than the most experienced and highest-educated engineer.

But perhaps more importantly, because he had grown up around them his entire life, Will respected the inmate workers. He treated them as equals and considered many of them friends. Learning how to respectfully and firmly, but fairly, interact with the convicts would serve Sandlin well in his railroading career. Of course, he had no way of knowing any of that then. Will Sandlin was simply bored and looking for new challenges. He was ready to follow his passion as a railroad man—and that's exactly what he did.

Now that we understand more about the background of this amazing Super Six railroader, let's fast-forward to how his formal railroad career began near Wesser, North Carolina, in 1882. After taking the train from Asheville to Canton, fifteen-year-old Will Sandlin got off in Haywood County and headed west by foot. He spent the next three days walking alone through the fifty miles of wilderness from Canton to Wesser. It was a hard hike through dense mountainous terrain—not for the faint of heart. Will Sandlin was barely a teenager, but he was a man on a mission.

Upon reaching the Wesser Creek Camp—not far from the present-day world-renowned mecca of whitewater rafting, the Nantahala Outdoor Center—Will located his father, George, and asked him for a job. George Sandlin was then the grading foreman in the Nantahala Gorge and oversaw the advanced corps of graders. He was ably assisted by Jim Bradley, who served as the walking boss, and Osbourn Long, who was captain of the convicts. Having clearly demonstrated the desire and passion for the job, George agreed to add his son to the team—albeit at the bottom of the ladder, doing manual labor with the crews. The youngster would get no preferential treatment from his father, and Will later said that he was a better man for it.

Will Sandlin and the work crews slowly inched their way through the Nantahala Gorge—so named by the Cherokee tribe as the Land of the Noonday Sun because sunlight only pierced the high canyon walls at midday. Sandlin continued to work hard, honing his skills and gaining further respect from the inmates and his co-workers. In 1884, only two short years after his arrival in the Gorge, young Will—still not yet eighteen years old—was promoted to the position of grade foreman and placed in charge of 150 convicts building the route through the gorge to Topton.

Not only was the Nantahala Gorge deep, with little room to work, but it was also renowned for being snake infested. Massive nests of copperheads and rattlesnakes populated both sides of the river and the steep rocky cliffs of the Nantahala Gorge. Workers remained on high alert, constantly in fear of being bitten, and even after the tracks were laid and trains operational, brakemen complained incessantly about the poisonous serpents, which lay on the rails at night seeking warmth.

This dangerous location was tailor made for an ambitious man like Will Sandlin to gain notoriety. Sandlin's promotion could not have come at a better time, as the Murphy Branch inched through the gorge and approached the infamous Red Marble Grade, with Topton near the crest. It was the place where Will Sandlin would become famous in railroad lore.

Colonel Thad Coleman had previously surveyed the Red Marble Grade and had managed to hold its gradient to 4 percent as the line ascended Topton. Sandlin and his crews were approaching this point and had begun laying track when upper management called in an outside consultant by the name of Hankins, who determined that Colonel Coleman's grade was far too steep. The engineer hastily ordered a new survey from Nantahala to Topton.

But like many so-called experts before him, the consultant failed to take soil content into consideration and instead ordered the construction foremen and their crews to return to the base of the mountain and start over. Sandlin and his men immediately disliked and doubted the outsider but had no choice but to follow the orders issued to them by their bosses.

Back at Nantahala, Will Sandlin studied the situation while comparing the old line proposed by Coleman to the new route endorsed by Hankins. The Hankins line traced a route around the hill that was only fifty feet below Coleman's original plan. Sandlin realized that this was sure to fail, as each new fill would undercut the old one, resulting in an avalanche roaring down the slope. Sandlin implored Mr. Hankins to reconsider his decision.

Hankins told the young man in no uncertain terms that he had no time or respect for uneducated hillbillies who knew nothing about the science of engineering. Sandlin bristled at the insult, but the young foreman did as he was told. Following these orders, Sandlin and his men dodged disaster every step of the way, as they were repeatedly forced to avoid landslides and then stop to clean up debris as they fought their way up the new route. Upon reaching the summit of the Red Marble Grade, Will met his father, George, who was busy blasting a five-hundred-foot tunnel near the highest point of the slope.

Hankins began to have doubts of his own concerning his proposed route. He ordered a crew to drill into the soil to determine its content—something he should have done long before this, and in fact, something he had been advised to do by both George and Will Sandlin before he ordered his ill-advised alternative route. The bore revealed a mountain railroader's worst nightmare: white mud.

Hankins's lack of geological knowledge proved to be his downfall. Colonel Coleman, a veteran of the legendary WNCRR Loops construction and the builder of five major tunnels between Old Fort and Swannanoa Gap, had already determined that the area was plagued with white mud and had wisely avoided it when he had laid out the original route. Will Sandlin had echoed these concerns as well.

Had Hankins taken the opportunity to consult with the local experts, the entire situation could have been averted. Instead, Hankins was forced to admit his mistake, and WNCRR officials ordered its crews to return to the base of the mountain for a third time—this time, they were ordered to follow Colonel Coleman's original route.

Surely young Sandlin was paying close attention to this, gaining further expertise in his already vast array of railroading knowledge. Now two years behind schedule and with its Ducktown copper mining objective already out of reach, the WNCRR goal, Murphy, remained twenty-eight miles away. The Red Marble Grade, a huge trestle project and another major tunnel construction job blocked its objective.

Will Sandlin took all these lessons and facts into account as his crews began a third ascent up Red Marble Grade as winter began to close in. Despite the weather and even in the worst of conditions, the WNCRR was renowned for almost never stopping work. But it had no choice in early 1885, as the worst winter in years slammed the region.

Many of the inmates struggled to survive in the same caves that Cherokee Indians had hidden in back in 1838 while running from the U.S. government during the Cherokee removal known as the Trail of Tears; 150 other inmates camped with Sandlin higher up the mountain, hoping to gain a little more warmth there. Sandlin hunkered down with his men and prepared for the worst.

Supplies, medicine and food were scarce, but Sandlin's crew managed to survive, thanks in large part to his rationing of supplies and wise management of available resources. Despite the dire weather, Sandlin had kept a supply route open between his camp and their primary supplier of provisions in Bryson City.

But tragedy struck once again on the Murphy Branch as the weather briefly thawed, unleashing a powerful flash flood that washed away trails, tracks and rails, followed by landslides that further blocked their escape in any direction. Sandlin's convict camp was landlocked with no means of escape and supplies running dangerously low.

Not only were they now cut off from assistance, but the cold weather also returned with a vengeance, blanketing the camp with additional heavy snow and frigid conditions. Supplies continued to dwindle. Inmates were freezing to death and dying of starvation and scurvy. At least nineteen inmates died of disease or exposure that brutal winter of 1885. And the toll would have likely been far higher had it not been for the leadership of Will Sandlin and the heroics of Steve Whitaker, a farmer employed by D.S. Russell to keep the camps supplied with provisions.

Unlike many of the bosses, Sandlin had been around these inmates most of his life. He considered them unfortunate humans caught in a bad situation, often not of their own doing, but he was also savvy enough to understand that there were legitimate criminals among them—hard cases who would readily kill to escape if given the chance, especially considering their dire circumstances.

Sandlin considered some of the convicts friends, but he treated them all firmly but fairly. And the inmates respected him for it. But even Sandlin was concerned that the most loyal of the convicts might mutiny if something wasn't done soon. Sandlin began leading hunting parties out onto the nearby mountain slopes to kill fresh game. But he remained ever on alert, fearing that the inmates might think he was out of ammunition and might try to escape or attack him if he had no ammo.

The truth was that Sandlin was down to his last few bullets, but he did his best to make the inmates believe that he had an almost endless supply, as he managed to keep their shrunken bellies full of squirrel and rabbit stew.

Steve Whitaker lived on the west side of the Red Marble Grade, not far from Andrews. As a regular supplier for the camps, Whitaker knew that they would all die if he could not deliver provisions to them soon. With the trails and rail beds blocked or washed away, Whitaker used sleds pulled by four oxen to deliver twenty bushels of corn, medicine, ammunition and other desperately needed provisions before the inmates rebelled. Sandlin later stated that unbeknownst to his men, he was down to his last bullet when Whitaker arrived.

Had Whitaker not arrived when he did, at the very least, more men would have died from sickness and starvation—as it was, nineteen died and many more were seriously ill. But it could have been far worse if Sandlin and others had been killed and a mass inmate escape ensued.

As the summer of 1885 finally began in earnest, Sandlin and his crews were back at work scaling the Red Marble Grade. Hankins's foolish orders and the terrible weather had put Will and his men another year behind schedule. But by following Colonel Coleman's original plan, while injecting a few ideas of his own, grading was completed and track laid almost to the summit of the 2,700-foot Red Marble Grade by the spring of 1887.

However, the job was far from done. Another deep cut was dug, a huge trestle built and another major tunnel project completed before Red Marble Grade was conquered. More on that shortly.

As mentioned earlier, the three steepest railroad grades ever built in eastern America are in Western North Carolina—that much is indisputable. But which grade is the second- and third-steepest remains hotly contested. Most experts agree that the Saluda Grade at 4.7 percent is number one, followed at number two by the Red Marble Grade at 4.4 percent and the Balsam Grade at 4.3 or 4.0 percent, depending on your source.

However, other equally competent experts make a good argument that the Balsam Grade should be number two, as it is steeper, thus making Red Marble number three. Kurt Newman, engineer of the 1702 on the GSMR today, takes the argument a step further when he makes the valid point that if track settling, equipment type and loads are taken into consideration equally, the Red Marble Grade is actually steeper and more difficult to scale than Saluda. And if anyone would know, he would.

We will leave that argument to experts much more knowledgeable than us. But suffice it to say, all three grades are incredible tributes to the men who designed them and the workers who often died or were permanently maimed during their construction.

However, as always, just laying track up the grade was only part of the problem. Sandlin was faced with another set of challenges, as he needed to build a major trestle project and a dig a deep cut near the crest of the grade, at Topton.

Instead of completing the tunnel that George Sandlin had begun in 1882, WNCRR management decided in 1887 that it was wiser to dig a forty-three-foot-deep cut right below the crest of the grade. As they dug into the cut, they found even more white mud. Will Sandlin and his crew worked to stabilize it, filling the foundation of the cut with boulders, railroad ties and logs. Finally, the cut was stabilized enough to lay track, and Sandlin and his men approached their next obstacle: building the bridge.

Surprisingly, engineer Hankins was still working for the WNCRR in late 1887 when he challenged Will Sandlin with building his first major railroad bridge: the double-decker Hawknest Trestle near the crest of the Red Marble Grade at Topton, North Carolina. Hankins had apparently learned his lesson and grudgingly sought Sandlin's assistance in supervising the project, bringing a set of blueprints of a trestle for Will's review.

Barely twenty years old, Will Sandlin took one of the first set of blueprints he had ever seen and went to work. Studying the plans carefully, Sandlin ordered a crew to go one mile below Topton and begin felling timber for the construction of the massive bridge, which was going to be four hundred feet long and forty-three feet high, with forty-three-foot sills.

But Sandlin had to carefully supervise the logging because the project required much more than just cutting down trees. Timber was carefully selected and measured to meet his meticulous specifications before cutting. A team of oxen pulled the hand-selected and cut timber to the construction site, where more measurements were done to create mortise-and-tenon joints required by the plans.

Having two decks caused more concern for the young engineer, as his calculations had to be perfect to ensure the proper alignment of the deck and guarantee that it could safely support an entire train weighing several hundred tons. While working on the project, Sandlin was, as usual, a hands-on manager and was severely injured at one point. His left hand was badly mangled, and the company doctor wanted to amputate it. Sandlin would have none of that and instead ordered the physician to set the broken bones as best he could. Ever the company man, the injured young foreman returned to work.

The bones never properly healed, and Sandlin fully lost the use of three fingers on his left hand. It would be the first of two major injuries that befell him while working on the Murphy Branch, but it never slowed him down.

With the Hawknest Trestle project done in late 1888, the Red Marble Grade was finally ready for trains on January 17, 1889. The wooden bridge would be admired and considered another engineering marvel of the Murphy Branch for more than six decades until it was finally destroyed and the cut filled in by Southern Railway in the late 1940s.

Will Sandlin and his men then moved on as they assisted other crews in the construction of the 346-foot-long Rhodo tunnel. The tunnel, also known as the Valley River Tunnel, is located five miles east of Andrews, North Carolina, about one mile from the small way station at Rhodo and nineteen miles from Murphy. The tunnel was later renamed the Will Sandlin Tunnel in honor of the iconic railroader and is still admired by engineers today.

With the tunnel completed by November 1889, the convict crews were making record time averaging about 2.5 miles per month throughout the latter part of 1889. Yet another convict camp was constructed near Marble in December 1889, and Will Sandlin was part of it all.

The bridge, cut and tunnel construction further enhanced the growing reputation of the young master railroader who had not yet reached his twenty-first birthday. But he was just getting started. Will Sandlin still had a lot more to accomplish.

With the tunnel, cut and bridge behind them, the WNCRR chugged into Andrews, North Carolina, in the spring of 1890. The community was then called Valley Town after an Indian trading post that was established there in 1837, and the Cherokees had lived there for centuries before that.

The tribe once had a large village here called Toonatla, which lay along the banks of the Valley River in the beautiful farming valley there. With the advent of the WNCRR, it was decided by locals that their community should be named Andrews after Super Six member Colonel A.B. Andrews.

Soon Andrews—like so many other stops on the Murphy Branch—would become a bustling village thanks in large part to the WNCRR. But that would come later. In the spring of 1890, it was time to celebrate the arrival of the WNCRR and the dawn of a new economic era in Western North Carolina.

The crews took a break in Andrews, where residents honored them with a complimentary barbecue dinner. This was exactly the type of event that Will Sandlin wanted to use as reward for his men. He never allowed his crews to play cards or participate in any games of chance involving betting that might increase the chances of fighting or tension among the ranks. He often allowed them to conduct shooting matches—in which he would supply the ammo and prizes at his own expense—as a reward for their work and good behavior.

Moreover, Sandlin wanted locals to see and appreciate what his men had achieved and that, for the most part, they were good people—just like the mountain folks who resided in the region. He saw this an opportunity for them to learn from and appreciate each other, but it was not to be.

As usual, politicians and dignitaries from all over the region gathered to sing the praises of the WNCRR and the hope it brought to the area. Sandlin and 150 of his men waited politely for the speeches to conclude as they anticipated a quality meal in appreciation for the work. Brass and string bands from nearby Bryson City and Murphy were hired as entertainment for the event.

Local hooligans were offended by the presence of the inmates at the gala and tried to stop them from taking their turn in the buffet line. A big brawl ensued, and Will Sandlin—despite his hand injury—pulled a knife and jumped in to defend his men and break up the battle. No one was going to disrespect his men, and Sandlin rushed to defend them.

Sandlin and other authorities finally broke up the melee, but not before several of the townies left with cuts and bruises. Totally disgusted with the actions of the residents, Sandlin apologized to his men and thanked them for how they handled the situation. Sandlin later reportedly stated, "I wish I had my pistol with me to back them off faster."

It was lucky for the rabble-rousers that Sandlin was armed only with his knife and that his convicts had only their fists for protection, or else the hellions would have likely been more severely injured or even killed. It was another example of Will Sandlin doing what was right—no matter what the cost—for his men. And it was why they loved and respected him.

With Andrews behind them, Sandlin and his men moved ever closer to their goal, but they were still about 14 miles from their final objective: Murphy, North Carolina. The crews made faster progress through the flat, wide river valley and passed locations that would soon be way stations on the Murphy Branch. They included Coalville at 11.6 miles from Murphy, Marble at the 9-mile mark, Maltby at 6.7 miles and finally Tomotla, only 5.3 miles from Murphy.

Surely the paid employees like Sandlin must have been excited to know that they were close to securing this monumental achievement. And it must have been especially satisfying to the twenty-four-year-old Sandlin. Will had been born into a railroad family—it was in his blood. He had literally lived near or worked on the WNCRR his entire life.

However, Sandlin's involvement paled in comparison to other Super Six Members, some of whom had been directly or indirectly involved in planning or building the WNCRR in some form or fashion since its inception in 1855—more than three decades! And all of them had been involved in some degree with the project since the late 1870s. Certainly, they must have been incredibly proud to see their dream nearing completion, and some of them—especially Colonel Andrews, Major Wilson, Governor Vance and Colonel Coleman—had gained not only personal satisfaction but also significant personal financial gain.

The same could not be said of the rank-and-file managers and paid employees of the Murphy Branch, and it certainly did not apply to the backbone of the entire operation: the inmate work crews. These convicts had worked and died under brutal conditions on the WNCRR for no pay since 1875.

The WNCRR likely never would have been built without them. Certainly, their emotions must have been bittersweet, realizing that their work was nearly done. Most had nothing to look forward to once the train reached Murphy. A few were due to be released, and still others would be farmed out for other projects with convict labor now the norm. But many returned to prison—a place probably safer than railroad work but still confined to four walls. It must have been difficult for them to reconcile what lay ahead in their future once the Murphy Branch was completed in just a few short days.

Their ultimate objective—Murphy, North Carolina—was only five miles away.

MURPHY, 1891!

The WNCRR rumbled into Murphy, North Carolina, on July 29, 1891. Thirty-six years after its initial charter, the WNCRR Murphy Branch was now completed. It was a stunning achievement of incredible engineering, stellar planning and backbreaking, dangerous work, the bulk of which was done by unpaid prison inmates.

But as usual, there was still more work to be done. The 123.1-mile route between Asheville and Murphy had to be constantly maintained and upgraded. Washouts, fallen trees, track repair, bridge maintenance and other obstacles had to be addressed daily, with regular improvements made to ensure that the railroad never stopped running.

More than sixteen years in the building and almost four decades since it was originally chartered, the WNCRR needed to make up for lost time and generate income to cover its missed budgets and rising costs. Keeping trains running from Asheville to Murphy and all points beyond in almost every direction was top priority. And no one wanted this more than the citizens of Western North Carolina. For the first time ever, mountain folks found themselves on a level economic playing field. There was money to be made, and it was their time to do it.

Stations, regular depots and smaller way stations were hastily built all along the line to accommodate the huge increase in freight and passenger business. Twenty-seven principal station sites were built between Biltmore and Asheville by 1900. But in 1891 and 1892, the focus of Will Sandlin and his crews that were still employed by the WNCRR was to simply make sure the trains kept running to generate income.

Sandlin was overseeing a major repair project near Andrews when he was seriously injured for a second time in late 1891. His crews were building culverts and abutments along the track right of way and then finishing them with stonework for reinforcement. These stones were massive and had to be carefully moved into place with a hoist.

Always in the thick of things, Sandlin supervised the project and watched closely as the hoist moved a huge rock, at least four feet long and two feet wide, into its proper location. The boulder unexpectedly slipped from the hoist and crushed Sandlin's right leg beneath it.

In agony, Sandlin ordered his crew to pull the rock from his badly broken appendage. Anyone else would have left the site for a trip to the nearest doctor, but not Sandlin. Instead, he instructed his men to set his leg with a makeshift splint made from nearby tree saplings. The crew then cut some crutches for Sandlin to use after the leg was crudely set and splinted. Sandlin finished the day on the job site before taking the next day off for a brief rest. He returned to work the following day on his normal schedule—hobbling around on crutches and working at his typical frenzied pace.

Eventually, after the job was finally completed, Sandlin went to a doctor about his leg. By then, the poorly set leg had healed badly and the damage was permanent. Will would remain partially crippled for the rest of his life, with one hand and one leg virtually useless, but he never allowed it to slow him down.

Ever conscious of lawsuits, and always taking care of big business, the WNCRR offered Sandlin a legal settlement. The railroad feared that Will might take legal action for his two major injuries and poor medical treatment of same. The WNCRR offered Will a contract guaranteeing him full salary and job for the rest of his life if he would agree not to sue. Sandlin, ever the company man, consented, but only if he could continue working. The RR agreed, and Will signed the deal. Sadly, the agreement would be voided just two short years later when the WNCRR was purchased by Southern Railway.

Let's briefly recognize what Sandlin and his fellow Super Six members had finally accomplished. After almost forty years since its inception, and more than two decades after citizens in the rest of the nation could travel by train from coast to coast on the Transcontinental Railroad, residents of Western North Carolina could *finally* ship and receive freight from anywhere in the United States or travel to almost anywhere in North America in record time, in relative safety, in any sort of weather and any time of year.

This was especially important to residents of the Land of Blue Smoke and, indeed, anyone residing anywhere in North Carolina. For the first time in recorded history, anyone in North Carolina could ride a train or send or receive freight from one end of the Tar Heel State on the coast across the coastal plain, sandhills and Piedmont, all the way to the other end of the state—Murphy—in the mountainous tip of far southwestern North Carolina.

We will examine this in more detail shortly, but this was an economic achievement of epic proportions. However, it came at an awful price, and not just financially. Before proceeding further, it is worth exploring the terrible human toll that was paid in order to achieve this monumental objective.

At any given time between 1875 and 1891, there were as many as 800 and as few as 270 convicts working at various locations on the WNCRR between Old Fort and Murphy. Keep in mind that prisoners were being constantly added to the work rosters as needed to replace injured, dead, paroled, pardoned or escaped inmates. And these numbers reflect only the numbers working at any given time, not a grand total.

Although we have been unable to confirm specific grand totals, taking into consideration the workload, the replacement numbers and, most importantly, the fact that more than 400 convicts died while working on the WNCRR, it is safe to estimate that 1,500 or more inmates worked on the Murphy Branch during that sixteen-year period between 1875 and 1891.

Think about that number for a second. More than four hundred prisoners died from injury, drowning, disease, exposure or gunshot wounds during those sixteen years while building 123.1 miles of railroad. Countless others were maimed for life in crippling accidents. And still others almost certainly died later from illnesses contracted while working on the railroad—most specifically lung diseases such as black lung or silicosis that may take years to develop but almost always eventually result in death. These workers were exposed to massive amounts of rock, quartz, sand and silica dust, all of which is deadly unless workers wear masks or safety gear.

None of the inmates on the WNCRR had safety gear, and in fairness, not much was known about this type of prevention or disease until it was too late. But even then, safety gear was issued to engineers in tunnels and other paid contract workers, so there is evidence that the WNCRR was at least somewhat aware of the issue. However, it should be noted that contract workers were not treated much better than the inmates—Will Sandlin is proof of that—but at least working on the railroad was his choice as a paid employee and one he never regretted.

However, even if the WNCRR was clueless about these issues, it doesn't make the situation any less tragic, and truthfully, based on the company safety records and management indifference to inmate conditions, it is doubtful it would have required any safety gear or taken any precautions regardless.

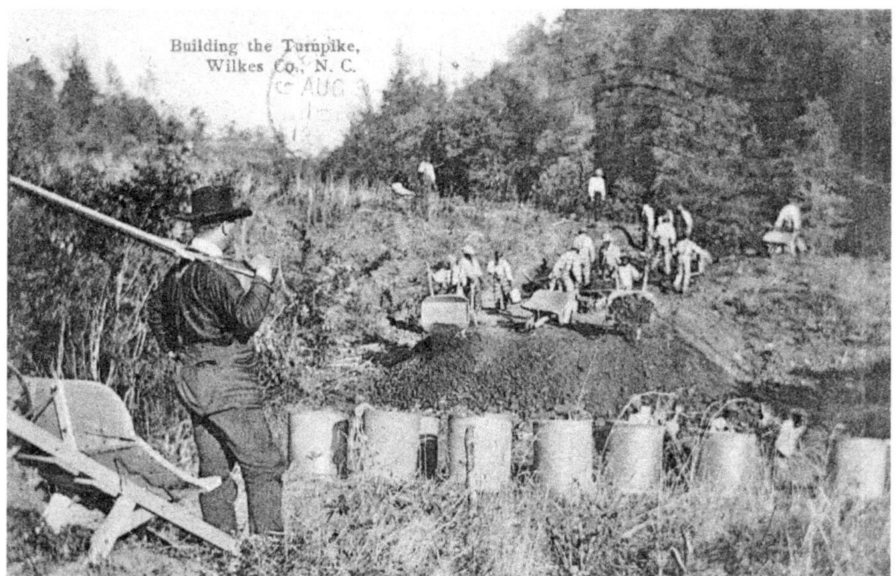

Convicts working on a Wilkes County road in early 1900s. *UNC Archives.*

But let's get back to those numbers. Assuming at least 1,500 inmates worked on the WNCRR between 1875 and 1891 and at least 461 of them died or were killed on the job, that would mean almost 31 percent of the inmate workforce died while working on the railroad during that period. And who knows how many other convicts died working on other projects throughout the state?

Thirty-one percent of the convicts, working as unpaid prison labor for sixteen years in the worst conditions possible, sacrificed their lives to build fewer than two hundred miles of railway along the WNCRR and the Murphy Branch. That is a sobering figure under any circumstances, but it is even worse when compared to similar statistics for the Transcontinental Railroad—easily the most famous railroad project in U.S. history, one that made it possible for passengers and freight to go coast to coast in just five days, at the cost of only $150 per passenger.

It took just six years (1863–69) and more than thirty thousand workers to build two thousand miles of track spanning the continental United States. Their working conditions were dangerous and terrible as well, but unlike the convicts on the WNCRR, for the most part they were a voluntary paid workforce.

Although it is hard to find exact numbers, experts agree that at least 1,200 of these 30,000 workers died on the job building about two thousand miles of track during that six-year period. That comes out to a death rate of less than 1 percent. Let that sink in for a moment. Less than 1 percent of a 30,000-man workforce died in six years while building two thousand miles of the Transcontinental Railroad line—a line that was also subject to attacks from hostile Indians and outlaws. Compare that to a 30 percent death rate for a 1,500-man workforce in sixteen years covering fewer than two hundred miles of the WNCRR!

In other words, the death rate was almost thirty times *higher* on the WNCRR versus the Transcontinental RR project, covering almost twenty times *less* distance and taking nearly three times *longer* to complete. Granted, the transcontinental project had twenty times more employees than the WNCRR, so it should have progressed faster and achieved a longer distance. But you would think those factors would have resulted in a much higher death rate as well, all things considered.

Despite less than ideal working conditions covering significantly more distance and utilizing far more workers in far less time, it was still *much* safer to work on the Transcontinental Railroad than the WNCRR. When you take all these statistical numbers into consideration, this truly illustrates the terrible human toll paid to build the WNCRR and the Murphy Branch.

Don't forget that these statistics do not include crippling injuries like those sustained by Will Sandlin and other non-inmate and inmate workers that left them permanently disabled, many of them unable to work again the rest of their lives. Nor are life-threatening diseases factored in that later occurred from working on the WNCRR. These diseases almost certainly resulted in scores of other deaths in years to come.

The figures we have included are also likely less than the actual totals, as dead inmates were routinely dumped in unmarked graves with no notification for next of kin, with little regard for their lives or accurately recording their losses. If one man died, another was brought in from the prison system with no questions asked.

The only thing that mattered was getting the job done. The building of the WNCRR and the Murphy Branch proves that. And even if the death toll percentages calculated here are incorrect and were lower, the numbers are still staggering to consider.

Nevertheless, the completion of the line remains an incredible achievement that was due in large part to the efforts of the Super Six. All six members of this roster lived to see their railroad vison completed, including Colonel A.B. Andrews, Governor Z.B. Vance, Colonel William Thomas, Colonel Thad Coleman, Major James Wilson and, of course, Will Sandlin. Sadly, three among their ranks would die shortly after the completion of the WNCRR: Colonel Thomas in 1893, Governor Vance in 1894 and Colonel Coleman in 1895.

The three surviving Super Six members—Sandlin, Wilson and Andrews—still had much work to do. Sandlin played a huge role in regional highway and logging railroad building that resulted in large part from the completion of the WNCRR.

Major Wilson was named the chairman of the State of North Carolina's first regulatory Railroad Commission in 1891 and remained a valuable ally and business partner to Colonel Andrews the remainder of their lives. The duo would later partner in building a famous but controversial hotel—the Round Knob Hotel—near the Round Knob site outside Old Fort, where the Mountain Division first gained notoriety. And as we shall soon see, Andrews would play a pivotal role in making the Murphy Branch relevant deep into the twentieth century.

Ecstatic with their success, the Western North Carolina Railroad and Murphy Branch would still need all the help it could get moving forward, because as usual, the operation found itself in serious trouble, teetering on the verge of bankruptcy in 1893. Yet again the business seemed cursed—maybe there was some validity to the curse that inmate Anderson Drake had placed on the WNCRR after the 1882 Cowee Tunnel tragedy.

Regardless of the cause, and despite achieving its near miraculous goal of reaching Murphy, North Carolina, and connecting the Land of Blue Smoke to the rest of the Tar Heel State and all points beyond, the future of the WNCRR appeared dismal at best.

SOUTHERN SAVES THE DAY!

The completion of the Murphy Branch unfortunately coincided with a national economic recession that adversely affected the railroad business. Between 1891 and 1893, seventy-four American railroads, running over twenty-seven thousand miles of track went bankrupt. The Richmond and Danville line, the parent company of the WNCRR, was among them.

It was a situation similar in some ways to what occurred when the R&D first acquired the WNCRR from William J. Best in late 1880, but the problem was further compounded by the terrible national economic downturn. Even though the WNCRR had managed to pay off its state debt and was finally generating daily operational income, the company remained plagued with high-interest loans and was continually over budget while still needing to upgrade its ancient rolling stock equipment—most of which dated back to the Civil War era.

The combination of these problems proved to be too much for even an astute businessman like Colonel Andrews to resolve. With his operation badly extended financially and unable to secure loans from even his most loyal of banking friends, the WNCRR was forced to enter receivership or bankruptcy in 1892.

However, Colonel Andrews had retained a management role as general agent of the company receivers and managed to keep the company operational until federal courts appointed Colonel Samuel Spencer, F.W. Huidekoper and Reuben Foster—all highly regarded businessmen and railroaders—as managers of the Richmond and Danville and the East

Tennessee, Virginia and Georgia lines in 1894. It is probably no coincidence that Andrews knew most if not all these individuals well and, like them, already had ties to Southern Railway. And it should be noted that tycoon J.P. Morgan and his banks provided the financing.

Colonel Spencer was an especially interesting character among this group and proved to be a godsend for the WNCRR. Like most of the Super Six, Spencer was a well-respected officer and veteran of the Civil War, having served in the Confederate cavalry as a colonel, reporting to one of the most famous cavalry officers in military history—General Nathan Bedford Forest—along with the well-known Rebel officer General John Bell Hood.

After the war, Colonel Spencer graduated from the University of Georgia and embarked on a successful career as a railroader. His star rose quickly, and by the late 1880s, Spencer had been named president of the Baltimore and Ohio RR line. He spent a little more than a year in this position, developing invaluable business relationships, before working with investment firms that focused on acquiring and managing railroads.

Spencer eventually became president of Southern Railway and launched a plan to combine at least thirty other railroads into one operation under his leadership as Southern president. One of these lines was the Richmond and Danville, which owned the WNCRR which was then still being managed by Colonel Andrews.

When the R&D declared bankruptcy in 1892, Colonel Andrews again saved the day by holding things together until Spencer literally purchased the company onto the local courthouse steps as the announcement was made of its foreclosure in 1894.

With the WNCRR safely under the operational umbrella of Southern Railway, Colonel Spencer—now the company president—named Colonel Andrews as a director, and Andrews would hold various high-level management positions with Southern until 1915. The two former Confederate officers proved to be a formidable team, as Spencer oversaw the entire operation, while Colonel Andrews now had the support and funding to properly run the beleaguered Murphy Branch.

Their first order of business was to spend as much money as needed to begin upgrading the existing line, build new depots, replace rotten trestles and buy new rolling stock. In the early 1900s, Spencer and Andrews made Bryson City the headquarters of the new and improved Murphy Branch.

Service improved drastically. Only one train ran per day in 1894 when Spencer took over the helm, but by the early 1900s, that number had increased to four trains per day. Daily morning train no. 17 ran from Asheville heading

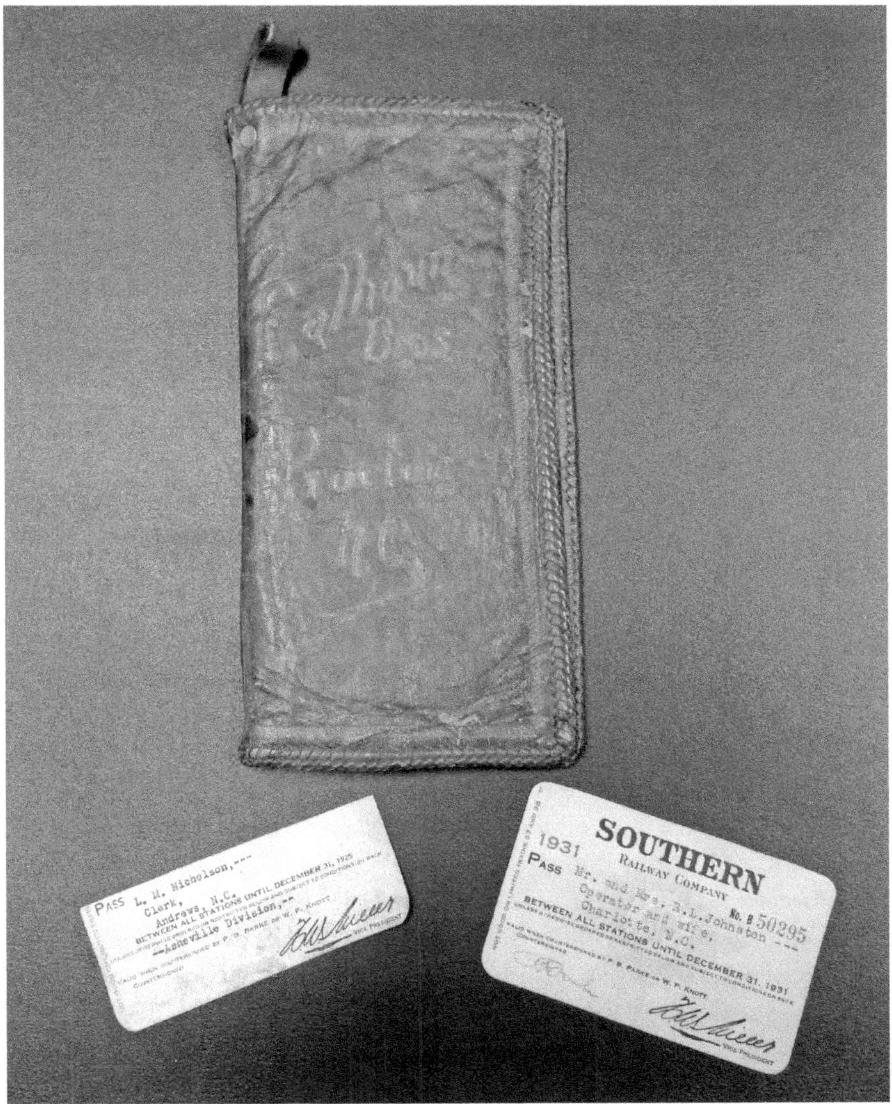

Granville Calhoun's wallet, along with two Southern Railway passes for 1925 and 1931. *Plott family photo.*

west at 7:30 a.m. and arrived in Murphy at 3:45 p.m. seven days a week. Another afternoon train, no. 19, left Asheville at 3:30 p.m. six days per week and pulled into Murphy at 9:50 p.m. on those days.

Running from west to east, train nos. 18 and 20 departed Murphy making the run to Asheville six days per week. No. 20 left Murphy at 7:30 a.m. and arrived in Asheville at 1:35 p.m., while no. 18 pulled out of Murphy shortly before noon and rolled into Asheville at 8:00 p.m.

Costs were reasonable and travel was fast. A one-way ticket from Murphy to Asheville cost $4.22. A ticket for the short run between Andrews and Murphy could be purchased for $0.34. An even shorter one-way ticket from Whittier to Sylva only cost a dime, and the trip took about fifteen minutes.

Each of the trains stopped briefly at the stations and flag stops along the 123.1-mile route to pick up or drop off both passengers and freight. Westbound and eastbound trains were carefully scheduled to avoid collision, as one stayed on sidetracks in Dillsboro and Willets, while the other passed in the opposite direction.

Business was booming and profits soaring, but problems still haunted the Murphy Branch. Citizens were overjoyed that the railroad had finally arrived and thrilled with all the economic advantages it brought to the region. However, that did not stop them from complaining about a host of wide-ranging problems.

Although Colonel Spencer and Andrews were doing a miraculous job making sure that services were improving, it took time to address all the issues and replace the equipment. Customers constantly complained about having to get off stalled trains near Canton and at Balsam to lighten the load and having to literally assist the railroad employees in pushing the train up the grade until they could re-board again.

But that problem was minor in comparison to others that made many speculate if the Murphy Branch was indeed cursed. In August 1906, according to the *Goldsboro Weekly Argus* newspaper, Allen Otter was arrested and convicted of trying to derail a train in the Indian Ridge Tunnel in Swain County.

One account says that Otter, a Cherokee Indian, had issues with the railroad and derailed the train for revenge, while another account says he "tried" to derail the train but failed to do so in May that same year. Regardless of which account is true, there was enough evidence for a jury to convict Mr. Otter and sentence him to three years in prison and charge him with a $200 fine.

The August 4, 1907 edition of the *Asheville Citizen Times* reported that another Cherokee man, Willistee Davis, also known as Black Wolf or Sanusky, was walking on the Murphy Branch tracks near Judson when he was struck by a westbound locomotive and thrown from the tracks—miraculously escaping serious injury.

Mr. Davis spoke no English, only Cherokee, and took his case before a local court to sue Southern Railway for negligence. Mr. Davis argued that because the train was late, and he had not expected it to come through then, that the railroad should be held liable. Mr. Davis was quoted by an interpreter as saying that he heard the warning whistle but thought it was on another track and ignored it. The court ruled in favor of the railroad of dismissed the case of Mr. Davis.

Two other residents were not as fortunate and were both killed by an oncoming train while standing on the tracks two miles east of Bushnell, in Swain County on August 20, 1906. The *Raleigh Times* wrote on August 20, 1906, that Mrs. Margaret Gibbey and her daughter, Sarah, were struck and killed by a work train on that date. The engineer stated that he rounded the curve and surprised them as "they stood there as if paralyzed by fear."

The October 8, 1910 edition of the *Atlanta Constitution* reported that there had been two trains derailed within a week on the Murphy Branch in early October 1901. One of the wrecks took place near Ela in Swain County and resulted in twenty injuries and two fatalities. The cause of the accident, which derailed three passenger cars, was attributed to faulty rails. The paper further stated that the Murphy Division has "an antiquated policy of providing as little information as possible despite the efforts of Southern main line officials to get the facts concerning the wreck."

If the newspaper is correct, there was tension between old-time Murphy Branch hands and newer Southern management. Nevertheless, without the assistance of Southern Railway, the Murphy Branch would have been shut down and the local employees left jobless.

Gene Adams was one of the earliest engineers on the Murphy Branch. He told the *Asheville Citizen Times* in 1931 that his first train crews often were two-man teams and included only a fireman to assist him. The fireman also pulled double duty as the conductor, collecting tickets and train fare. Adams added that these early consists only included the engine, one coach and a box car.

He stated that he often had to stop the train to avoid colliding with people, livestock, wild turkeys and even bears. Unlike some of his co-workers, he said he never actually hit anyone or anything on the track but recalled stopping to collect chestnuts occasionally before they became extinct.

Perhaps the most ironic mishap of all, and one that led to further speculation pertaining to the alleged Cowee Curse, was the cave-in of the Cowee Tunnel that took place on July 1, 1909. The specific cause of the mishap is not listed, but based on the problems with white mud and soil stability encountered while building the tunnel, it surely was not unexpected.

Fortunately, no one was injured, but the tunnel disaster effectively shut down the railroad for several days. And until the tunnel was cleared, trains were forced to operate in opposite directions, stopping at the western and eastern portals. They then transferred any passengers willing to climb over the mountain to the waiting train on the other side. As usual, mountain folks made do, regardless of the situation.

These are just a few of the tragic incidents that took place as the Murphy Branch began full-time operations serving the Land of Blue Smoke under the new leadership of Southern Railway. Meanwhile, despite these tribulations, the entire Southern line was enjoying record profits and incredible success under the leadership of Andrews and Spencer.

Southern Railway more than doubled its track mileage and increased the company's annual profits from $17 million per year to $54 million yearly while serving more than 12 million passengers on Spencer's various lines, which included the original WNCRR and Murphy Branch along with twenty-nine others. Most impressively, this superior performance all took place in a little more than a decade, from 1894 until 1906.

Tragically, the stellar career of Colonel Samuel Spencer would be cut short in a November 29, 1906 railroad accident that took place near Friendship, North Carolina. Celebrating their recent business success, Colonel Spencer invited several of his friends and business associates to join him on a quail hunt in Eastern North Carolina.

As the train approached their hunting lodge destination in Wake County, the private passenger cars in which Spencer and his friends slept, along with two other cars, became detached from their engine due to a faulty connection.

Oblivious to what had happened, the engine continued with the rest of the consist toward their destination. Meanwhile, the detached cars, with their sleeping passengers, rolled slowly to a halt in the opposite direction. The missing cars were slammed by an oncoming freight train coming behind them at a rate of about forty miles per hour.

The cars were shattered into splinters and burst into flames. Eight people on board died, and ten more were seriously injured. Colonel Samuel Spencer, a survivor of battles with the hard-charging Confederate cavalry legend General Nathan Bedford Forest, was ironically among the victims killed in the collision, dead all too soon at the age of fifty-nine. But perhaps it is fitting that the railroad legend—like a ship captain—went down with his respective ship—or, in this case, a train.

Colonel Samuel Spencer would be rightly remembered as "the father of the Southern Railway system," and appropriately, the Rowan County town of Spencer, North Carolina, and the nearby Spencer Shops—the site of the

North Carolina Transportation Museum today but originally the hub for Southern Railway operations in the southeast—are named in his honor.

Despite his untimely death, like all great leaders, Colonel Spencer left behind a solid management structure for Southern Railway that included Super Six member Colonel A.B. Andrews, among others, as well as his successor to the Southern Railway presidency, William Finley; he also left the company in superb shape financially. Thanks to his foresight and the stellar management of Southern officers who followed them, Southern Railway was destined to become one of the most profitable and largest railroad lines in the United States. And because of them, the Murphy Branch not only survived—it flourished.

After Southern acquired or consolidated its primary operation to include the Murphy Branch or WNCRR, along with twenty-nine other bankrupt railroad lines, management budgeted to replace its ancient rolling stock and continued to do so after Spencer's death. The original engines were 4-4-0 locomotives, also known as the American type locomotive. It was arguably the most popular steam engine of its era but was considered antiquated by 1894 when Southern took over.

Between 1894 and 1912, Southern's top priority was to replace these nearly obsolete engines, which dated back to the Civil War. This new roster included the following engines: G Class 2-8-0 no. 154, a F Class 4-6-0 ten-wheeler; Ks and Ks-1 Class 2-8-0 nos. 722 and 630; MS and MS-1 Class Mikado 2-8-2, a larger engine that could only be used on the eastern portion of the Murphy Branch; and a PS-2 Class 4-6-2 Pacific locomotive.

The railroad employees began to refer to all these new engines as "Consolidations" because they were acquired when Southern Railway consolidated these additional thirty rail lines under the Southern corporate umbrella.

In later years, the Murphy Branch would run Santa Fe or Pacific types of engines before eventually converting entirely to diesel electric locomotives in the 1950s. More on this shortly.

Better crossties and improved track maintenance and trestles, along with heavy-duty one-hundred-pound rails and multiple newly constructed depots and way stations, became standards for the line. The moves resulted in safer, better-quality service and made the line more efficient and profitable. Southern Railway and its leadership were indeed having a positive impact on the Murphy Branch.

No longer burdened with inadequate funding to improve and maintain its operation, and with ancient equipment finally updated, the stage was

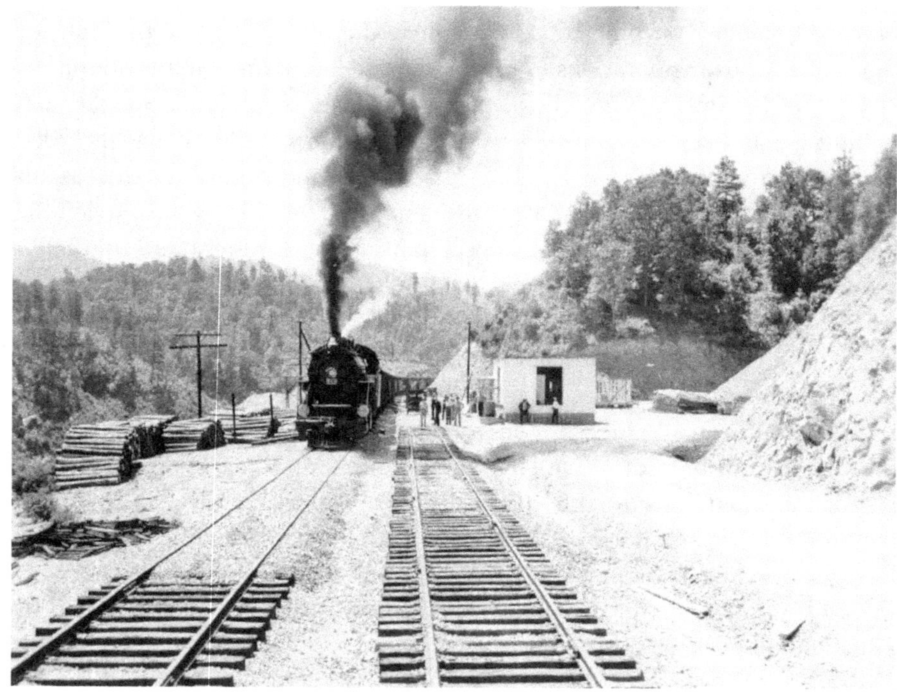

Siding being built outside Bryson City, with no. 711 in the background. *Thanks to Tom Plott and Ashley S. Hawkins.*

set for the Murphy Branch to do its part in leading an industrial and economic renaissance in Western North Carolina. The region was finally on a level economic playing field with the rest of the nation, ushering in a boom in all sorts of businesses—ranging from industrial to agricultural to tourism—unlike anything ever seen before or since in Western North Carolina history.

A BRAND-NEW DAY

A new day—indeed, a new economic era—dawned in Western North Carolina with the completion of the Murphy Branch in 1891. The management intervention of Southern Railway ushered in the "glory days" of the steam operation in the Great Smokies from 1900 until 1952. Despite two upcoming world wars and the Great Depression, which economically devastated most of the nation, life was better for most Western Carolinians.

After all, hard times were nothing new to them, and the railroad provided them with all sorts of opportunities never seen before in the region. What had been a remote and isolated area for almost two centuries was now directly connected to the rest of North Carolina as well as the rest of the nation. A new economic era had begun.

By 1900, twenty-seven depots or stations, as well as a handful of smaller way stations, had been built along the Murphy Branch between Asheville and Murphy. All of them became centers in varying degrees for different types of commerce, ranging from farming, logging, mining, tanneries and manufacturing to the newest market: tourism. Most of them were also federal mail distribution hubs as well as telegraph stations, thus providing enhanced communications for the Land of Blue Smoke.

Moreover, these depots and the railroad itself became the commercial and community focal point in each of their locations. The county seat in Jackson County was literally moved from Webster to Sylva, due mostly to the Murphy Branch running through Sylva.

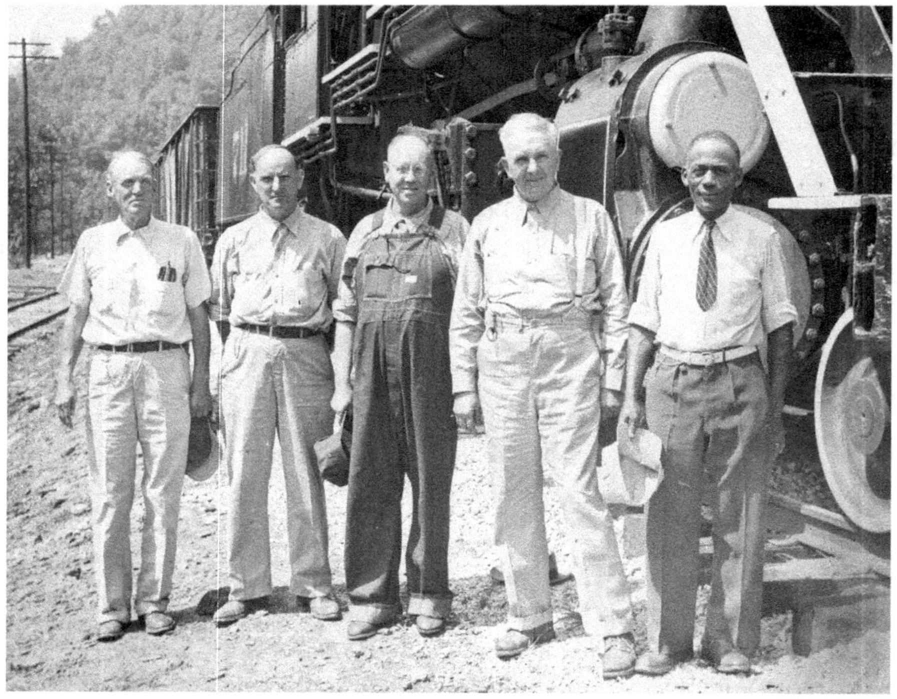

Southern Railway no. 711 and crew at Bryson City. *Thanks to Thomas Plott and Ashley Swenson Hackshaw.*

Populations and business opportunities exploded throughout the area as well. Asheville was a sleepy country town with only 2,500 residents in 1861, but by 1900, it had become the largest city in Western North Carolina and the third-largest city in the entire state! The city also became the southeastern hub for Southern Railway. Southern Railway divisions running from Salisbury and Eastern North Carolina, as well as from Upstate South Carolina and East Tennessee, all intersected in Asheville. And anyone living in the area could easily travel or ship anything to all points nationally to the east, west, north or south.

Canton had fewer than three hundred residents in the early 1890s, but by 1910, it was home to one of the largest pulp mills in the United States, Champion Fiber, and claimed more than five thousand citizens in the 1910 census.

To give you a better idea of the dramatic impact the Murphy Branch had on the region, let's briefly take a more specific look at each of the twenty-seven primary stations and what they meant economically to their respective locations, starting with Biltmore.

The Biltmore Station was basically built to service the Biltmore mansion, the largest privately owned home in the United States, completed by owner George Vanderbilt in 1895. The station also supported the business interests of the vast estate, which included one of the largest nursery businesses in the nation, several factories and dairy operations; of course, the station also provided access for all incoming and outgoing tourists, as well vendors, workers and support staff for the operation.

The next stop heading west was Asheville, the largest city in the region and the county seat of Buncombe County. In addition to being classified as a Southern Railway hub, Asheville was already a renowned tourism location, with first-class hotels, resorts and a state-of-the-art electric railway public transport system.

The Candler Station, in the western suburbs of Asheville, was the junction for the Knoxville Division of Southern Railway and was a major shipping terminal for local farming communities such as Hominy, Acton, Emma and Sulphur Springs.

The first station in Haywood County was Canton, a boomtown for the logging and paper industry. Champion Fiber employed more than six hundred people in 1910 and operated several standard- and narrow-gauge logging spur railroads to communities such as Sunburst in northern Haywood County and Quinlantown and Crestmont in other parts of the county.

Moving farther west into Haywood County, we come to the Clyde Station. In 1916, Clyde claimed three hundred residents and a rapidly expanding tourist business, with eight hotels and several boardinghouses, along with a bank, three churches, a railroad depot and a high school.

The Tuscola Station—also in Haywood County—was the mail distribution center for northern Haywood County and was the gateway to the Methodist Assembly Center, now commonly referred to as Lake Junaluska. Opened in 1913, it was, and is, a beautiful Christian lake resort and yet another hot spot for tourism.

Waynesville, the county seat of Haywood County, was home to the next station. Waynesville was a bustling town of almost 2,500 residents in 1913, built around a big lumber business; a growing tourism and farming industry as well as several factories—all serviced by the Murphy Branch—further supplemented its economy.

The nearby Hazelwood Township (and depot) was well known for its fast-growing furniture manufacturing businesses such as Unagusta Manufacturing and Waynesville Furniture Company. Junaluska Leather Company, with one hundred employees, was another large local employer and Murphy Branch customer too.

Another division of Champion soon opened there, as did Dayco Industries in 1941; a state prison unit began operations in the early 1930s. And it was the nearest town to the Quinlantown logging operation, located along Allen's Creek. Few if any of these businesses would have survived, much less began, were it not for easy railroad accessibility.

Our next stop begins by climbing the steep Balsam Grade as the Murphy Branch enters Jackson County. The Balsam Depot was the highest point on the Southern Railway (later Norfolk Southern) system at 3,348 feet and the home to a famous tourist resort still in operation today: the Balsam Inn. The iconic inn has one hundred rooms and was opened in 1908. The Balsam depot was also home to a post office and serviced the shipping needs for local farmers.

The next three stations—all in Jackson County—were Willits, Addie and Beta. All three were smaller operations, considered developmental depots, based on the potential business for logging and mining, as well as farming.

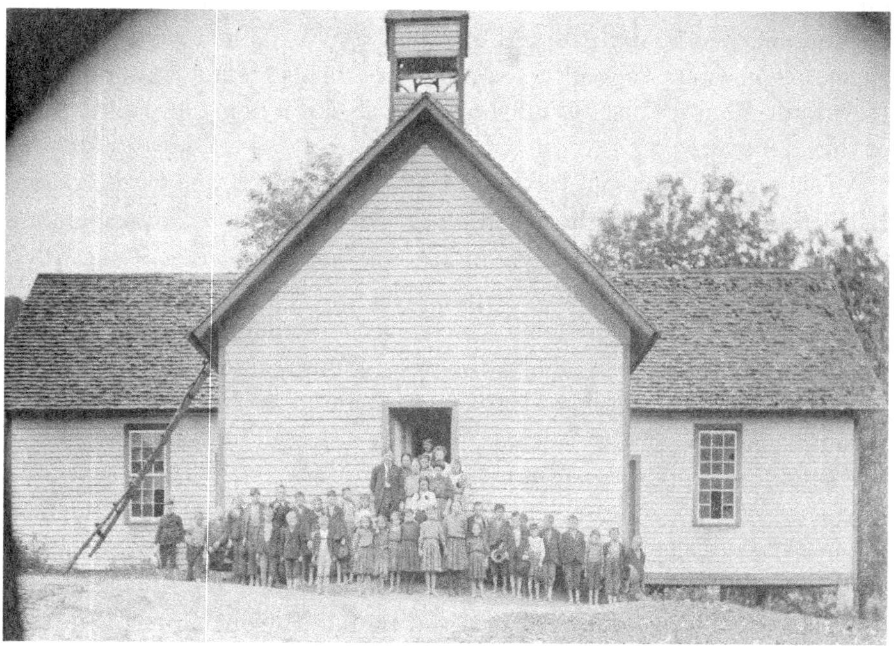

Above: Willits School, 1910. *Hunter Library Archives at Western Carolina University (WCU).*

Opposite: The 1908 grand opening announcement for the Balsam Inn. *Hunter Library Archives at Western Carolina University (WCU).*

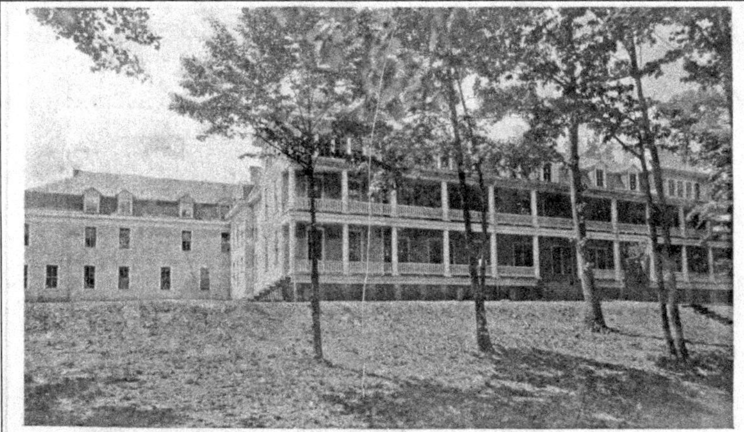

THE BALSAM, BALSAM, N. C., HIGHEST R. R. POINT EAST OF THE ROCKIES. ALTITUDE 3551 FEET

THE BALSAM

Opens June 10th

Is located at Balsam, N. C., 36 miles west of Asheville, on the Asheville and Murphy Division of the Southern Ry.

It has the distinction of being the highest railroad point east of the Rockies, with an elevation of 3551 feet above the sea level.

Many new features have been added to this noted resort for the season of 1909, and several thousand dollars expended to make this hostelry superior to many and second to none in this part of the country.

With the improved condition of the grounds and its large groves of beautiful shade trees, it is the most attractive and delightful place to spend the summer in the mountains of Western North Carolina.

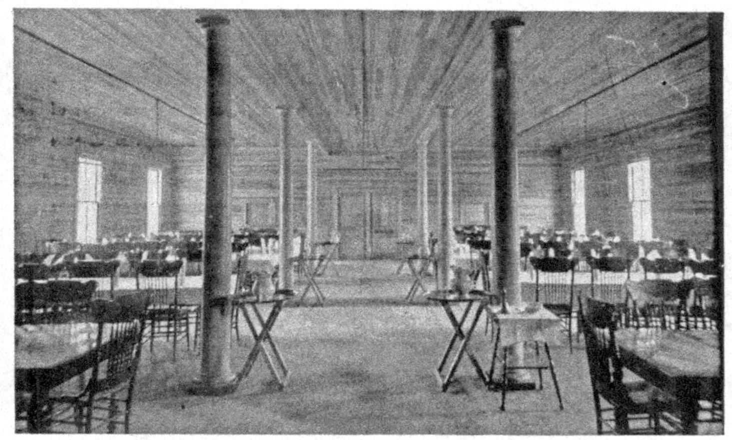

DINING ROOM, THE BALSAM, BALSAM, N. C., HIGHEST R. R. POINT EAST OF THE ROCKIES. ALTITUDE 3551 FEET

Sylva, the next stop, was the county seat of Jackson County. It is a vibrant community with an iconic courthouse, (now the county library), hardware store, meat market, dentist, tannery, two livery stables and two blacksmith and wagon shops, as well as two pharmacies, five general stores and a robust bank. Sylva was surrounded by farms, orchards and a kaolin mining operation, while also enjoying a growing tourism business. The town took great pride in generating the second-highest volume of freight on the Murphy Branch, and Southern built a new depot there in 1913 to further facilitate these services.

Continuing westward, the next depot was in Dillsboro, a Jackson County village that was already enjoying a strong tourism business, along with thriving lumber and mining operations and a lucrative farming market. Blue Ridge Locust Pin Company, the Harris Clay Company and the T.H. Hastings Company—a purveyor of telephone poles, shipping them by the thousands out of the station—were three of the more prominent companies in Dillsboro in 1913.

Following the picturesque Tuckasegee River, the Wilmot Station was located at the confluence of Camp Creek, Bradley Creek and the Tuckasegee River, and it was the last stop in Jackson County for the Murphy Branch.

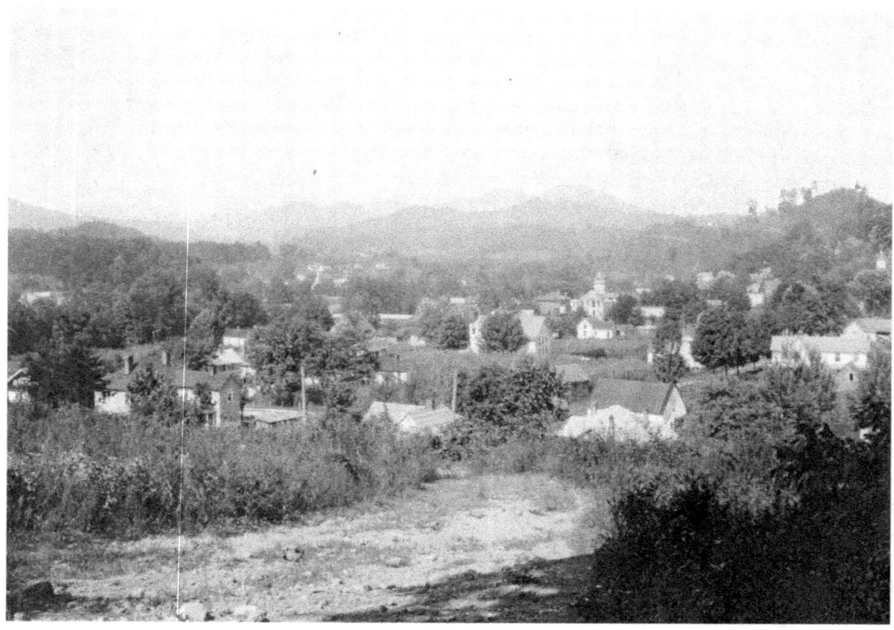

Sylva, North Carolina, late 1800s. *Hunter Library Archives at Western Carolina University (WCU).*

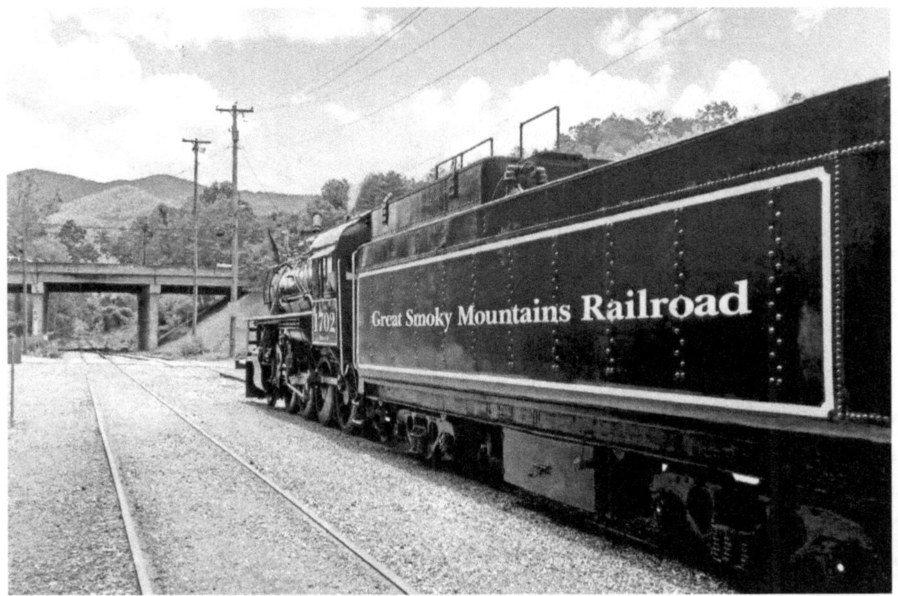

Rear view of GSMR no. 1702, westbound from Dillsboro. *JMP Photos.*

Wilmot was primarily a freight and shipping source for farmers and the logging industry.

The first Swain County station was in Whittier, a community that was about the halfway point for the 123.1-mile Murphy Branch—65 miles from the western terminus in Murphy and 58.6 miles eastward to Asheville. The village sits near the Jackson and Swain County lines. Whittier was truly a railroad town, as it was designed with the depot being the center of the town limits, which extended 0.5 mile from the station in all directions. And it was both a passenger and a freight station capable of sending and receiving telegraphs.

Southern Railway upgraded the station and the surrounding railway in 1910. The community was a center of commerce for the lumber industry, with several large sawmill operations nearby, and the lush river valley shipped tons of produce and livestock from local farms, including mass quantities of cabbage and later tomatoes, both primary crops for the area.

Bryson City—the county seat of Swain County—was the site of the next station and today is the home of the Great Smoky Mountains Railroad. But in 1913, Bryson City was the headquarters for Southern Railway's Murphy Branch operation and was the home to several lumber and woodworking operations, as well as a shipping terminal for local farmers, livestock owners

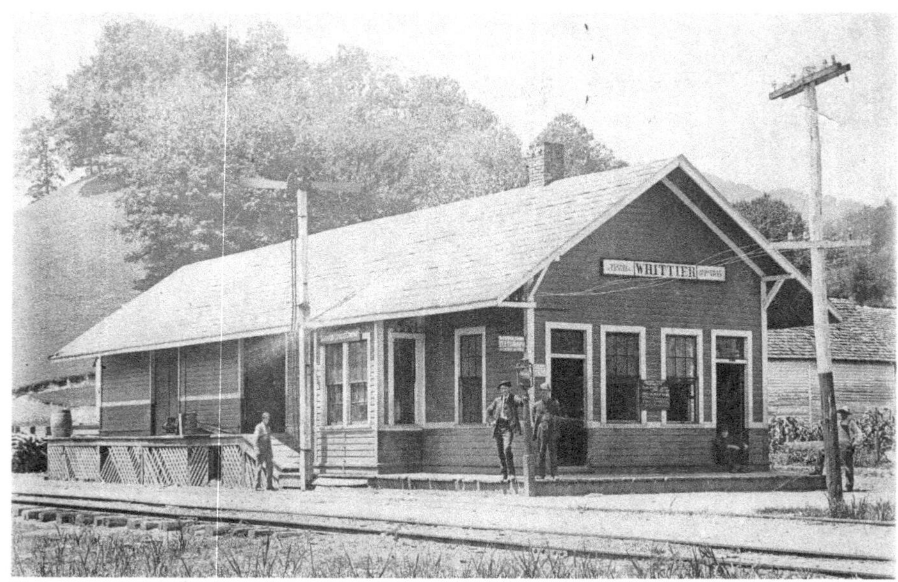

Whittier, North Carolina depot, early 1900s. *Hunter Library Archives at Western Carolina University (WCU).*

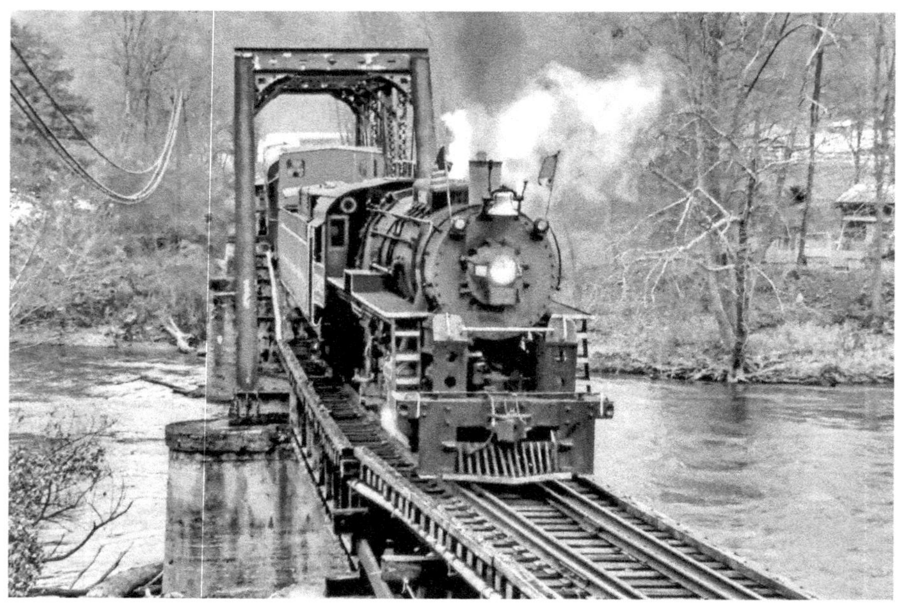

No. 1702 at Ela Trestle. *JMP Photos.*

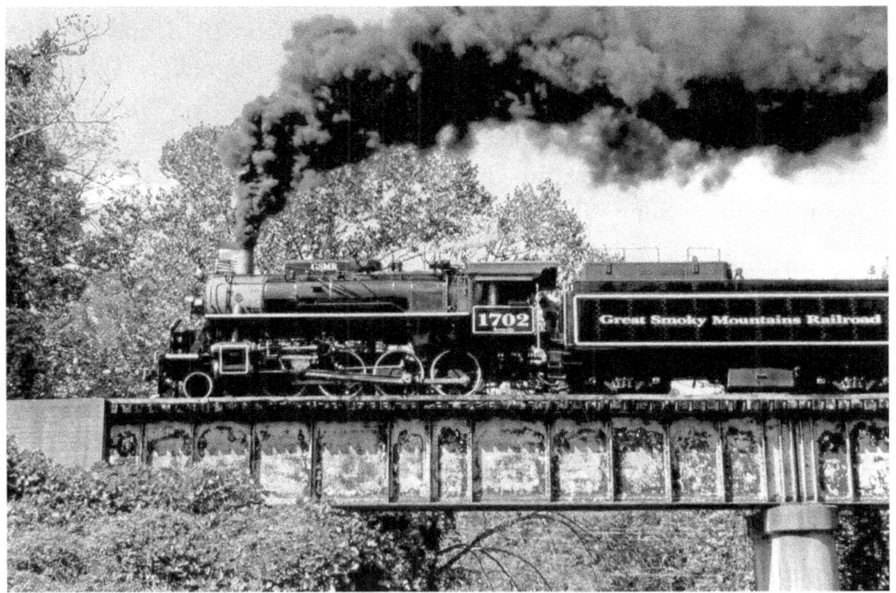

GSMR no. 1702 westbound on bridge west of Bryson City. *JMP Photos.*

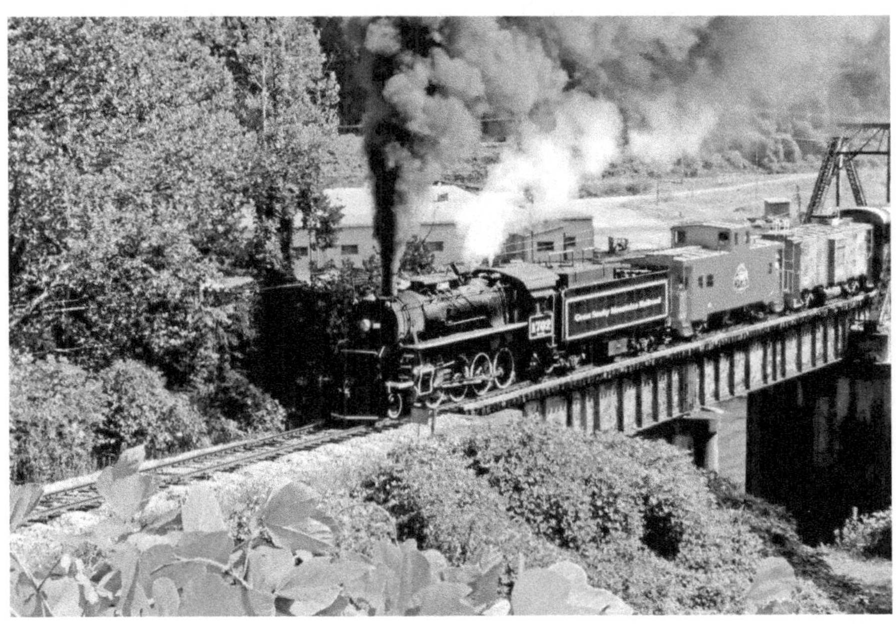

Another angle of no. 1702 crossing bridge west of Bryson City. *JMP Photos.*

and logging operations. Tourism was already growing in 1913, and the area was a mecca for hunters and fishermen from across the nation. When the Great Smoky Mountains National Park was formed in 1934, Bryson City would become the North Carolina gateway to the park.

Moving deeper into Swain County, the Forney Station was located three miles from Siler's Bald and served the logging industry and rural regional farmers.

The next stop was Bushnell. Although under the waters of Fontana Lake today, Bushnell was an incorporated town of more than five hundred residents in 1913 and was the primary hub for several logging railroad spur lines that connected various Ritter Lumber Company outlets to the Murphy Branch at Bushnell.

An eight-mile spur line ran to the biggest of these subsidiaries, Proctor, another community of more than five hundred citizens that is also now mostly under the waters of Fontana Lake or else in the GSMNP. The spur line ran deeper into mountains from Proctor northeast into Bone Valley. The legendary Granville Calhoun—whom author Bob Plott knew as a boy and wrote about in several of his books—was the railroad agent in nearby Proctor.

Southern Railway and Ritter Lumber also operated a twenty-three-mile stretch of logging railroad for Southern's Carolina and Tennessee Line (and Ritter's own Smoky Mountain Railway) that began at Bushnell and went through Ritter and Proctor before terminating at Fontana. Between 1909 and 1926, the Bushnell Station likely shipped as much lumber as any

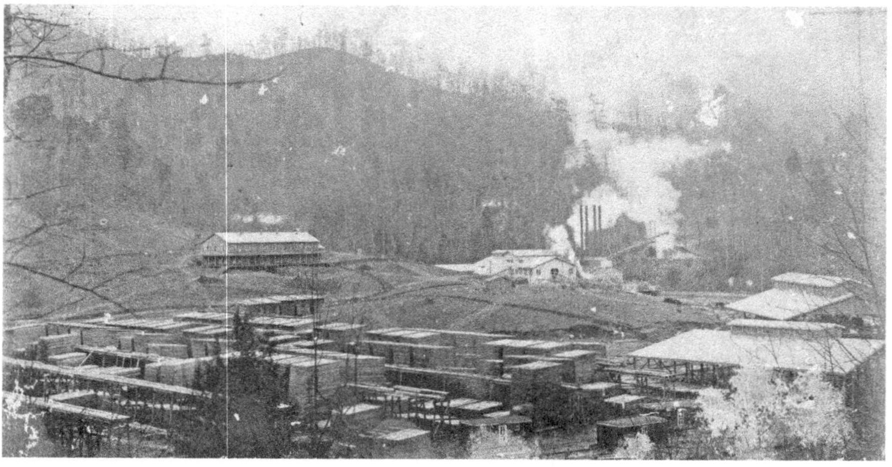

Proctor, North Carolina, early 1900s. *Plott family photo.*

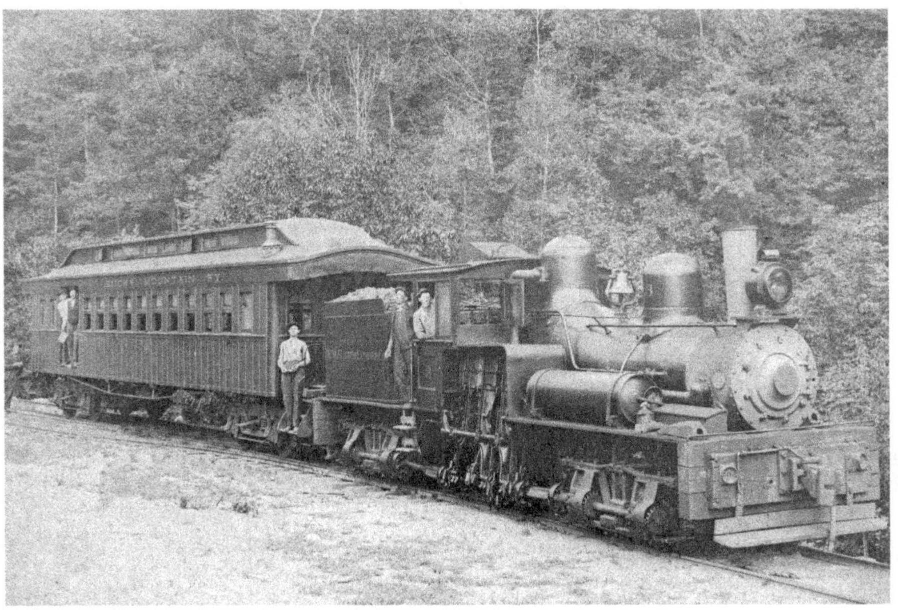

The Smoky Mountain Railroad, a privately owned logging railroad that connected with the Murphy Branch in Bushnell. *Hunter Library Archives at Western Carolina University (WCU).*

station in the region or perhaps even in the Southeast aside from the massive Champion operation in Canton.

Still in Swain County, the next depot, Whiting—also known as Judson—was near the Indian Ridge Tunnel and, like Bushnell and Proctor, is now underwater. It was mostly a small developmental station serving locals, with hopes that it would turn into a large lumber hub.

There were even bigger hopes for our next stop: the Almond Station. Prior to the formation of Fontana Lake, Almond was the site of a post office and hub for several mining and logging operations, as well as a shipping terminal serving local farmers. But Almond never took off like Bushnell, and like Bushnell, it was later adversely impacted by the lake.

The next stop, still in Swain County, was Hewitt, located deep in the western end of the Nantahala Gorge. It was an area renowned for its mining operations, primarily talc, China clay, marble and granite, along with some logging, and it was a popular location for fishermen and hunters.

As the railroad began to slowly climb out of the Nantahala Gorge, the Murphy Branch's last stop in Swain County was the Nantahala Station, known mostly for servicing nearby granite and marble quarries and local farmers.

Navigating the famous Red Marble Grade, the Murphy Branch climbs precariously into Cherokee County, the location of the Topton Station—at 2,700 feet in elevation the fourth-highest station on the line. Topton's primary function was serving as the only source of mail for the town of Robbinsville, which had no direct railroad access. In 1925, the town would be connected by the Graham County Railroad to Topton. Mail for the town was delivered to Topton twice daily. Topton was also a minor logging terminal and hot spot for tourists looking for great hunting and fishing.

Heading back down the mountain, the railway enters a beautiful nine-mile-long valley before arriving in the town of Andrews—named for Super Six member Colonel A.B. Andrews. The Andrews depot was a mail stop and the center of commerce for this booming community. Woodworking, lumber and tannery industries were the primary businesses in Andrews, which was the home of Graham County Lumber Company and the Snowbird Lumber Company, both of which built miles of logging spur lines that connected to the Murphy Branch in Andrews.

Going deeper in Cherokee County, the next station was Regal. It primarily served the marble mining, farming and logging industries, but it was best known as being the shipping hub for the Regal Marble Company, the largest local employer with sixty employees. The company specialized in high-grade

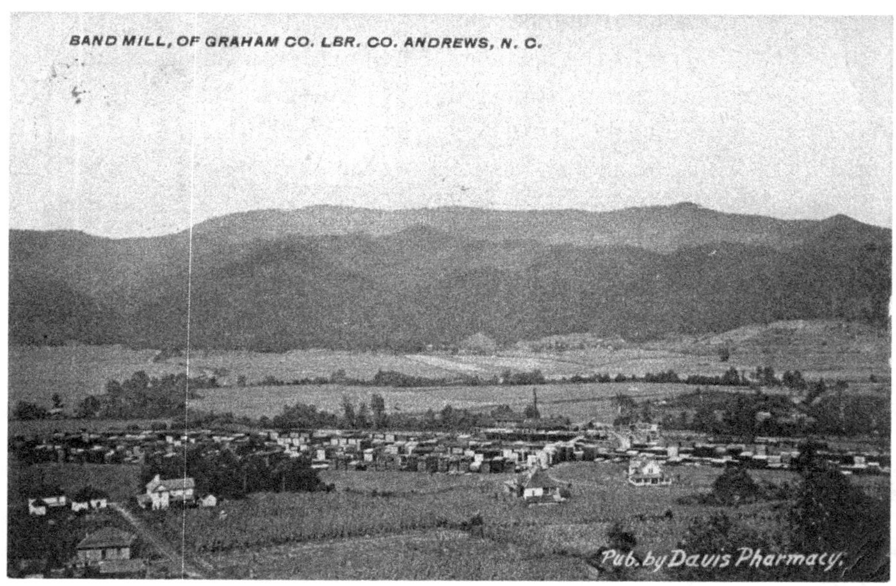

Band mill of Graham County Lumber Company, Andrews, North Carolina. *Hunter Library Archives at Western Carolina University (WCU).*

marble products. It processed one thousand cubic feet of marble per day and shipped a full train carload of products to nine different states weekly.

The operation was renowned for the ornate marble grave markers that were sold in every state of the union, as well as Canada and Mexico. Coal deposits were also found near the community of Coalville, but to the best of our knowledge, no substantial amount of coal was ever mined there.

The Regal Depot was also a popular jumping-off point for hunting and fishing expeditions in the Snowbird Mountain range, as well as nearby way station villages such as Tomotla, Maltby, Coalville and Marble.

The western terminus of the Murphy Branch was the Murphy Station, located in the town of Murphy, the county seat of Cherokee County. Thanks to the Murphy Branch, the town of Murphy became the commercial center of southwestern North Carolina and was the terminus for both the Southern Railway and Louisville and Nashville lines, while also being the hub for several logging spur lines that extended from Murphy deep into Cherokee and Graham Counties.

Murphy was home to several woodworking and lumber operations, a beautiful courthouse that was twice destroyed by fire and a luxurious three-story brick hotel, the Regal Hotel, along with a highly regarded department store and bank.

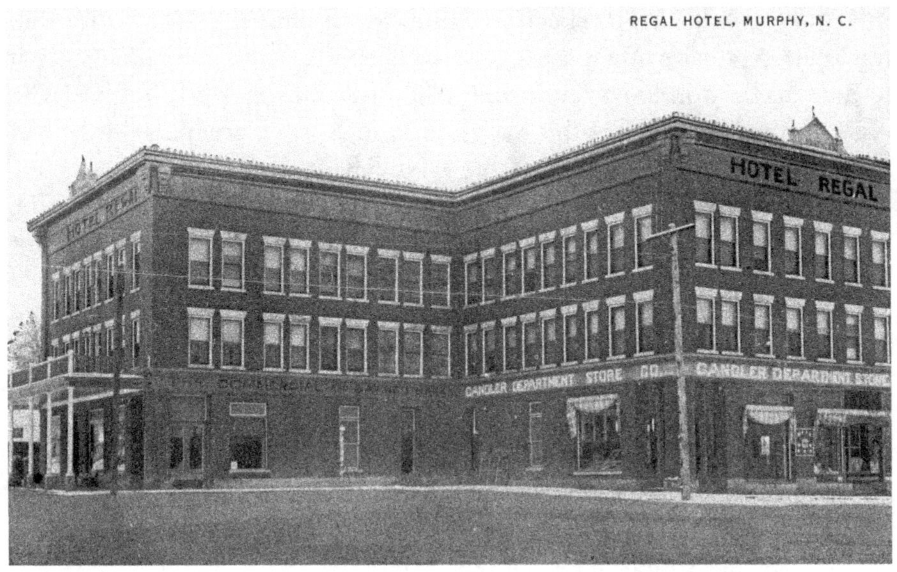

Regal Hotel and department store, Murphy, North Carolina. *Hunter Library Archives at Western Carolina University (WCU).*

To better illustrate the dramatic economic impact that the Murphy Branch had on the towns of Andrews and Murphy, consider the following facts: Murphy only had a population of 170 in 1880 and almost no commerce aside from farming. Yet by 1930, 1,612 people lived there, and the town was flourishing with business opportunities; it was also the intersection for two major railroads and several logging railroad spur lines. Andrews was not even incorporated until 1905 and was not much more than a trading post prior to the arrival of the Murphy Branch. But by 1930, it was home to 1,748 residents and variety of businesses.

The same could be said for most of the other twenty-seven station locations, aside from the obvious cities or towns such as Asheville, Waynesville, Sylva, Canton and Bryson City. But even these latter four towns either did not exist at all until the late nineteenth or early twentieth centuries, or if they did, they were very small. Only Waynesville, with a population of 225, existed in 1880, yet by 1930, all four of these towns had at least 1,300 citizens and thriving economies thanks to the railroad.

The city of Canton is perhaps the best example of explosive growth, as it went from being nonexistent in the late 1880s to becoming the home of almost six thousand people and one of the nation's largest pulp mills in 1930—an astounding 98 percent increase in population. But it took the Murphy Branch to make it happen.

As noted, Asheville has been in existence the longest—since 1797—but remained a small trading crossroads with only a stage line connecting it to the outside world and fewer than 2,600 residents in 1861. Yet by 1900, Asheville had become the third-largest city in North Carolina, with 14,694 residents, thanks to the arrival of the WNCRR.

Nor should we forget the impact that the Murphy Branch had on the temporary logging boomtowns such as Bushnell, Sunburst and Proctor—all with more than five hundred residents and thriving economies between 1900 and 1930. They are now all long gone but would never have grown to that level without Murphy Branch and Southern Railway.

Perhaps most importantly, we should not forget that the Murphy Branch proved to be a literal life saver to the residents of Western North Carolina who lived near these twenty-seven stations during the catastrophic flood of 1916.

On July 16, 1916, the entire state of North Carolina was bombarded by a rainstorm of biblical proportions. Almost two feet of water fell in less than twenty-four hours in some places and resulted in more than eighty deaths and the destruction of countless roads, homes, pieces of equipment, railroad lines and bridges. There were seventy-seven railroad tracks washed out between Salisbury, North Carolina, and Ridgecrest alone.

All major Southern Railway lines running east, west, north and south in or out of Asheville—by then the crown jewel city of the Smokies—were closed or destroyed. That is, all except for the Murphy Branch. Perhaps because it was built so well or because it was somehow better protected from the fierce storm—or a combination of both factors—the Murphy Branch somehow survived basically unscathed.

It seems poetic justice of sorts that the line considered to be little more than an afterthought to many Southern executives suddenly became their lifeline as the only route in or out of Asheville. Southern rerouted all trains normally going to Asheville instead from Atlanta to Marietta, Georgia, and on to the Southern terminal in Murphy, North Carolina, where they headed east to Asheville.

Dozens of engines pulled hundreds of relief freight cars to stranded region. Old-timers recalled seeing trains rolling down the Murphy Branch heading to and from Asheville every thirty minutes daily for about nine months. Without this relief, many more would have died, and the rebuilding process would have taken years. The Murphy Branch saved the day.

Let's move on and take a closer look at what was initially the most important industry on the Murphy Branch: the logging industry.

THE LOGGING BOOM

Although many would find it hard to believe today, almost every town or station previously listed among the twenty-seven stops along the Murphy Branch, as well as several smaller way stations, would have been categorized as a logging town or community from about 1900 until 1936. And for good reason, as logging and lumber-related industries were integral parts of the economic boom that took place in Western North Carolina during this period.

Before proceeding further, we'd like to say that we are not logging experts or logging train experts regarding the logging business or logging industry railroads in Western North Carolina during any era. We are amateur historians, and our focus is a brief history of the building of the WNCRR/Southern Railway and the Murphy Branch, the GSMR, steam operations along this line and the stories behind them, as well as the dramatic impact they had on the Smokies.

However, if you would like to learn from the definitive experts in this field, we suggest you read *If Rails Could Talk*, the superb series of books written by train expert Ronald Sullivan and edited by the foremost train expert in the field, Gerald Ledford. The series consists of several volumes, each focusing on a specific location. But we would be remiss in our efforts if we did not at least briefly review the amazing impact the logging industry had on the Murphy Branch and Western North Carolina in general. So, let's get to it.

Logging was nothing new to Western North Carolina in 1900. In fact, it had been done for decades prior to the arrival of the WNCCR, albeit in much smaller volume. Before the 123-mile Murphy Branch was completed, as well as the hundreds of miles of logging spur lines built to connect with the line between 1900 and 1930, logging operations were terribly inefficient, incredibly dangerous and brutally difficult under the best of conditions.

However, lumber companies remained determined to tap into this vast new resource, as typically one large tree harvested in the Smokies produced eighteen thousand board feet of lumber after processing at the sawmill. The challenge was getting these massive trees to market.

Basically, the only way to transport timber cut from the remote and steep hollows of the Smokies was to drag the logs out—pulled by draft animals—to the nearest passable wagon road, of which there were few. Logs were then loaded manually into wagons to transport to market. A wagon could only carry five or six logs to the sawmill, and it often took as long as a month to transport them there.

Another popular and faster but even more dangerous method of logging the deep mountains ridges was to use flumes to funnel pulpwood to a nearby stream and then float them to market. The concept was simple and involved first building a wooden log flume powered with water from the closest water source. Pulpwood was then floated down the flume. The flume ran into a big creek or river, and the logs were then floated downstream, often to a splash dam, where they could be sorted and sometimes branded to identify their owner. The timber was then floated to an even bigger tributary such as the Little Tennessee River and taken to the nearest sawmill market in large piles.

If flumes were not built and there was enough open land to allow it, another less complicated method was to simply roll the logs down the steep ridge into the stream and repeat the aforementioned process. Either way, throughout this process, tough, nimble mountaineers (known as "river jacks," "drivers" or "river pigs") herded the logs with long poles, jumping from log to log keeping them from jamming as the pile moved downstream. The iconic Mark Cathey—whom Bob Plott profiled in two of his previous books—was a renowned river jack. Other loggers would follow along the banks or in whale boats to assist and rescue downed drivers.

Injuries and death were well-known to loggers, but this was generally the least worry of the company executives. From the perspective of the logging barons, it was an inefficient and costly method, and logging areas were limited due to lack of major stream accessibility. As a result, thousands of acres of prime timber were eliminated from logging consideration.

But the advent of the Murphy Branch and its joining spur lines that reached deep into the Land of Blue Smoke changed all that. Seemingly endless acres of primeval forest were now open for business. And it took the timber magnates and their companies only a short time to take advantage of the opportunity.

By 1915, almost all of the twenty-seven stations along the Murphy Branch, and the town or community where a station was located, could truly be classified as a legitimate logging town, as could communities or towns like Sunburst, Quinlantown, Ravensford, Smokemont, Noland Creek, Proctor, Fontana, Medlin, Kitchenvale—just to name a few—all of which were located on logging spur lines that connected to the Murphy Branch.

And companies like Little River Lumber Company, Chilhowee Extract, Crestmont Lumber, Quinlan and Monroe Lumber, Boice Hardwood, Suncrest Lumber, Parsons Pulp and Lumber, Norwood Lumber, Bemis Lumber, W.M. Ritter lumber, Montvale Lumber, Kitchin Lumber, R.E. Woods Lumber Adams and Westveldt, Stikeleather Lumber and Mining and, most notably, Champion Paper and Fiber were among the timber industry leaders that dominated the local economy for decades—and not just the logging economy, but the entire region's economy.

These operations—owned by master businessmen such as Reuben Robertson, J.G. "Jim" Stikeleather, Jack Coburn, E.E. Quinlan, Charlie Quinlan, E.W. Monroe, R.E. Woods and W.T. Mason among many others—accrued massive fortunes, thanks in large part to the logging industry and the Murphy Branch/Southern Railway.

In some cases, these individuals owned or had stock in logging operations; in other instances, they were land speculators reaping the timber and mineral rights from their property. But often they were both, and J.G. "Jim" Stikeleather was a perfect example of that.

Stikeleather owned interests in his own lumber and mining companies but also owned vast amounts of mountain timberland. For instance, he once purchased almost twenty-three thousand acres of forest land deep in the Great Smokies in the Hazel Creek watershed, the region referred to by author Horace Kephart as "the back of beyond." Stikeleather reportedly paid no more than $5 per acre for the property and probably far less than that, more likely $2 or $3 per acre. But even at $5 dollars per acre, his purchase cost totaled, at most, $115,000.

Stikeleather made the best of his acquisition, as he cut and sold tons of timber from the property, as well as derived a significant amount of income from mining. He also had a hunting lodge on the property, where he entertained friends and clients from across the nation for years and profited from that as well.

Best of all, when the GSMNP was formed, Stikeleather—a staunch advocate for the formation of the GSMNP—sold that same property to the government for $11 per acre (or $253,000), more than doubling what he had originally paid for it.

But Stikeleather's deal, and fortune that resulted, pales in comparison to the incredible story of Champion Paper and Reuben Robertson. Champion Paper Company was formed in Ohio in 1893 by Peter Thomson, whose son-in-law, Reuben Robertson, moved south in the early 1900s to develop the Champion Fiber Company in Canton, North Carolina.

The companies merged in 1926 and became known as Champion Paper and Fiber Company. By 1908, Robertson's mill in Canton was open for operation and soon became one of the nation's largest paper manufacturers, home to the first book mill in the South and the world's largest machines producing white paper. Canton, due to Champion Paper and Fiber, became the center of the regional logging industry for decades to come.

By 1913, the operation was employing more than one thousand people at its Canton facility and in the coming years would employ as many as eight thousand in its local plants, as well as in nearby logging operations scattered along the Murphy Branch and throughout the region. Like Stikeleather, Robertson was constantly acquiring logging land needed to sustain his business, but his timber needs were far greater than Stikeleather's, as were his landholdings.

In 1931, Champion sold 90,000 acres of Champion property to the U.S. Forest Service for $3 million. The land eventually became a large segment of the almost 520,000-acre Great Smoky Mountains National Park. That financial windfall, along with its logging and other business profits, allowed the company to upgrade equipment, survive the Great Depression and continue to flourish as the largest employer in Haywood County.

Consider the following mind-boggling numbers that were generated by Champion during the heyday of logging. At the height of the boom in the 1920s, Champion owned or had logging rights to 420,000 acres of timberland—most of it very remote locations deep in the Smokies. During this period, the company cut 25 to 40 million feet of lumber annually. It took 1,140 tons of coal per day to fuel the massive boilers in its Canton facility, and in 1924 alone, the company handled 83,200 freight carloads of incoming and outgoing freight while shipping about 130,000 tons of paper to customers.

Today, almost a century later, and despite several ownership changes and new name, the Canton company remains the counties' largest employer. It is truly an American success story—albeit one that has had to address several major environmental concerns over the years; however, that is another story.

But again, none of this happens without the Murphy Branch and the Southern Railway. The logging spur lines also played an integral role in this economic boom, and their success required the introduction of some steam equipment new to the region. Let's take a quick look at a few of these logging operations and what it took to run them.

The remote, steep and rugged ridges of the Land of Blue Smoke often required a special engine—known as a geared engine—to pull the load, and these locomotives often required narrow-gauge branch lines, which did not require as much room to build for their engines. The geared locomotive is a type of steam engine that used reduction gearing in its drive train to increase pulling power and traction as opposed to the typical direct drive (or rod) steam engines described in the first chapter.

The Murphy Branch was a standard-gauge railroad line and ran rod engines. But most, if not all, of the logging spur lines used three types of recently developed geared engines to pull their loads: the Shay locomotive, the Class B Climax and the Heisler.

The Shay engine was the first geared engine developed and was the most popular of the three types. Multiple Shays have been documented as operating along the Murphy Branch logging lines between 1900 and 1936. Since the Shay was so popular in the Smokies—and across the nation as well—we will focus mostly on the Shay engine as we explore their development and their impact on the logging industry along the Murphy Branch.

Ephraim Shay, an Ohio native, was the inventor of the locomotive that would be named after him. The Shay engine was designed and developed by Mr. Shay in the later 1800s, and he was awarded a patent for the engine in 1881.

Shay was a multitalented man who, during his career, wore many hats. He was an inventor, a merchant, a teacher, a railroad owner and a logger. And it was during his logging career in Michigan that he designed the Shay locomotive out of necessity.

In the Smokies, logs were usually found on steep, inaccessible and rugged terrain that conventional railroads could not climb. In order to access them with steam equipment, loggers were forced to build railroads and engines that could navigate these incredibly harsh grades and sharp curves. And it was Ephraim Shay who built the first and the best of them.

Frustrated with the performance of standard rod locomotives, Shay set out to develop a two-cylinder unit that he felt could better harvest his timber,

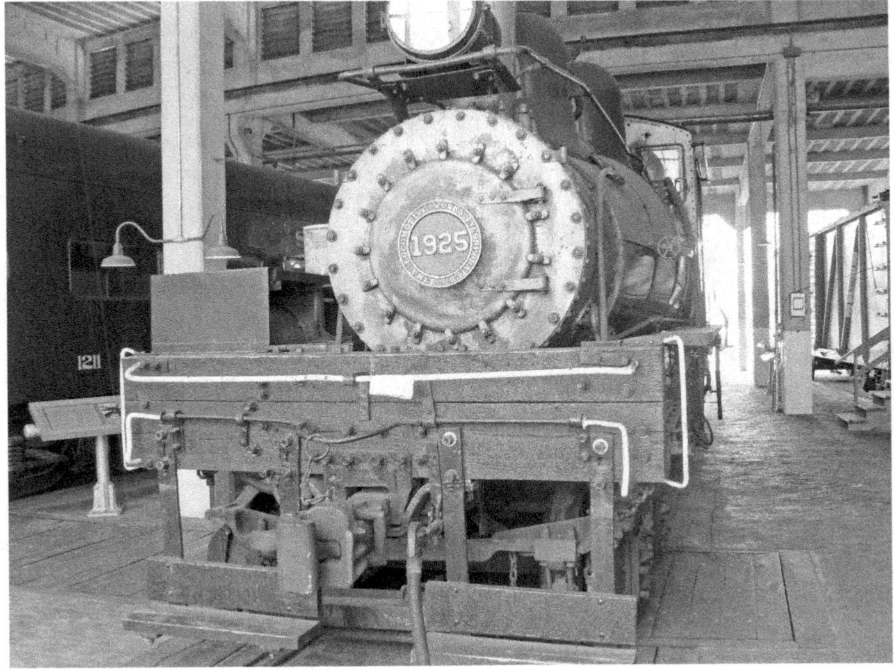

Shay no. 1925 in the roundhouse at Spencer Shops. *JMP Photos.*

and that is exactly what he did. Satisfied with his design after successful field testing, Shay contracted the Lima Locomotive Works of Lima, Ohio, as the official manufacturers of his engines. The company built 2,761 of them between 1880 and 1945, and likely 20 of the locomotives ended up working along the Murphy Branch or nearby at some point during that time.

These locomotives were easy to differentiate from the other conventional rod engines on the Murphy Branch due primarily to the location, type and arrangement of the cylinders and pistons that were used to drive the wheels, along with the location of the wheels' line shafts.

The Shay had two or three vertical steam cylinders positioned only on the right side of the engine near the front of the crew cab. (Rod engine cylinders were horizontal.) Piston rods were attached to a crank shaft—like those used in a car engine. Drive shafts were attached to either end of the crank shaft, while the drive shafts extended to a gear box on the outside of each wheel. The left side had no visible gearing or cylinders. Because of the cylinder location, the boiler had to be located to the left center of the entire frame.

The high ratio of piston strokes to wheel revolutions allowed the wheels to run at what was called a partial slip, creating increased rail traction for the Shay and better value in pulling loads. Conventional rod engines would often spin their drive wheels, burning the rails and losing traction.

Shays—also called "sidewinders" or "stemwinders" due to their side-mounted drive shafts—could be fueled by wood, coal or oil and came from the Lima factory outfitted with either two or three cylinders; the three-cylinder model was the most powerful and most popular. The engine offered various truck set wheel options as well, including two, three or four truck sets.

Shay engines were categorized in four classes or models—A, B, C and D classes—and depending on their number of cylinders, drivers and wheel sets, they weighed between 13 and 150 tons each. Class A weighed 13 to 20 tons, Class B weighed 20 to 70 tons, Class C weighed in between 70 and 125 tons and Class D was the heaviest at 150 tons, with three cylinders, four trucks and sixteen drivers.

What the Shay lacked in speed, it more than made up for in pulling power and its ability to handle steep grades, tight tracks and sharp curves—all qualities that made the Shay popular throughout the logging industry and especially along the Murphy Branch.

It should also be noted that these powerhouse Shay engines were used to pull other large steam-powered pieces of logging equipment such as skidders and log loaders to logging sites. A skidder—sometimes called a steam donkey—was a type of logging equipment used to drag logs to the loaders, where the loader would then place them in the freight cars for the trip to the sawmill. Draft animals such as oxen, mules and horses were also used to drag timber to the cars, but the machinery—unlike animals—could handle heavier loads around the clock if needed.

Arguably the most famous, and almost surely the longest running of the Shay engines working along the Murphy Branch, was the Graham County Shay no. 1925. The 1925's story is so remarkable and plays such an important role in the history of the Murphy Branch that we should take a moment to share it.

The Graham County Shay no. 1925—so called for its association with the Graham County Railroad Line, a company chartered by Southern Railway in 1905 to run to and from Topton to Robbinsville—is a Class C seventy-ton, three-truck locomotive. The engine's number comes from the year it was built and the year it first became operational to Robbinsville.

The Delaware-based Bemis Lumber Company was late entering the logging game. It built a big operation based in Robbinsville, North Carolina, in 1926 and began using the 1925 Shay that same year, as well another, the

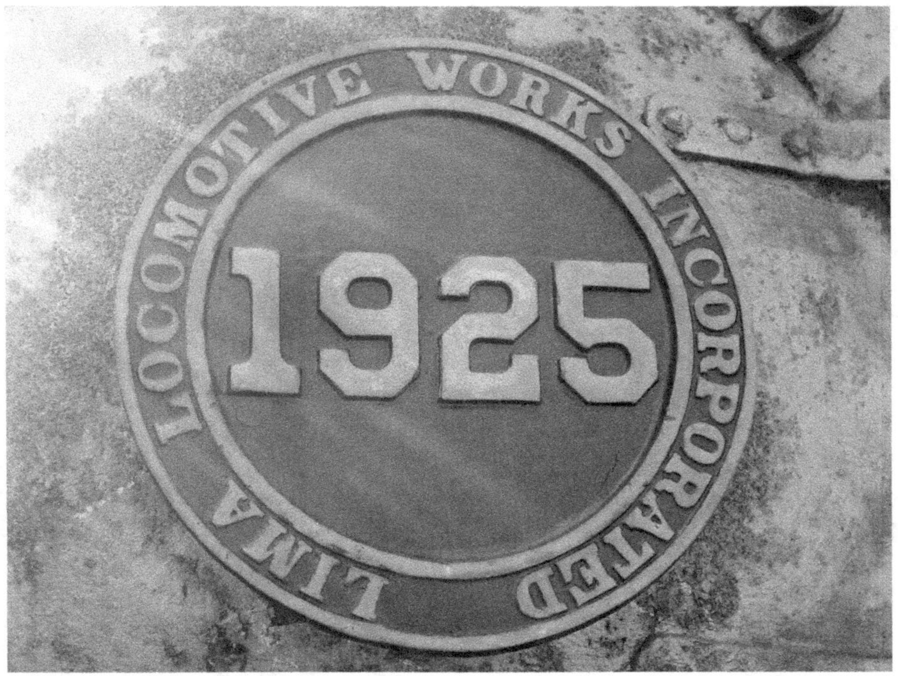

Manufacturers plate on the Shay no. 1925. *JMP Photos.*

1926, in 1926. Because Robbinsville—the county seat of Graham County—had no rail service, the 1925 and 1926 were used to take both freight and passengers to and from the Murphy Branch Southern Railway connection at Topton, as per its 1905 charter agreement.

And unlike most of the other logging spur lines, which were out of business by the later 1930s or before, Bemis continued using its logging rail line and the 1925 and 1926 until 1967. But both engines carried on as freight carriers and, later, for one of them, as a tourist train for years after that.

The tourist train was known as the Bear Creek Scenic Railroad. In 1968, the 1925 was involved in a terrible wreck when it suffered brake failure and derailed in the Nantahala Gorge. No one was killed, but several people were injured and the 1925 was badly damaged. The company was able to rebuild the 1925 using its original parts, combined with new parts salvaged from the 1926, thus putting the 1926 out of business.

The 1925 resumed operation and ran (along with a modern-day diesel engine) until the Bear Creek Railroad closed in 1970 before enjoying a brief resurgence as a tourist and freight line under new ownership in 1973. The line ran for two years before closing permanently in 1975.

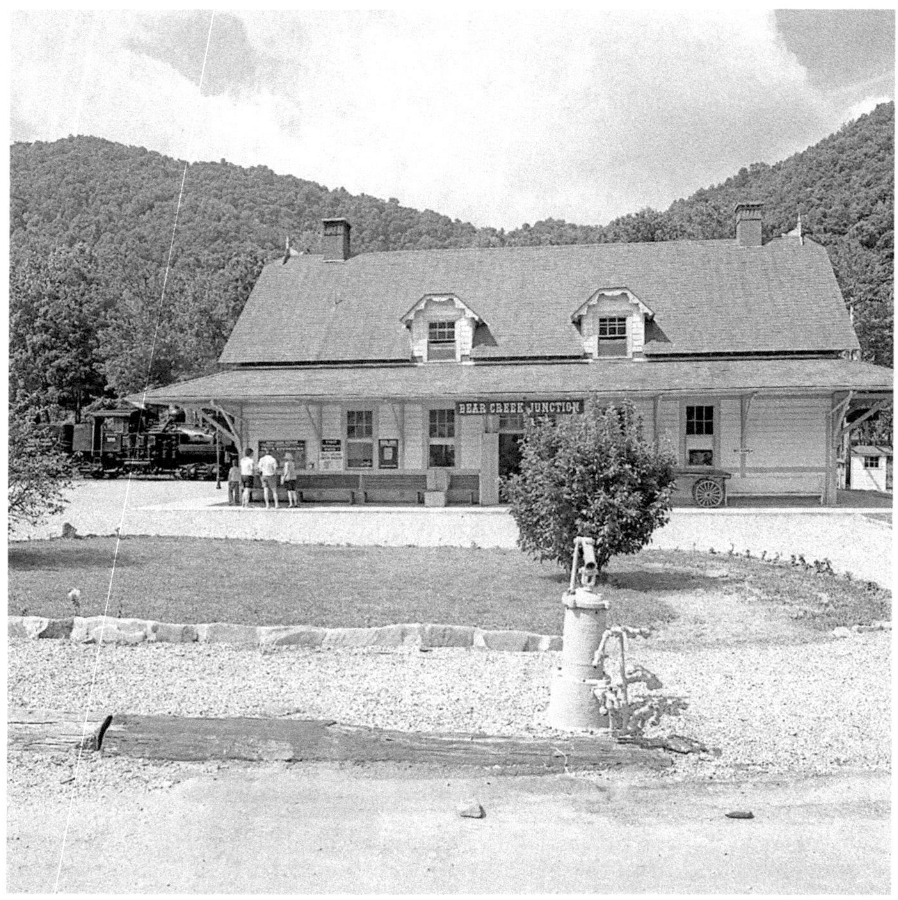

Bear Creek Junction Scenic Railroad in Graham County, North Carolina. *UNC Archives.*

The 1925 was donated to the North Carolina Transportation Museum in Spencer, North Carolina, in 1987 and was briefly brought back into operation as an on-site ride there from 1997 until 2005. The 1925 remains on display at the Roundhouse there today. Hopefully it can be rebuilt again as a prime example of glory days of logging in the Land of Blue Smoke.

But let's get back to logging and the Murphy Branch. It should also be noted that while the logging lines were known mostly for their Shay engines and narrow-gauge lines, there were also quite a few standard-gauge rod engines used by the lumber companies as well, particularly in getting loads to and from the main line headquarters such as Champion in Canton to its surrounding subsidiaries. For specific details on those, we would suggest reading the books by logging experts Gerald Ledford and Ronald Sullivan.

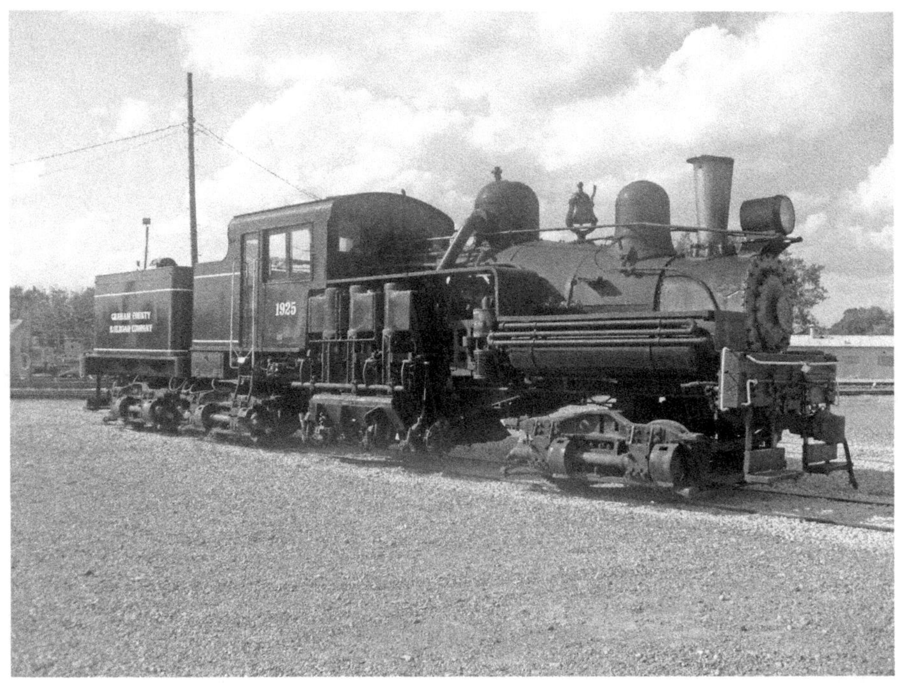

Graham County Shay no. 1925 and tender. *JMP Photos.*

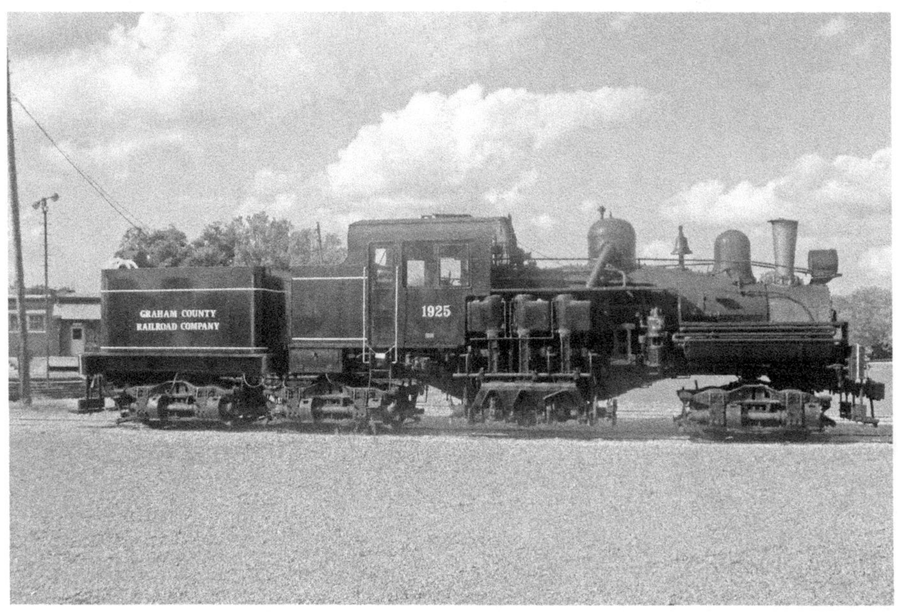

Side view of the 1925. *JMP Photos.*

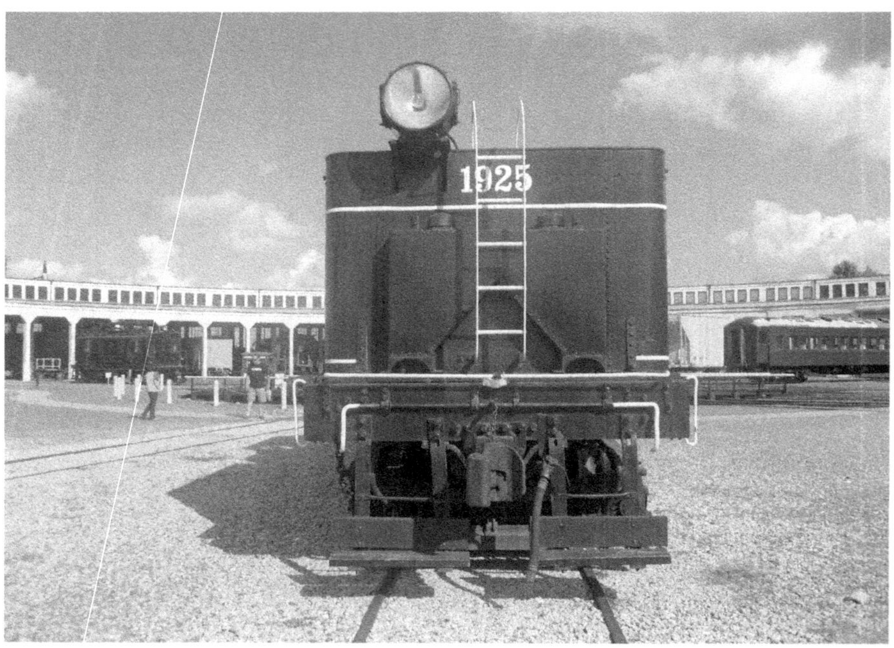

Rear view of 1925's tender. *JMP Photos.*

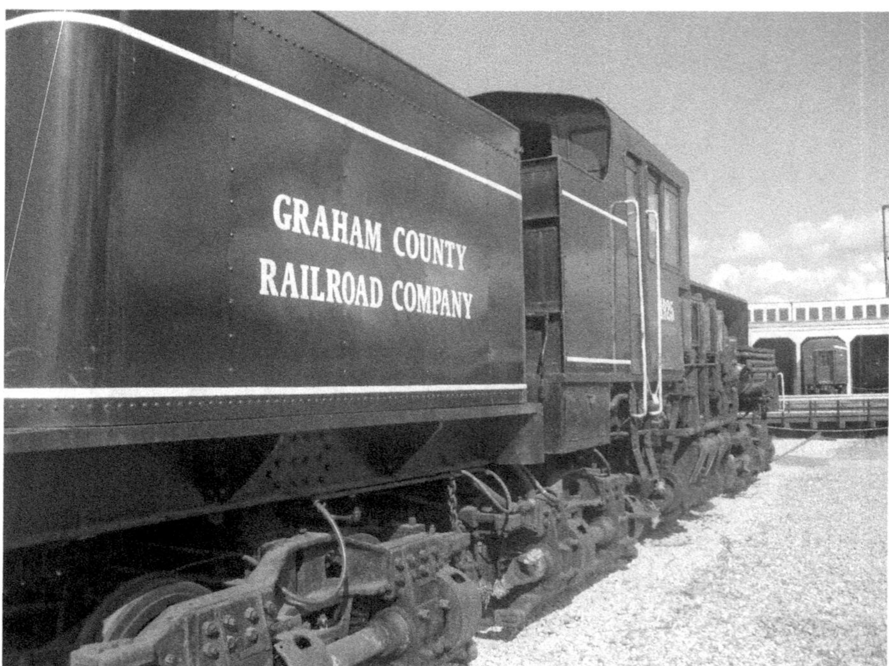

Another view of the 1925. *JMP photos.*

Most of these engines, to the best of our knowledge, have been scrapped. Champion, of course, was by far the largest and longest-running operation—still in business today as Blue Ridge Paper Products—and had more equipment and employees than most of these operations combined. But the same types of equipment were used at most, if not all, of these locations.

While the Shay was indeed the preferred narrow-gauge geared engine in the Western North Carolina logging industry, the Snowbird Valley Railway, which was owned and operated by Kanawah Hardwood Lumber Company, used the Climax engine. It was built by the Climax Locomotive Works located in Corry, Pennsylvania. The Climax was the second geared engine to enter the market in 1888.

The Snowbird Railway went from Andrews to Little Snowbird, and loads were pulled by Climax engines no. 1 1 and no. 2. Unlike the Shay, the Climax has diagonal cylinders on both sides of the engine. The driving rods are in the center of the engine and power the crankshaft, which turns the wheels.

To the best of our knowledge, there were likely no more than ten Climax engines working on Murphy Branch spur lines, if that. But we can document at least six of them. In fact, Climax only built a little over one thousand of these engines during its existence between 1888 and 1923. And of that number, there are only ten that still survive today in North America. One of them is the Climax no. 1323 narrow-gauge B-40, which is now on display at the Cradle of Forestry Museum in Brevard, North Carolina. Champion first purchased it in 1914 and used it at its Quinlantown operations and possibly others as well.

The Heisler was the third type of preferred geared logging locomotive. Heisler was the smallest-geared engine manufacturer and the last to enter the market in Dunkirk, New York, in 1891. Only a few hundred of these engines were sold, and only a handful were used in the Smokies—probably no more than five, if that. Like the Climax, it had one cylinder on each side of the boiler and centrally located drive rods powering the wheels.

Now that we understand the equipment and narrow-gauge lines needed to operate these logging spur lines along the Murphy Branch, let's take a look at some of the towns that sprang up along these lines, as well the people who built and worked on them.

Although Champion was the biggest, it was not the first major logging operation to operate along the Murphy Branch. That honor goes to the W.M. Ritter Lumber Company, which originated in Welch, West Virginia, in 1901 before eventually moving its headquarters to Roanoke, Virginia. Ritter had logging operations in six states—including North Carolina—

and grew at such an explosive rate that the company eventually split into four divisions to manage them. Ritter was involved in the coal mining industry as well.

In 1902, Ritter Lumber convinced Southern Railway to extend a spur line from its Bushnell terminal to its huge logging operation in Proctor. It was the earliest logging spur line in the Hazel Creek Watershed and one of the first, if not the first, on the Murphy Branch.

The twenty-three-mile line ran from the Murphy Branch in Bushnell nine miles upstream to Proctor and then another nine miles up Hazel Creek, with connecting lines to Sugar Fork, Bone Valley and Walker Creek before eventually terminating at Fontana. The Ritter spur line was known as the Smoky Mountain Railroad.

In 1910, Ritter Lumber announced record production totals in its North Carolina operations, and Montvale Lumber Company had joined the fray and extended its business to Eagle Creek, near the Tennessee border. Never one to miss an opportunity for profit, the Ritter-owned Smoky Mountain Railroad allowed passengers to ride in the cabooses of log trains to and from the main line junction in Bushnell.

By 1927, Ritter was no longer operating in the Hazel Creek Watershed and had, for the most part, closed its operations in North Carolina. However, the company continued to prosper in multiple states until 1960, when it was sold to Georgia Pacific. It is estimated that between 1900 and 1960, Ritter Lumber sold more than 3 *billion* feet of lumber to its clients.

As noted, before the demise of Ritter, Bushnell, Proctor, Medlin and Ritter were all substantial communities. Proctor and Bushnell both had more than five hundred residents, and Proctor took pride in being the home to two post offices, a church, a school, several retail outlets and even a movie theater, owned by Granville Calhoun, who sometimes used a handcar to run errands on the railroad.

Granted, some of these communities were there before the logging boom and likely would still be there today were it not for the formation of the GSMNP and Fontana Lake. Their residents were solid citizens, many of them well-educated, articulate and savvy businesspeople—the superb businessman and stellar outdoorsman Granville Calhoun being a classic example.

Others preferred living in the back of beyond and living off their own hook by hunting fishing and farming and avoided modern encumbrances if possible. They detested the logging magnates, but it was hard to turn down good money working for them.

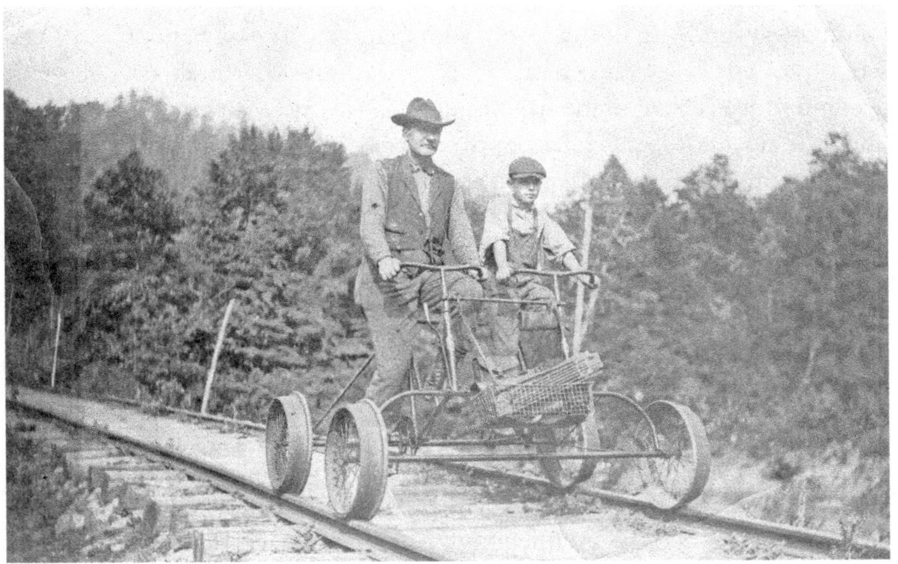

Granville Calhoun and son in a bicycle car on Murphy Branch, early 1900s. *Plott family photo.*

But no matter what their stance, none of this economic boom and explosive growth would have occurred without the railroad and the logging industry. Many felt that these changes were not necessarily better.

Even Granville Calhoun, who benefited greatly from them, admitted as much and lamented that he missed the old days, saying, "Then came the lumbermen. Why, it was just like a revolution, and I guess it was. Folks who understood a rifle trigger and fishing pole saw things they had barely heard of, much less seen. There wasn't much time left for hunting and fishing."

All these lumber spur towns are gone now—some under the waters of Fontana Lake, others burned down or destroyed when the park was formed or left to ruin when the timber boom ended. Most all of them were company towns. They were similar in many ways to the textile towns in the Piedmont of North Carolina such as Kannapolis or Gastonia, where the textile mill owners not only provided their employees with a job but also rented them homes for as long as they were employed, thus basically controlling their lives.

In these cases, particularly with towns like Sunburst, Crestmont and Quinlantown—all in Haywood County—Champion Lumber Company controlled almost everything. In fairness to it, Champion treated its employees well for the most part. It provided company doctors, a commissary and, in the case of Sunburst, a Forestry School, a public school, a church—with a dance hall and skating rink built over it—and a community center or banquet hall that was used for public meetings and as a lodge for local civic groups such as the Masons and Odd Fellows. Sunburst also had a barbershop, a town jail, a forty-room hotel and a boardinghouse.

At its peak, Sunburst claimed 550 residents, including 100 African Americans, which was an oddity at most of the logging communities in the Smokies—the only other logging town with any significant number of Black employees was Proctor, whose Black residents were segregated on the north side of town.

Almost all these Sunburst residents worked for Champion in some form or fashion. The citizens took pride in their home and their treatment by Champion. However, it must be said that it wasn't like these folks had a lot of other employment options either, even if there were several private business owners such as Granville Calhoun in Proctor and Zeb Knotts in Sunburst.

Knotts, like Calhoun, was a colorful character who owned a store on the outskirts of Sunburst. Knotts' Store was a community gathering place and renowned for its wide selection of candy and vending machines for candy and gum, which made the business especially popular with children. On the wall above the counter in the store hung a sign that perfectly summed up Zeb Knotts and his business philosophy: "We have been in business since 1910. We have been cussed and discussed, we have been pillaged, lied to and cheated. The only reason we stay in business is to see what the hell will happen next!" You can't beat the mountaineer sense of humor.

But there was another, more brutal side of the logging business too. Author Bob Plott interviewed Dewey Sharp, a lifelong resident of Graham County, in 2008. Sharp was almost ninety-nine years old then and had worked on one of the Graham County logging spur railroad lines that connected with the Murphy Branch when he was twenty-one years old in 1930. This is how he described it:

> *The pay was bad, and the working conditions were worse. We seldom made more than a dollar day but it was during the Depression so we took what we could get. Worse part was that most of what we made went right back to the company to pay for housing, food, clothing and supplies. They didn't give you nothing but a hard time. We worked six days a week in all kinds of weather from daylight until sundown and often ended up owing the company money!*

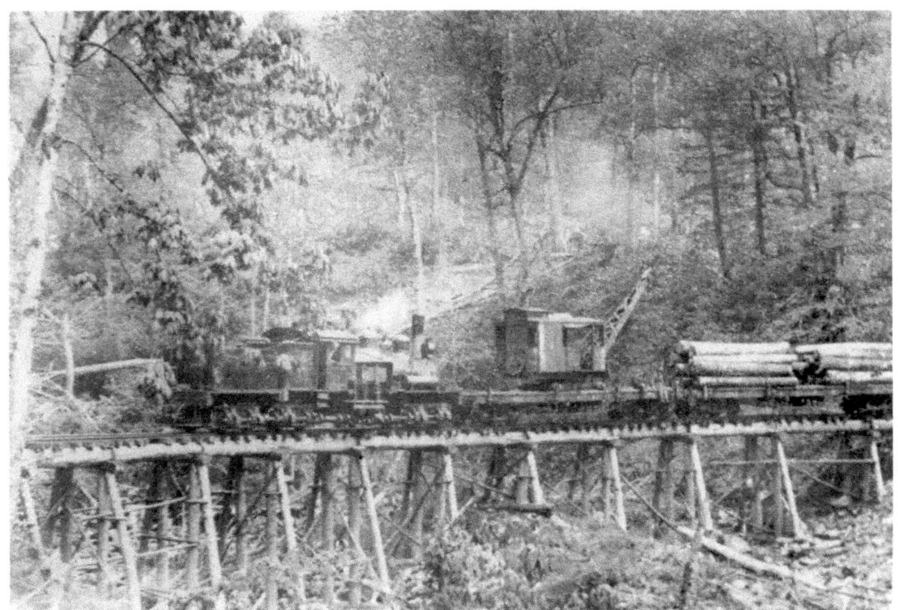

Graham County logging train. *GSMNP.*

Sharp paused, laughed sadly and continued:

> *There were no benefits, men were injured or killed almost daily. And if you got hurt or killed and your family was living nearby, they threw everyone out and sent you on your way. There was always plenty of folks lined up waiting for work, replacements were easy to come by. It was bad, son, real bad, and the work was brutal. Not only did you have to worry about a tree or limb falling on you, you had to be careful about getting cut. It was hot as the devil in the summer and you had to always be on the lookout for rattlesnakes, copperheads, hornets and yellow jackets. Winter wasn't much better, there were no snakes and insects to deal with then, but it was terribly cold and snowed a lot which made conditions even harder to work in. I saw many a man killed or get maimed for life. And like I said, those that were injured, just got fired, there was no compensation.*

When asked how bad the living conditions where, Sharp noted:

> *We lived in company houses that really were nothing more than wooden boxes—with a door cut out and maybe a window or opening for a stove pipe for the wood stove to heat the place, but some of them did not even have*

that. Several single men bunked in one box and married couples with kids were allowed their own box. And when I say boxes, well, that's exactly what they were. They were just big wooden crates that could be loaded on flatbed cars whenever we moved. You usually could get two boxes per car, but sometimes they loaded four to a car.

When asked what he meant by "moving," Sharp replied:

I mean just that—move them. We only stayed in one place long enough to clear cut it before we moved on to the next one. As we cut all the timber down, they had crews building more railroad track to the next big stand of trees and then they would get a crane to load the boxes on the cars, chained them down and moved on to the next stop.

When asked how long it took to move, he responded:

It did not take long. We would move only on a Sunday—never during the work week because they were not going to miss cutting any logs. I was lucky that they let me keep my hunting dogs as long as I fed them, and they didn't bother anyone. Plus, I would hunt on Sundays, and brought meat in—and they liked that. I didn't own nothing but those dogs and the clothes on my back. So, no, it didn't take long for us to move. I just pissed on the fire, called the dogs and moved on to the next place they wanted us to work.

Sharp concluded his logging interview by adding that he cut plenty of original timber growth during his five years working as a logger and described the difficulty of it all:

I get tired just think about it. The trees were huge, I remember some Poplars that were bigger than 25 feet around. And we cut all of them by hand with a crosscut saw or axe, there wasn't no chain saws back then! It was the mountain boys like me, the locals, that did all the dirty, dangerous work. They brought in their own managers, engineers, mill wrights and such—the so-called skilled labor—and they got the best and highest paying jobs. But what could we do? We needed work and they provided it, such that it was.

The logging companies were often not fair in their land negotiations. They offered terribly low prices, and if an owner refused to sell their property or relinquish timber rights, the companies had the power to have the land condemned and foreclosed on. Owners basically took what they could get and in most cases were glad to get it. This was an all-too-common negotiation technique used by the Tennessee Valley Authority and the National Park Service in coming years when they came calling to acquire land from locals for the GSMNP and Fontana Dam.

You could do a similar, more in-depth case study of each of these logging communities, and you would probably find remarkably similar stories in each of them. Progress was considered by most to be a good thing, as it provided jobs and regular incomes, and it came in large part because of the railroad or access to it.

But like most forms of progress, there was a price to pay. Sometimes that price came in the loss of human lives, or crippling injuries or diseases incurred while working there, as noted in the actual building of the WNCRR and Murphy Branch, along with the dangers associated with the logging industry.

In other cases, there was a terrible environmental toll to be paid, as these early logging operations gave no thought to replanting trees after clear cutting. Instead, they left the land fallow and susceptible to erosion. Silt issues and landslides destroyed many mountain streams and farms. Waste emitted from industrial operations into mountain tributaries played havoc with these waterways. The Pigeon River is a notable example of a once pristine stream riddled with toxic waste that, many believe, resulted in the deaths or illnesses of many mountaineers. Government-mandated cleanup efforts have been successful, but the damage was done.

Perhaps the most eloquent description of the impact that progress had on the remote parts of the region was written by Florence Cope Bush in her book, *Dorie: Woman of the Mountains*:

> *The lumber companies had opened the door to the outside world. We became aware of things—things that money could buy, things that made life easier (or harder), things to see, things to do. They had opened a door—a door we were forced to use as an exit from our ancestral homes. Then after the exit, the door was closed to us. We were given visitors rights to the land—to come and look, but not to stay.*

Writer Horace Kephart, a strong advocate for the GSMNP, was equally as succinct in his disgust for the havoc incurred by the loggers. During his first visit back to Hazel Creek after a massive clear-cutting operation, Kephart described the situation as being "wrecked, ruined, desecrated, vile and mean."

Yet just as many other folks took pride in their families having worked for multiple generations and making a good living with a company like Champion (now Blue Ridge). And they still do today. No one can dispute that the company had a positive impact on the local economy, not just in providing company jobs for local residents but also in the form of businesses that opened and flourished in the region, such as retail stores, restaurants and medical and legal offices that served these Champion employees and those in the surrounding area.

So, as always, there are two sides to the story. But like it or not, the damage was done, and times were indeed changing—some would say for the worst, some for the better. But either way, the Murphy Branch and Southern Railway was right in the middle of it all and, as usual, was charging full speed ahead.

YOU CAN'T KEEP A GOOD MAN DOWN

Before we conclude our brief study of the logging industry on the Murphy Branch, we would be remiss if we did not first revisit Super Six member Will Sandlin and discuss his impact on the industry as well as his continued impact on the Murphy Branch and southwestern North Carolina between 1905 and 1940.

Although Will Sandlin had played an integral role in the completion of the Murphy Branch and recognized the need for intervention by Southern Railway, it nevertheless signaled the end of the young railroader's career working as an employee for the operation.

As noted in the eighth chapter, Sandlin had been repeatedly severely injured on the job, and the WNCRR was so concerned that Sandlin might sue for damages that in 1891 it guaranteed him a job for life if he would promise never to file a liability suit against the company. That agreement, however, came to a sudden halt once Southern Railway took over ownership in 1894. The agreement was declared null and void by the new ownership, and Sandlin, badly maimed from his railroad career, was out of a railroad job at the tender age of twenty-seven.

A lesser man would have been bitter and angry. But not Will Sandlin. Instead, the young mountaineer saw it as another great career opportunity. Still three years shy of his thirtieth birthday, Sandlin took a Civil Service exam and received certification to bid on and build state road projects, while also utilizing his railroad skills in building miles of spur lines for local logging operations in Graham and Cherokee Counties that connected to the Murphy Branch.

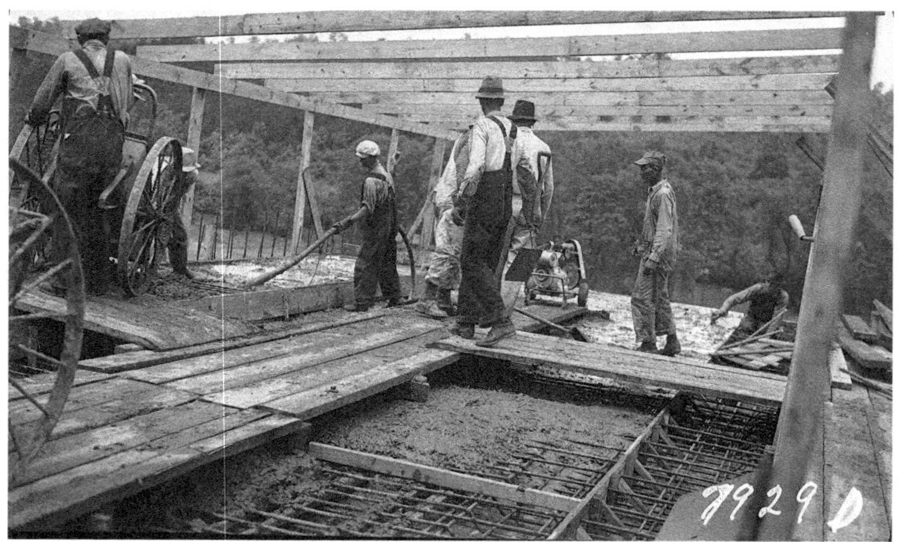

A bridge building project near Murphy. *UNC Archives.*

With his highway certification completed, Sandlin worked on various smaller road projects when not working on logging railroad jobs. For instance, he designed and surveyed a wagon road, known as the Barker Wagon Road, from Andrews to West Buffalo. But his crowning achievement building and designing highways came in about 1922, when county commissioners asked him to bid on building a road in northwest Macon County.

The road—originally an ancient Indian trail referred to by old-timers as "the cat's stairs" due to its steep and winding grade—wound out of the Nantahala Gorge between Queens Creek and the Swain County line and climbed about five miles over the top of the mountain into Macon County.

The politicians wanted a connecting route suitable for automobile or wagon travel between Swain and Macon Counties but could not find a builder willing or capable to master the 8 percent grade. Having mastered similar railroad gradients on the Murphy Branch, Will Sandlin's bid was accepted, and he was just the man for the job.

Just as with his previous railroad projects, many college-educated engineers scoffed at the idea of anyone—especially "a dumb hillbilly"—building a road like this. The experts deemed it impossible. But the experts did not know Will Sandlin.

By the end of 1923, he had miraculously completed the project. The gravel road—masterfully designed like a set of stair steps, suitable for a vehicle to safely navigate—was deemed an engineering marvel. The route became known as the Winding Stairs Road and is still in use today. Despite this stunning accomplishment, Will Sandlin's first love as an engineer was building railroads, and the logging boom allowed him to follow his passion as a railroader. Let's flash back to 1905 and examine his success in the logging field.

As noted in the eleventh chapter, lumber companies like Ritter, Whiting, Bemis, Kanawha, Snowbird, Champion and many others all built booming lumber businesses along the Murphy Branch, along with hundreds, probably thousands, of miles of railroad spur lines deep into the mountains between Canton and Murphy to transport timber from the dark hollows to the main line depots along the Murphy Branch. And again, it was Will Sandlin who led the charge in building many of these logging spur lines in Swain, Macon and Cherokee Counties.

Snowbird Lumber Company executives were exasperated with the incompetence of their college-trained engineers and hired Sandlin for various projects to design and build miles of narrow-gauge railroad deep into the Snowbird and Unico Mountain Ranges at different times between 1905 and 1916. While working on an especially difficult eighteen-mile stretch of track from Andrews to the Snowbirds, Sandlin fired five of the six company engineers, later saying, "I figured I couldn't do any worse myself."

He was exactly right. Sandlin's first obstacle was constructing a four-hundred-foot trestle over a steep gorge. He had difficulty matching the grade levels on each side of the gorge, and it was here that he first used a transit. Once he had mastered the basics of the instrument, he designed the bridge using the proper specifications. Sandlin sang the praises of the transit as a valuable tool for the remainder of his career, while the lumber companies provided Sandlin with their own accolades for his stellar work.

As usual, the logging companies went to Sandlin for the toughest jobs crossing the steepest grades, and there was no shortage of them. On one project for Champion Paper at Cold Spring Mountain, the bed grade was so steep that steps had to be hung in the mountainside to allow workers to stand straight.

A twenty-eight-ton engine hauled 8,600 feet of steel cables that were installed over two sets of tracks, along with a GS-HP loading machine. One track was built to help pull that same huge engine up the grade, as cars filled with timber or pulpwood went down the second track built beside it. The massive six-thousand-foot peak was clear-cut within twelve months. From an environmental perspective, this was a disaster, but from an economic perspective it was a huge success and never would have happened without the WNCRR and men like Will Sandlin.

In 1925, Sandlin butted heads again with professional engineers on his next project in building ten miles of railroad line from Robbinsville to the Southern Railway junction in Topton. It was a homecoming of sorts for Will, as he was right back to where he first became legendary as a railroad man and working with the company that had unfairly fired him. And as usual, Sandlin completed the project despite criticism from his more educated peers.

Will Sandlin continued to design and build logging railroads and state highway projects the remainder of his career, while also working as a civil engineer for ALCOA and the TVA. And in doing so, Sandlin further perpetuated his legacy as a legendary railroad builder and proud member of the Super Six. Like with the other members of this iconic roster, it is impossible to say that the Murphy Branch would never have been built without them. However, it's hard to imagine it happening without their collective efforts working as team and individually, or at the very least, the WNCRR would not have been finished in the nineteenth century and maybe not until after World War II, although that is highly speculative. Nevertheless, the fact that a statement like that could even be considered viable is proof positive of the incredible skills and contributions of the Super Six.

Will Sandlin's personal life was equally as successful as his professional career. He and his beloved wife, Nannie, had one daughter and two foster children, all of whom enjoyed successful professional careers of their own. Sandlin also took pride in his fifty-year membership in the local Masonic Lodge.

Will not only lived to see the Murphy Branch completed, but he also saw the WNCRR line and the economy in Western North Carolina improve as a result of his efforts in ways that probably not even he could have imagined. Will Sandlin died on March 27, 1947, just short of his eightieth birthday. His death came only a few years after the line he had worked so hard to build was forced to be partially rerouted due to the formation of Fontana Lake. But first let's examine the dramatic impact the Murphy Branch had on the common man.

CHANGING LIVES

While much has been written about the dramatic economic impact that the logging and mining industries had on the Smokies and the role that the Murphy Branch played in both, let's not forget that these booms were both relatively short-lived.

The logging boom began in about 1901 and was done for all practical purposes by 1930, largely due to the formation of the GSMNP in 1934. Mining at its height in Western North Carolina never was done on the same scale as logging and was basically finished by the early 1900s, except for a few notable exceptions such as the Regal Marble Company. But even so, mining in Western North Carolina was never done on the scale of the coal industry in other southern Appalachian states, such as West Virginia, Kentucky and Tennessee.

Our economic focus related to the Murphy Branch should be on two areas that have remained strong and steady from the start: farming and tourism. But maybe instead of emphasizing all the explosive growth both in population as well as economics that took place along the Murphy Branch between 1900 and 1940, perhaps we would be better served to examine the impact that the Murphy Branch and Southern Railway/Norfolk Southern had on the common man, most notably local farmers.

It also might be a good idea to allow some of the old-time railroaders to weigh in with their perspectives on the changes they witnessed and what life was like at the helm of an iron horse. However, let's start with exploring things from the farming perspective.

Dewey Sharp provided us with a classic example from the perspective of the common man logger earlier, but there is no better illustration of the common farmer's point of view than the Gibson family of Whittier, North Carolina. The Gibsons can trace their roots in the Smokies back to 1830, when family patriarch John Baxter Gibson was born in Graham County, North Carolina, before later moving to what is now Jackson County, not far from present-day Whittier.

Gibson fought in Colonel Will Thomas's Cherokee Legion during the Civil War and bought 303 acres of land from the State of North Carolina in 1874 (the state had taken it from the Cherokee Nation). In 1881, Gibson purchased 300 adjoining acres from the estate of his former commander, Colonel Thomas, giving him a total of 633 acres.

Over the years, some of that acreage was sold, but Gibson family members have lived and worked at least 125 acres of that same family farm in Whittier since 1874—and still do today, as the farm is now honored as a Heritage Farm.

The Gibson clan, better than most, understand what it means to be a true native of the Land of Blue Smoke. Moreover, William Gene Gibson, now ninety-three years old, and his wife of seventy-three years, Estella, along with their son Billy Gene Gibson, are the current owners of the property and are uniquely qualified to understand the dramatic impact that the Murphy Branch, Southern Railway and the GSMR has had on their native homeland.

Author Bob Plott is friends with the family and first interviewed them for their take on this subject in 2015. Their perspective is especially interesting to us, as William can vividly recall how the coming of the railroad changed his life as a boy in the 1930s.

His son, Billy, better known as Bill, served for thirty-seven years as executive director of the Southwestern North Carolina Planning and Economic Commission and understands the impact that the Murphy Branch had on the region. Moreover, as we will later see, Bill Gibson played an integral role in the Murphy Branch's resurgence as the GSMR and knows what that has meant to the region in recent years. But let's start with William G. Gibson and let him share his insight on the impact the railroad had on local farmers:

> *I was born right here on this farm in 1927. My great-grandpa was John Baxter Gibson, and his house was at the head of the hollow up on the ridge—where Bill is restoring it today. He fought in the Civil War with Will Thomas and is buried here on the farm in the family cemetery. When*

I was a boy, this was still a remote area. We were self-sufficient; we had to be. We grew or killed most everything we ate; my mother was an expert seamstress and made our clothes. Our water came from a hand-powered well pump—there was no running water indoors. We cut wood to heat and cook with. Grew and canned our food, raised livestock, hunted and fished. There was plenty to eat, but there were no frills. Money was spent only on the priorities—stuff we could not grow or make ourselves, like hardware, sugar or coffee. We even built our own coffins out of curly chestnut—we made one for my grandmother. I remember a horse-drawn wagon taking my grandmother's body to burial in the family cemetery.

Bob Plott asked Mr. Gibson if he found that life to be hard and, if not, if he missed it. Gibson replied:

Yeah, those were good days. It's hard not to miss them—although I appreciate what we have today too. We had to work hard, but everyone did. I didn't mind it. We worked hard from dawn to dusk. In many ways, I guess it was no different than the frontier days. I remember once seeing some of our Cherokee friends going to the train depot in an ox-driven cart. We traded a lot together. We were one of the earliest white families here and got along well with the tribe. They were good people and had been badly mistreated. But even in those days, the railroad had been here for almost forty years and played a huge role in our lives. It'd hard to put into words just how important it was to us.

But it was somewhat limited too, especially before the train came and it got harder during the Depression, but we made do. Heck, I was twelve or thirteen years old in 1939 before my family owned a car. It was a T-Model Roadster that my daddy paid forty dollars for. And it would take over two hours to drive one way to Waynesville. You pretty much were limited as to where you could go. People tended to stay here their entire lives, and many had not been far outside the county until the train came. Mind you, I had never seen a car or truck of any *kind until I was ten years old in 1937. I will never forget it. It was 1934 International Harvester truck, and it had green and red wheels. That really stuck with me. Until then, the only vehicles I knew of or had ever seen was a wagon or cart pulled by a horse, mule or oxen—except for the steam train. And let me tell you something, that train was a* big *deal to us in a* lot *of different ways.*

"How so?" Plott asked.

Obviously I wasn't born when the train first came through in the 1880s, but my folks saw it firsthand. Before then, they had no way to take crops or livestock to market except by wagon, so it was mostly just subsistence farming. We grew and raised enough to eat and maybe trade a little, but before the train, you really had no way to take any crop to market in volume. My daddy and my grandpa told me about their Cherokee neighbors coming down from their nearby farms on Soco and spending the night at our place before they went on to Whittier to pick up supplies delivered by the train at the general store in Whittier. My wife's family ran it. That train was a lifeline for their business. It was, in many ways, a lifeline for all of us.

It's hard to even imagine now, but for the first time we could have heavy farm equipment delivered to the depot so we could farm on a larger scale and be more productive. Think about something as simple as a wood stove. Houses were hard to heat with just a fireplace. And a big metal woodstove was almost impossible to transport any significant distance—especially on those old rough wagon roads. But the train could deliver most anything of any size to us to pick up at a depot just a few miles away.

But it was much more than that too. Trains ran everything; life sort of revolved around them. Before the train came, we would have to waste a day driving a wagon team just to get to Sylva to pay a bill or go see a doctor or pick up something we needed. Once the trains were running, it took only about 15 to 20 minutes to make that same trip. And the trains ran multiple times daily, so you could get your business done in a half a day in most cases and still get some work done. Southern had a flagpole at each of their stops. If it was raised, that meant they needed to stop and pick you up, if it wasn't, they went on. It cost ten cents each way—twenty cents total—to make the trip.

The 10:15 a.m. train ran to Sylva daily, and another headed back this way at 12:30 p.m. Two passenger trains ran daily east to west, along with four freight trains. They usually stopped in Wilmot, Barkers Creek, Dillsboro, Whittier and Sylva, and of course, you could go on further east or west if you needed. And that *was a big difference that is hard to describe, but it gave you a sense of freedom.*

Mr. Gibson paused again to reflect before continuing.

For the very first time, we were truly connected to the outside world in every way, when less than fifty years earlier we could not even get to Asheville or any point east, west, north or south except by wagon, although by 1937 folks were starting to get cars. We had options for the first time. We had a way out to get more education or find other work most anywhere in the country. Let me give you an example of that. When things got bad, my daddy boarded the train in Whittier and found a job working for Henry Ford in Detroit, Michigan—making fifty cents a day. My wife's grandparents got on the train in Whittier and went all the way to Centralia, Washington, on the West Coast—just like a lot of folks here in Western North Carolina who went out there looking for work in the logging industry. The Murphy Branch connected us to the outside world; we could go anywhere! It was life changing!

"What else do you recall about the train?" Plott requested. Mr. Gibson responded:

The passenger train always had two passenger cars and a baggage car and caboose. There was a steam engine pulling it, I think it was number 722 or 711, but I might be wrong. I have seen freight trains that were much bigger, so big that they needed two engines to pull them and one engine to push them—I can't recall their numbers, but they were big engines. Another

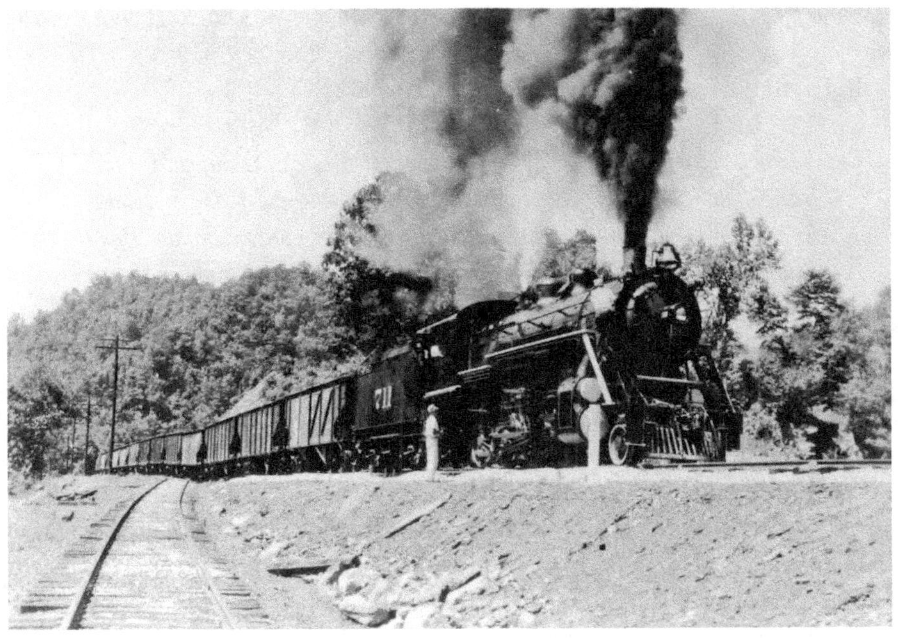

No. 711 at Murphy Branch siding, west of Bryson City. *Thanks to Thomas Plott and Ashley Swenson Hackshaw.*

thing I can remember is that there was a distinct difference in the sound of their whistles. The passenger train had a deeper-throated sound, while the passenger train was higher pitched. It tickles me to hear that old steam whistle blowing again today on the tourist train. I grin every time I hear it—brings back a lot of good memories. Memories of going away on the train, and even better memories of coming back home.

"Please elaborate on leaving and coming home," Plott asked. Mr. Gibson answered:

Like most mountain men my age, I went off to fight in World War II. I was in the Merchant Marine and then got drafted by the army in 1944. I rode the train out of here to basic training. It was sort of scary, but it was our duty and we were excited too. After Japan surrendered, I ended up being stationed in Japan and serving as driver for officers there. We were stationed in the Emperor of Japan's former palace, and I drove an officer to meet General Douglas MacArthur. I will never forget that. But I had to take a hardship discharge in 1948 to come home and take care of the farm. My daddy was a diabetic and one of the first people ever to take insulin shots. My wife was waiting for me too. We had gotten married while I was home on leave in 1947. And guess how I came home? On the train. On the Murphy Branch.

Reflecting a moment, Mr. Gibson quickly added:

Think about this son. I have seen a lot of changes in my life. From traveling in ox carts to space travel and a man on the moon and everything in between—including two atomic bombs being dropped on Japan. But I doubt any of it meant more to us in the long run than that train.

That about says it all doesn't it? William Gene Gibson returned home and carved out a solid career working his family farm and supplementing his income by working for the State of North Carolina while raising three children with his beloved wife, Estella. The couple still live there today, and their son Bill and his partner, Kristen, have a home on the ridge.

Let's wrap up this chapter by allowing a few old-timer railroaders to offer their perspective on what it was like working for the railroad in those early days and the impact it had on their lives and others.

An *Asheville Citizen Times* reporter interviewed Gene Adams in 1931 about his time as a Southern employee on the Murphy Branch. Mr. Adams began his career in the early 1880s as a teenager working for the WNCRR. He did the dirty work in the shop, where he learned firsthand "the why, wherefore and when of railroad machinery." When he was eighteen in 1885, Adams was promoted to fireman and, not long after that, achieved his dream of becoming a steam locomotive engineer. He would continue in that role for the next thirty-four years, and his remarkable career included several landmark events.

Adams was the engineer for the very first complete passenger train that rolled into Murphy, North Carolina, on June 1, 1898. It was called the Smoky Mountain Special and consisted of a seventeen-cylinder steam engine, a tender car, one combination mail and baggage car and one passenger coach.

And before the steam engines were converted to oil, Adams also fired the last wood-burning locomotive on the line in 1886. The old-timer recalled in the 1931 interview that he was at the throttle of at least one passenger train daily for thirty-two years and once worked twenty-nine straight Christmas day holidays piloting the engine.

Mr. Adams rightfully noted, "Railroading in the good old days, just as today, required men of brains and brawn, men with cool heads and steady nerves. You still need those traits today, but it seems like you had to have even more of those qualities to get by back then." Adams further added these life-changing points:

> *I have witnessed many changes in communication and transportation. Not only with the trains and what they meant to us but also in communication. My father told me of seeing the first telegraph lines being strung from Salisbury to Old Fort and how one old woman complained that she could no longer whip her children without everyone for miles in all directions knowing of it!*

Author and journalist John Parris described Murphy Branch engineer Bob Christopher as "a railroading man from a railroading clan." Christopher, son of a steam engineer, began working in the Murphy Branch at the tender age of fourteen in the early 1900s and eventually became an engineer himself. He ran both steam and diesel engines during his long career and shared his thoughts about the importance of the line with Parris in 1958:

> *Back in the early days of the steam trains, the passenger train and freight trains were institutions. People depended on them. Folks along the route reckoned time by the passage of the passenger trains. The trains kept a strict*

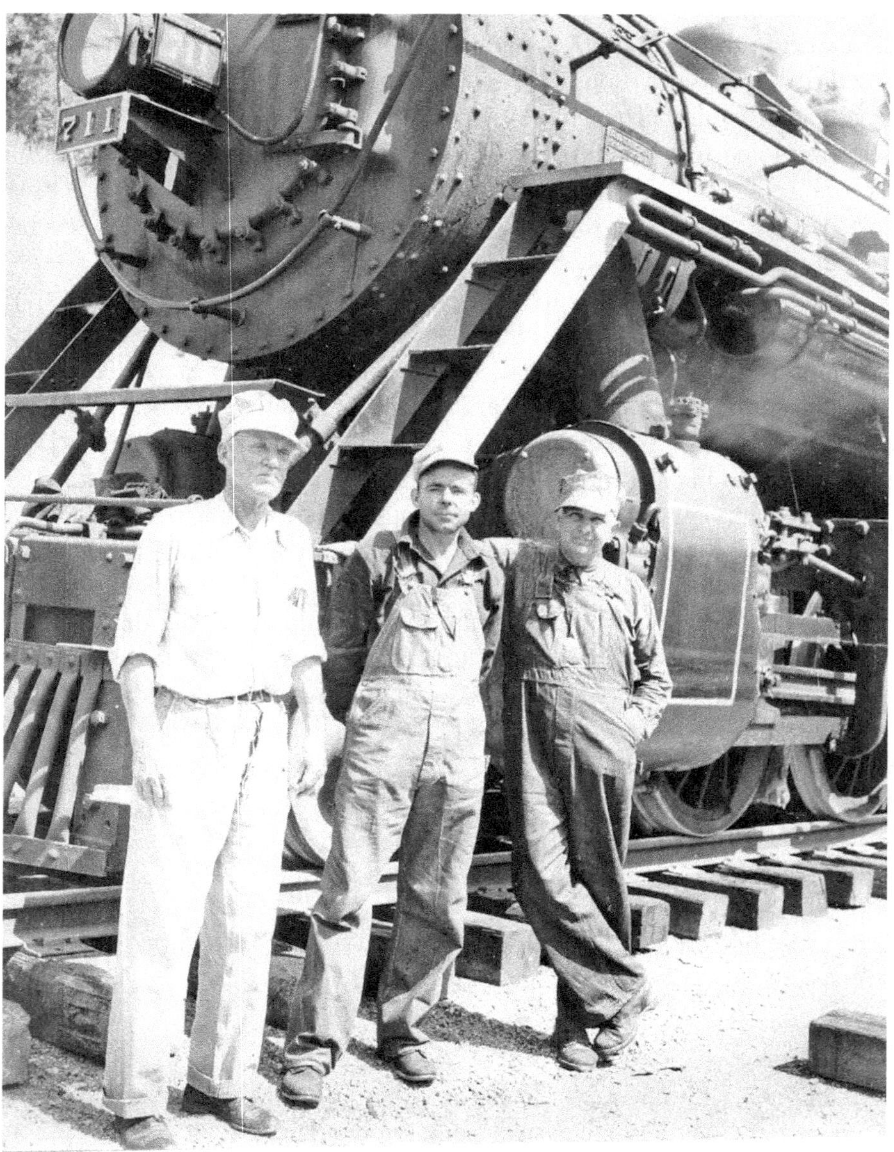

From left to right: Tom Sandlin, unknown and Joe Sawyer, with no. 711. *Frank Clodfelter photo. Thanks to Thomas Plott and Ashley Swenson Hackshaw.*

schedule and the blasts of their whistles clocked the hour of the day—even the minute to the hour. They were important. Life revolved around them. The depots were gathering places—not only to board passengers or pick up or ship freight—but also to congregate to talk and gossip. Trains were

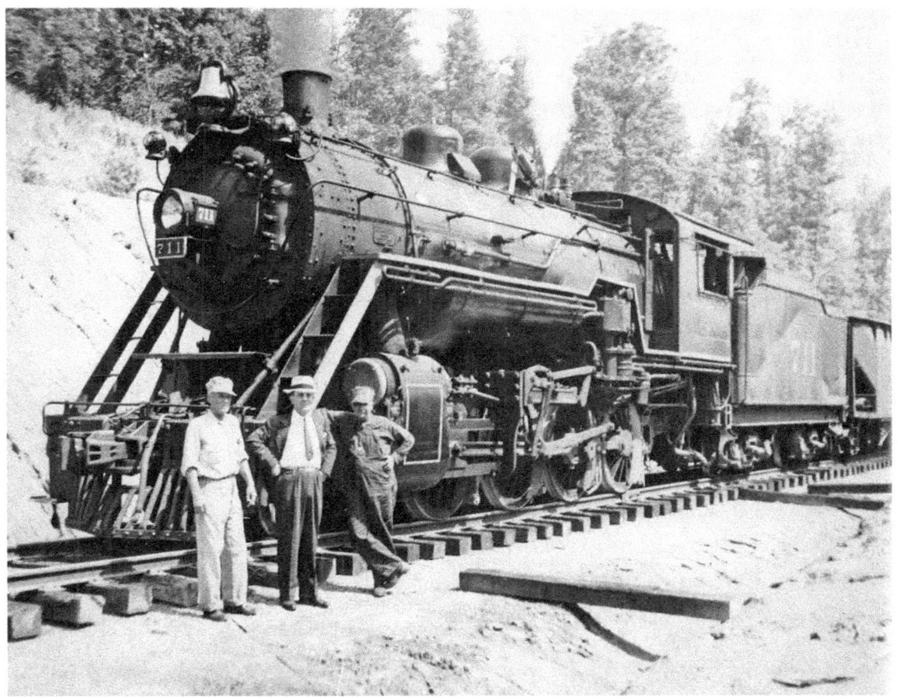

No. 711 crew with railway official. *Thanks to Thomas Plott and Ashley Swenson Hackshaw.*

> *friendly, important things to local folks. They were a big deal. Back then engineers were thought of in the same trinity as Santa Claus and God and all the kids wanted to grow up to be engineers!*

Bryson City native James Fox got his start on the Murphy Branch after serving as a solider in World War II. He began his career working as a fireman in 1943 and later became an engineer for eighteen years on both diesel and steam locomotives until his retirement in 1961. Fox began his career on hand-fired steam engines, which usually required that you go wherever the job required—basically most anywhere on the Southern line all the way to Greensboro, but mostly on the Murphy Branch. Here are some comments that Fox made to author Mead Parce:

> *I began work during the last days of the steam era. The steam engines of that time were the 600 Class, I was at the helm of both the 711 and the 722. The 722 stayed at Andrews back then and ran 220 pounds of steam pressure. Later, they put bigger cylinders on them to cut the pressure back to 185 pounds which was not quite as dangerous.*

Fox once pulled one hundred cars of cement on the 711 to Fontana Dam when it was being built and drove passenger trains as well. Fox told Parce that he believed he was at the throttle for the last steam passenger train to Murphy in 1948, adding:

> *The track was better back in the steam days. It was elevated. The diesels flattened it. Diesel engines are a lot cleaner, but it was more about real railroading with the steam engines. The grades were tough, we had some of the steepest in the county right here on the Murphy Branch. Cowee was hard and it got hot, Balsam wasn't that bad. I think Red Marble was the worst. It was all hard work, but I enjoyed every single minute of it. I miss the old times, but I believe we made a difference.*

Indeed, you did, sir. Well done.

Let's next take a glimpse of the impact that tourism had on the Land of Blue Smoke—thanks in large part to the Murphy Branch.

TOURISM

Today, tourism is widely recognized as the primary source of income for many residents of the Land of Blue Smoke. And understandably so, as the GSMNP is the most visited national park in the United States, and outdoor recreational options such as hiking, skiing, whitewater rafting, mountain biking, hunting, fishing and golfing are limitless.

Almost every town along the modern-day Murphy Branch is filled with world-class restaurants, museums, hotels, art galleries, breweries, bookstores, boutiques, wineries and many other entertainment options, including concerts and gambling at two huge casinos, as well as one of the most popular tourist railroads in America.

It is estimated that $65 million of tourist money is spent *daily* throughout the state of North Carolina, and according to the Blue Ridge National Heritage Council, more than $2.3 billion in tourist dollars are spent annually in Western North Carolina.

But the truth is that tourism in the mountains goes back to the days before the Civil War, long before the WNCRR, when wealthy Lowcountry planters sought refuge from the oppressive heat and insect-borne tropical diseases by seeking refuge in the high country. Their servants and slaves loaded the supply wagons and carriages as they accompanied their masters to vacation homes or resorts. Granted, these folks were the rich elite. They were in the minority and had little impact on local economy, but it was nevertheless an early form of tourism to the region.

However, that all changed with the advent of the WNCRR and the Murphy Branch. The railroad opened the flood gates for a national tourism market that still flourishes today. But even in the first half of the twentieth century, tourism proved to be a big boost to the regional economy and laid the foundation for the massive industry it is today. An entire book could be devoted to the places and people who pioneered this industry. But let's take a glimpse into that early tourism industry and the impact that the Murphy Branch had on it.

Once regular passenger trains were running in the late 1800s, visitors had easy access to the Smokies from anywhere in the United States. Just as today, some came seeking solace and healing in the wilderness, such as writer Horace Kephart, who first arrived in Dillsboro in 1904 and spent a few months there studying the Cherokee Indians before moving on to Hazel Creek in 1905 and, still later, to Bryson City, where he would spend the remainder of his life. Kephart's two most well-known books, *Our Southern Highlanders* and *Camping and Woodcraft*, are still in print today.

Kephart also wrote many articles and gear reviews for national outdoor magazines such as *Outdoor Life* and *Field and Stream*, in which he extolled the superb hunting and fishing in the land he called "the back of beyond." Kephart often field-tested camping gear and firearms for manufacturers and wrote about them in various publications.

Another notable early outdoor writer was Raymond Camp, who wrote a regular column for the *New York Times* and wrote glowingly of the Great Smokies and their ample outdoor resources, along with their colorful characters.

Readers of these two writers alone numbered in the hundreds of thousands and resided all over the country and around the globe. These same readers would become intrigued with the area and schedule trips there via the Murphy Branch to pursue various forms of outdoor recreation or to purchase hunting dogs such as the Plott bear hound from the Plott clan. These pursuits also included guided hunting or fishing trips for clients and celebrity friends to multiple regional lodges owned by affluent local businessman or logging companies.

Hunting camps for locals such as the Waynesville Rod and Gun Club near Sunburst, the Panther Flats Camp in Graham County or Granville Calhoun's Appalachian Hunting and Fishing Club on Hazel Creek were common.

But the bigger, more affluent clubs with larger access to privately owned land—serviced by cooks, guides and even private game wardens—

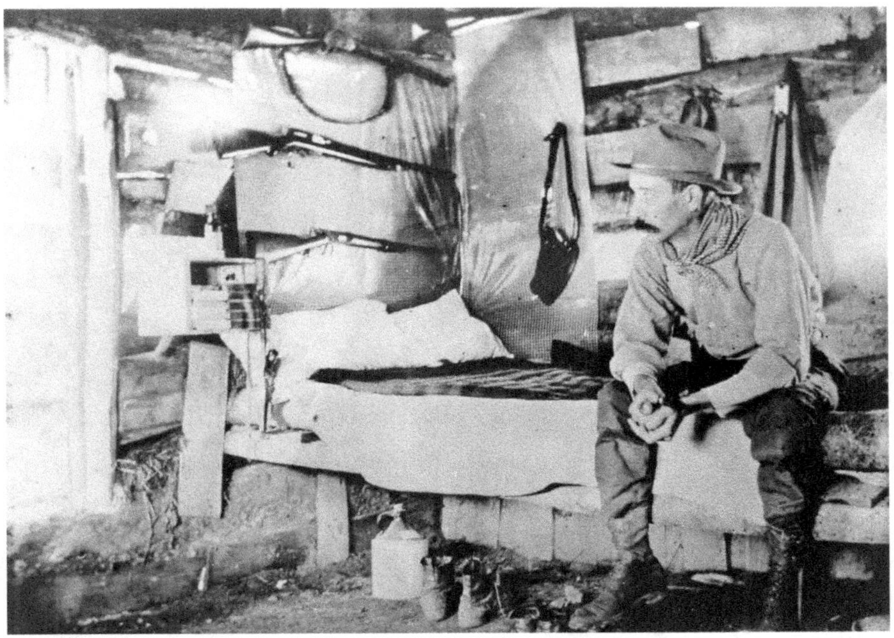

Horace Kephart at camp in the Smokies. *Hunter Library Archives at Western Carolina University (WCU).*

were especially popular as forms of entertainment for customers and friends. These clubs were usually owned by large companies such as Champion, Whiting or ALCOA or by individual businessmen like J.G. "Jim" Stikeleather. Stikeleather's nephew, Jim Gasque, was yet another prominent writer who wrote eloquently about hunting and fishing in the region, thus encouraging others to visit.

Most, if not all, of these camps could only be accessed from the outside world via the Murphy Branch. Let's look at some of these more famous locations that author Bob Plott described in detail in his fifth book, *Plott Hound Tales*.

Arguably the most famous of these clubs was the Hazel Creek Rod and Gun Club. The club was called various names over the years, but it was owned by a group of affluent Asheville businessmen that included Jim Stikeleather, W.M. Smathers and P.H. Branch, among others. The exact date the club was chartered is unknown, but it operated for more than two decades and did not close until after the formation of the GSMNP. It was located one mile upstream from the mouth of Bone Valley Creek on the east bank of Hazel Creek.

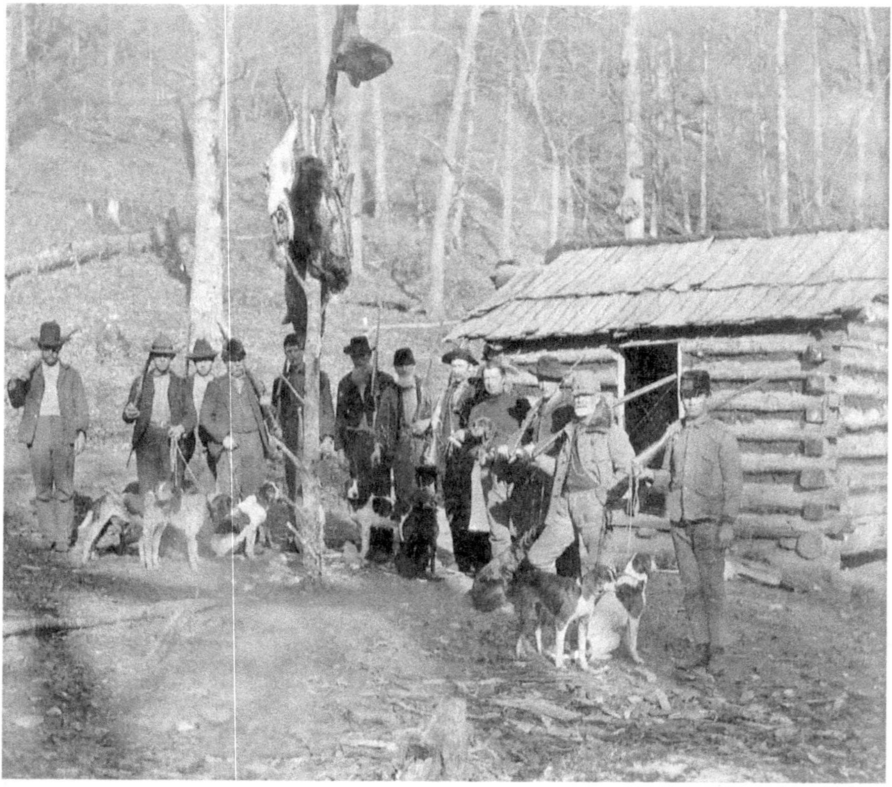

John Denton party at Panther Flats Camp. *Denton Family photos.*

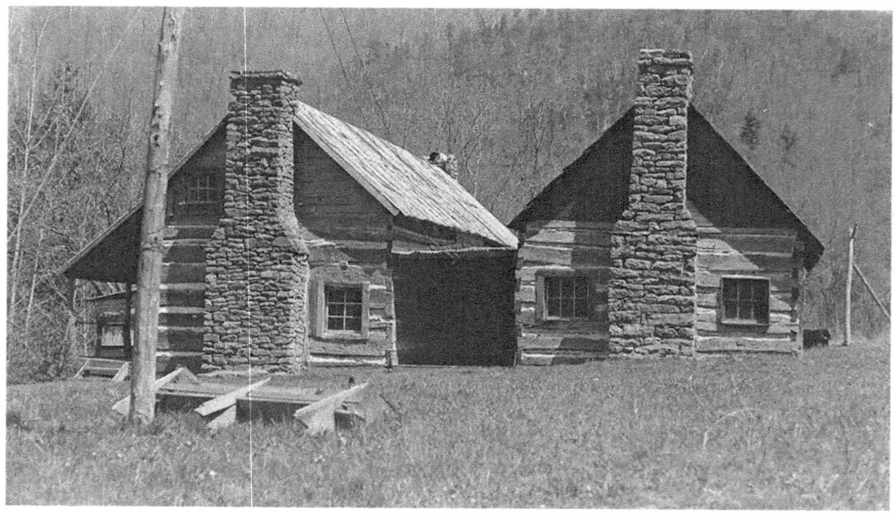

Hazel Creek Lodge after GSMNP was formed and before the lodge was relocated. *GSMNP.*

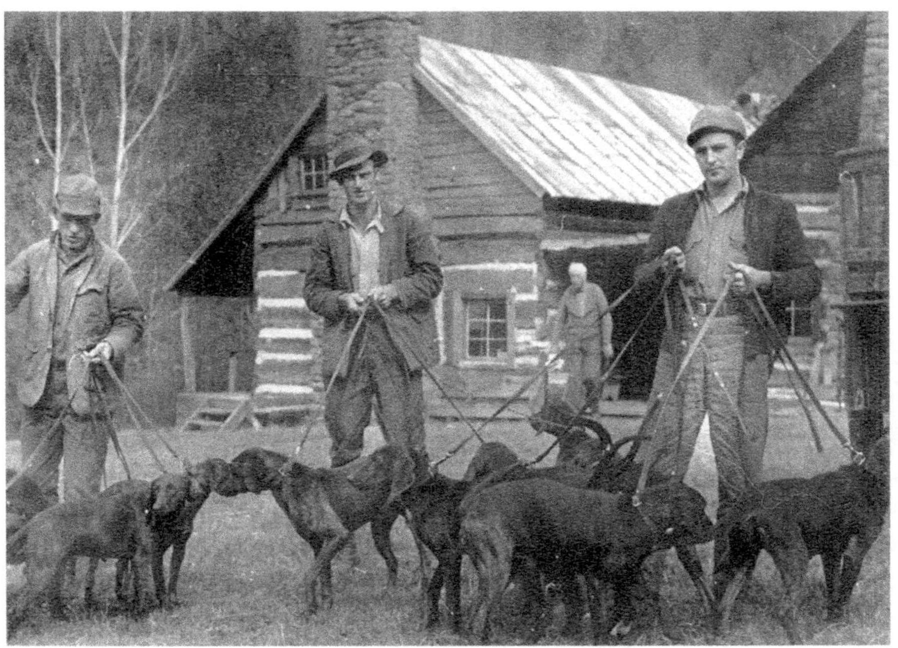

A 1935 photo of Hazel Creek guides and Plott hounds. Little George Plott is on the far left. *Plott family photos.*

The club employed iconic local hunting guides such as Mark Cathey, Von Plott, Oliver Laws, Jim Laws and many others. The guide provided not only hunting expertise and guidance to the club's guests but also hunting dogs, including the legendary Plott hound, the official state dog of North Carolina.

Over the years, the owners entertained many well-known guests at the club, including the most famous of them all, Baseball Hall of Famer Branch Rickey, the man credited with integrating professional baseball when he signed Jackie Robinson in 1945. Rickey also first established minor-league professional baseball in Asheville, and the Asheville Tourists still play there today.

Rickey was an avid outdoorsman and especially enjoyed hunting and fishing. He visited the Hazel Creek Lodge multiple times in the 1930s and '40s, taking the Murphy Branch train from Asheville to Bushnell. But his most famous visit was the October 20–21, 1935 hunt during which his party jumped twenty bears and killed eight bruins in less than forty-eight hours. News of this hunt was reported nationally and drew further attention to the region and even more tourists.

Other large, privately owned clubs or lodges included the Deep Creek Rod and Gun Club, owned partly by Champion Fiber, near Bryson City, and the Tapoco Lodge near Robbinsville that was built in 1930 as a retreat for employees and guests of the American Aluminum Company (ALCOA). The sites of the Deep Creek and Hazel Creek Clubs are now in the GSMNP. Both the Tapoco Lodge and the nearby Blue Boar Inn remain popular tourist destinations today.

Author and historian Lance Holland recently made a stunning discovery when he learned that the Hazel Creek Lodge was not burned down or destroyed by the park service, as originally thought. Instead, Mr. Stikeleather had the building dismantled and reassembled in the backyard of his Asheville home, and the family still uses it for a guest house today.

We would be remiss if we did not share an especially interesting connection of one local hunting club to the Murphy Branch—the Hooper Bald Lodge, built by Whiting Manufacturing. Its story is told in detail in Bob Plott's second book, but a brief recap is required here. The company purchased the 5,429-foot Hooper Bald and most of the land surrounding it in western Graham County and built an elaborate hunting lodge on the summit of the peak in 1908.

The plan was to fence the property entirely and stock it with exotic game animals, thus creating a private hunting preserve for company friends and clients. By 1911, the lodge had been completed, and the fencing was in place. The next plan of action was to ship the animals to the site.

Southern Railway was the freight carrier and delivered multiple loads of exotic and domestic animals to the Murphy Branch depots in Murphy and Andrews in the spring of 1912. Surely the railroad engineers and employees were amazed by their task. Since July 29, 1891, these men had hauled every sort of freight, equipment or livestock imaginable to and from Asheville to Murphy and all stops in between. But never anything like this. Their loads included hundreds of domestic animals, ten thousand pheasant eggs, two hundred wild turkeys, eight buffaloes, fourteen Russian boars, fourteen elk, six Colorado mule deer and thirty-four bears, including nine Russian brown bears, just to name a few.

As challenging as it must have been to ship them by train, the overland trip to Hooper Bald would have been worse. Whiting hired a tough ex-cavalry officer named Captain Frank Swan for the job. The wily veteran arranged for ox-drawn wagons to transport the animals to the resort.

It took more than four months to complete the task, and by late 1912, all the animals had been delivered to the company lodge, which had telephone

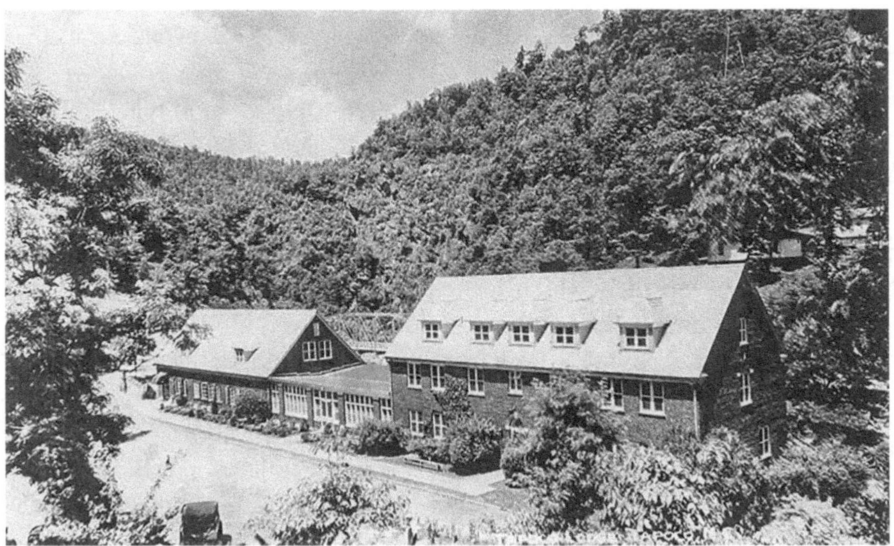

Tapaco Lodge. *Hunter Library Archives at Western Carolina University (WCU).*

lines strung across the Snowbird range from Marble to the Lodge. Although the project did not end well, that's a story for another day. Southern completed its task in the delivery of what surely was the most unusual freight delivery in Murphy Branch history.

Thanks to all the stories written about these hunting lodges and many others, as well as word of mouth references by famous clients such as Branch Rickey, these clubs brought great national attention to the region and were the beginning of large-scale commercial tourism via the railroad.

But not everyone was interested in hunting and fishing. Others flocked to the region by train on the advice of their doctors seeking relief for lung disorders in the cooler, dryer air or to soak in the numerous hot springs at local resorts renowned for their healing powers. All these folks needed places to stay, and resorts began to pop up nearby the twenty-seven stations that dotted the Murphy Branch in the late 1930s. As the logging boom declined, these same cities and villages that were once considered logging towns now became known as tourist havens. Most still are today.

One of the earliest examples is the Jarrett House in Dillsboro, North Carolina. The three-story, twenty-two-thousand-square-foot hotel, capable of seating 125 diners, was built by William Dills, the founder of Dillsboro, in 1884. It was originally known as the Mount Beulah Hotel, and not only was it considered a prime tourist destination, but the WNCRR also scheduled daily twenty-minute lunch stops at the hotel, which was renowned for its fine country cooking.

When the train stopped at Balsam, the agent there would telegraph the lunch reservations for passengers and crew so the food would be ready upon their arrival in Dillsboro. The depot was a short walk from the hotel.

In 1894, Dills sold the operation to Franklin businessman Frank Jarrett. Jarrett renamed the business the Jarrett Springs Hotel to capitalize on a nearby Sulphur Springs, which he felt would further increase his profits. The business later became known as simply the Jarrett House and remained a beloved tourist destination famous for its food and lodging until Jarrett's death in 1950. In the coming years, the business changed ownership multiple times but remained a community staple until closing recently.

Another famous resort that is still in operation today is the Balsam Inn, located near the original site of the Balsam Depot on the Murphy Branch. The one-hundred-room hotel boasted a 250-guest capacity and fine dining all-inclusive at a reasonable price. The Inn opened on June 10, 1909, and charged $2.50 per night, or $12.50 per week. The higher elevation made it a popular stop for those escaping the heat of the lowlands and a haven for folks suffering from lung problems.

Tuberculosis remained a serious and common health issue in the early 1900s. Many doctors advised their patients to seek relief in the Smokies. Arguably the most famous of these patients was the artist considered by many to be the father of country music, Jimmie Rodgers.

Rodgers, a former brakeman on the New Orleans and Northeastern Railroad (a division of Southern Railway), as well as a switchman for Southern Pacific, was known as "the singing brakeman." Rodgers spent almost a year in Asheville in 1927 seeking relief from the disease. Rodgers also recorded some of his most famous music in Asheville and nearby Bristol, Tennessee, during this time.

Complications from tuberculosis finally killed the iconic musician in New York City in 1933. Rodgers was so beloved that Southern Railway arranged for a special train car to carry his body back home to Meridian, Mississippi, for burial. Fans lined the railroad in every town from New York to Meridian to bid a final farewell to their hero taking his last train ride home.

The train also brought many other famous celebrities and politicians—including multiple U.S. presidents—to Asheville to stay at the Grove Park Inn. The beautiful forty-thousand-square-foot rock building built on the western slope of Sunset Mountain opened on July 12, 1913, and remains a world-class resort today.

Farther west in Haywood County, the Murphy Branch brought customers to multiple resorts, including the Eaglesnest Hotel near Waynesville, built in 1900. Before it was destroyed by fire in 1918, the hotel was Waynesville's most popular resort.

The Lake Junaluska Methodist Assembly, which opened in 1913, was another favorite destination, and the Lake Junaluska Assembly remains a beloved resort today. Visitors to Lake Junaluska arrived and departed from the Tuscola Station on the Murphy Branch. There were no fewer than eight other hotels or boardinghouses located in the nearby tiny hamlet of Clyde.

Bryson City was the headquarters of the Murphy Branch and home to the Fryemont Inn, which opened in 1923. The lodge remains in operation today as one of the town's most popular resorts, and a big part of its popularity then and now is the Inn's proximity to the GSMNP and the GSMR.

The terminus of the Murphy Branch—Murphy, North Carolina—was home to what many considered the finest hotel in far Western North Carolina, the Regal Hotel. The luxurious three-story resort also housed a bank and a department store.

The list is endless, but you get the picture. Tourism was rapidly becoming king in Western North Carolina, particularly with the demise of the logging industry. But all these examples pale in comparison to the Biltmore. Millionaire businessman George Vanderbilt arrived by train to Asheville in 1887, only seven years after the WNCRR line was first completed to the city. He decided that he wanted to build a home here and began buying land in 1888. Construction started in 1889 on his 250-room mansion, and it was completed in 1895.

The estate not only housed his family in their palatial mansion but also was the home to several businesses, including a large dairy operation. The Vanderbilt family opened their home to tourists in 1930. Today, the almost seven-thousand-acre Biltmore estate attracts 1.4 million visitors annually.

A good argument can be made that Vanderbilt would never have visited Asheville without the railroad, and it is unlikely that the estate would exist today without it. It is almost impossible to consider the construction of such a mansion without nearby railroad access for incoming and outgoing freight. And undoubtedly the Murphy Branch was a primary source of transportation for tourists first visiting the resort in the 1930s and '40s.

To be fair, it is safe to say that a tourism boom was inevitable even without the railroad. New highways being built—including later a nationwide highway interstate system—and old roads being improved, combined with increased personal mobility (as almost everyone later owned cars), would have resulted in an influx of tourism at some point.

But it would likely have been at least a half a century later before it occurred, maybe longer. And that would have been a huge economic setback for the Land of Blue Smoke. Who knows what would have happened to the region economically during these fifty years had there been no train?

Imagine the region not only without tourism as a primary economic source but also, just as importantly, without all the other commercial, industrial and personal advantages that the Murphy Branch brought to Western North Carolina. Even with the problems some of these businesses introduced to the area, life without them, and life without the Murphy Branch, would have been devastating to many mountain residents and most definitely to the economy here.

Now that we have a better understanding of the huge economic impact the railroad had on the Land of Blue Smoke, let's resume our history of the Murphy Branch line in the late 1930s.

THE END OF AN ERA

The golden era of steam engines on Southern Railway's Murphy Branch was relatively short-lived. As noted, Southern Railway purchased the line in 1894 and, thanks to superb management, took the railroad to new heights in a very short time. But arguably the best and most profitable years for the line came during the logging boom from 1900 until about 1930, followed by a brief resurgence when Fontana Dam was built in the early 1940s.

It was during this time that Southern Railway's Murphy Branch had the best of both worlds: a lucrative freight *and* passenger business. It appeared that the Murphy Branch had finally emerged from the shadows that had seemingly cursed the line since the earliest days of the WNCRR and throughout the construction and operation of the railroad.

However, the Great Depression, which devastated the national economy between 1929 and 1933, along with the demise of the logging industry were crushing blows to the Murphy Branch. Nevertheless, as usual, the operation found new ways to survive.

With the bulk of the logging business gone—at least on the western end of the line—the announcement of a major dam construction project by the Tennessee Valley Authority (TVA) proved to be a short-term blessing for the line—and a long-term curse.

In 1942, the TVA began construction on a 480-foot-tall, 2,365-foot-long dam on the Little Tennessee River in Swain and Graham Counties. The dam impounded what would become the 10,230-acre Fontana Lake. At the

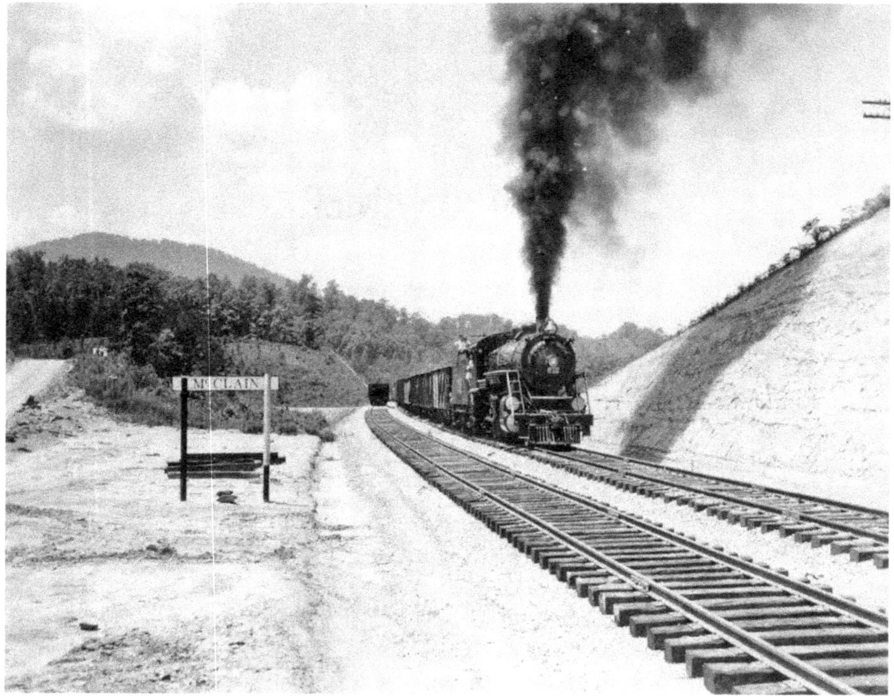

No. 711 going past McClean. *Thanks to Thomas Plott and Ashley Swenson Hackshaw.*

time, the dam was the fourth-tallest dam in the world and still today remains the tallest dam in the eastern United States. It was built by the TVA to provide power for the war effort at the nearby Oak Ridge, Tennessee federal nuclear facility and to supply an additional source of electricity to customers in East Tennessee.

The massive project required the TVA to purchase 68,292 acres of land, along with the relocation of 1,311 families and more than 1,000 graves. Sixty miles of highway and eight miles of the Murphy Branch were submerged or inaccessible once the lake was formed.

Multiple towns, communities, logging spur lines and depots (including Proctor, Fontana, Forney, Japan, Brock, Welch and Tuskeegee, among others) were lost in the process. One of the Murphy Branch's most prominent terminals, Bushnell, would be under two hundred feet of water when the lake was completed.

The charter of the 522,419-acre GSMNP in 1934 also adversely affected the railway in that many of its customers who resided in the park were relocated. Entire towns, businesses, lodges and hunting clubs disappeared

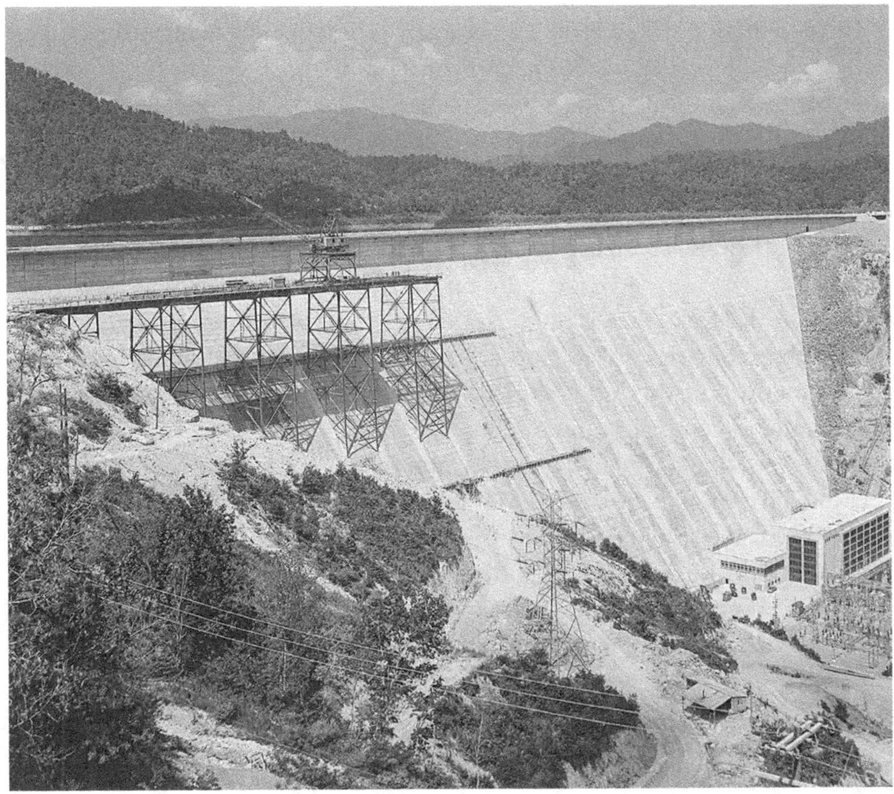

Fontana Dam construction nearing completion. *TVA Archives.*

once the GSMNP and Fontana Dam were fully operational. These losses were personal to those relocated, but they also adversely affected bottom-line profits to Southern Railway.

While these issues were long-term problems for the Murphy Branch, the construction of Fontana Dam was indeed a short-term blessing for the operation. Special spur lines connected the dam project to the Murphy Branch—these were later torn down upon completion of the dam.

More than fourteen thousand box cars of construction materials, concrete and other freight were shipped to the site via the Murphy Branch between 1942, when the project began, and its completion on November 7, 1944. This was the heaviest freight usage ever seen on the Murphy Branch. The construction freight was further supplemented by large loads of copper being shipped from copper mines in Western North Carolina to smelters in Copperhill, Tennessee.

In anticipation of part of the Murphy Branch soon being underwater, Southern Railway began construction on a rerouting of the line in September 1943. It took about two months to complete the revised fifteen-mile route, which reduced the original route by eight miles. The TVA sweetened the deal by agreeing to build a bridge that was 791 feet long and 179 feet high over what was then the Little Tennessee River but later became Fontana Lake. The bridge, located near Almond, remains one of the most popular spots for tourist railroad excursions on the GSMR today.

Despite the reduction in total distance, the revised route was also much steeper than the original line. It made the grades far more difficult for freight shipments, thus further reducing freight tonnage by 40 percent—yet another blow to the railroad's bottom line.

Upon the completion of Fontana Dam, the record-setting freight business was lost forever, as was the bulk of the copper mine shipments. To make matters worse, with so many people being relocated by the park service, passenger train business had dwindled to almost nothing. Improved mountain highways, along with a huge increase in automobile ownership, resulted in fewer people using the train as their primary form of transportation. This

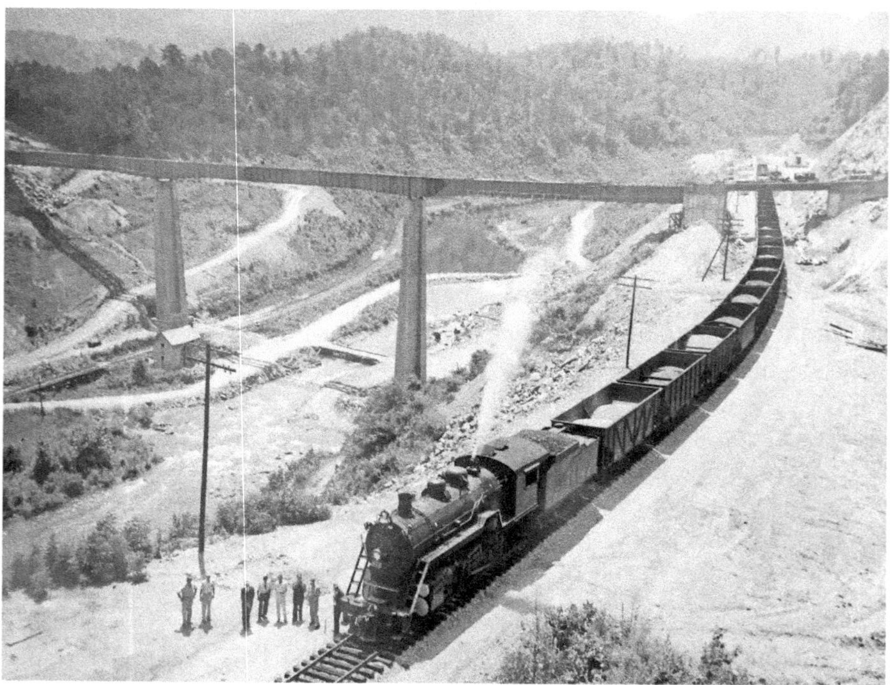

No. 711 pulling first freight train under the new Almond trestle in 1944. *Thanks to Thomas Plott and Ashley Swenson Hackshaw.*

was especially true after the end of World War II, as the nation enjoyed a boost in the economy.

Moreover, many of the Murphy Branch's former biggest freight customers were now utilizing the improved highway systems and delivery trucks as the primary resources for their shipping needs. Passenger and freight trains were a dying market on the Murphy Branch.

Ever vigilant of maintaining and improving its profits, Southern Railway was forced to reduce the number of passenger trains ran on the Murphy Branch. Yet despite these cutbacks, the railroad continued to upgrade and add new engines for the line. These engines were known as the P-1 and PS-2 Class Pacific steam locomotives, utilized a 4-6-2-wheel arrangement and were used only for passenger trains.

Ironically, less than a year after obtaining these PS-2 engines, Southern Railway terminated all passenger train business on the Murphy Branch. The last steam-powered Southern Railway passenger train of any kind on the Murphy Branch completed its final run on July 16, 1948.

More than half a century of steam railroad passenger service on the Murphy Branch had come to an end. It was a sad day for many residents of the Land of Blue Smoke, and the news would only get worse in coming years.

Just four years later, in August 1952, the no. 722, a 2-8-0 Consolidation 214,000-pound steam-powered locomotive built at the Baldwin Locomotive Works in 1904, pulled its last load of freight on the Murphy Branch. It was the end of an illustrious era of steam-powered engines on the Murphy Branch. The year 1952 marked the end of almost a century of steam service initially on the WNCRR, and later the Murphy Branch/Southern Railway, dating back to the original charter of the WNCRR in 1855.

Southern sold the no. 722 that same year to the ET&WNC Railroad. The mighty engine remained in service until 1985 under various owners before being taken out of service in 1985. The 722 is now once again owned by the GSMR, which hopes to someday restore the engine back to its original glory.

Five years into the second half of the twentieth century, Southern Railway had totally replaced its Murphy Branch steam engines with more powerful and cost-effective diesel engines, including models F-7, GP-7 and later GP-30, GP-38 and the GP-38-2, all of which were built by the Electromotive Division of General Motors. Other diesel models used included the U23-B and the B23-7, both built by General Electric. These diesel engines were only used for freight runs. Since our emphasis is on steam engines, we will not focus on this topic, other than to say that most people believed that steam engines would never again run on the Murphy Branch.

Even though freight shipments along the Murphy Branch continued to decrease at an alarming rate, Southern did its best to find new ways to service longtime customers with its diesel engines. Probably the most creative example of this took place on October 31, 1958, when passenger service was resurrected for one charter trip to transport football fans from Bryson City to Sylva and back.

Then, as now, high school football reigned supreme in Western North Carolina, and few rivalries were more competitive or harder fought than the games between perennial state champions Swain County High and Sylva-Webster High. The two bitter rivals were scheduled to play on October 31, 1958, in Jackson County, but a massive road construction project made it almost impossible for Swain County fans to make the trip by car or bus.

Bryson City residents asked Southern Railway if it would consider chartering a special train for the event. Southern agreed, but only if there was a guaranteed minimum of 250 ticket sales, requiring a train of five cars. This was no problem for these rabid football fans, and tickets for the excursion rapidly sold out, eventually selling more than 800 tickets.

Bob Christopher, whom we met earlier, had worked for Southern since the early 1900s and was the son of an original Murphy Branch engineer. Christopher had piloted the next to last steam passenger trip on the Murphy Branch in 1948, and he was at the helm of Southern diesel no. 89 pulling the football fan train. There were seventeen passenger cars in the consist, making this special charter the largest passenger train—steam or diesel—to ever run on Southern Railway's Murphy Branch.

It was momentous occasion, never to be forgotten. Only eleven years after passenger service had been terminated on the line, it had returned in one final blaze of glory. But as great as it was, it was not enough to make a difference in the future of the operation.

In 1978, only 2,223 freight cars traveled the Murphy Branch, what was then an all-time low. It would only get worse in the coming decade. However, a brief respite occurred in 1982, when two of the biggest railroad lines in America—Southern Railway and Norfolk and Western—merged to become the massive railroad conglomerate now known as Norfolk Southern.

Mountaineer Harold F. Hall was CEO of Southern at that time and skillfully negotiated this merger. A native of Nantahala, North Carolina, Hall was born into a family of railroaders that included his father, three brothers and two uncles. He graduated from Andrews High School in 1943 and later served in the Pacific Theater as gunner on a bomber during World War II.

When he came home after the war, he became a telegrapher at the Bryson City Depot on the Murphy Branch. Known for his keen mind and stellar work ethic, Hall rose quickly through the Southern managerial ranks and became president of Southern Railway in 1980. Under his superb leadership, Southern Railway enjoyed gross profits of $3 billion annually, all while developing a vast railway network stretching eighteen thousand miles and providing jobs for forty-one thousand employees.

Having begun his distinguished railroading career on the Murphy Branch, and descending from a long line of railroaders, Harold Hall had a vested interest in the Murphy Branch and undoubtedly wanted to see it succeed. But Hall was a businessman too and had to do the right thing for his company. He publicly stated on numerous occasions that he was constantly looking for ways to cut costs.

Hall was faced with a difficult decision, the same decision that he had wrestled with for years: what to do with what remained of the Murphy Branch line? In 1986, Norfolk Southern hauled just 817 cars on the historic line and ran only three freight trains per week to only ten major customers.

These record low shipping totals, combined with rising operations costs of more than $1 million annually, as well as the earlier elimination of the passenger business, could only mean one thing: the end was near for the Murphy Branch.

In 1986, Norfolk Southern management made the decision to close the line entirely from Dillsboro to Murphy. However, it still planned to keep the route east from Dillsboro to Asheville open for freight business, due in large part to the higher volumes of freight still running there—most notably at Champion in Canton.

As required by federal law, on April 6, 1986, Norfolk Southern Railroad filed an official petition with the Interstate Commerce Commission for closure and abandonment of the sixty-seven miles of track from Dillsboro west to Murphy. This meant that all the towns and businesses along the abandoned route were being notified in advance of the decision and that Norfolk Southern planned to either sell the abandoned track to investors—likely for no less than $1.7 million—or else abandon them entirely for salvage at an undisclosed cheaper price.

However, who could secure enough money for even a bargain price? And even if some local investors could be found, could a deal be made with Southern before it was too late? Or would Southern even consider a deal at a lower rate? Southern also made it clear that while it would prefer selling the line, the window to do this was rapidly closing. Furthermore, if a deal could not be made quickly, Southern intended to tear up the line and sell the rails for salvage before the end of 1988.

The answers to all these questions were not promising. The clock was ticking, and it seemed certain that an illustrious era of railroading on the Murphy Branch had finally come to an end.

RAILROAD RESURGENCE IN THE LAND OF BLUE SMOKE

Just when it appeared that the Murphy Branch was done for good, a miracle of sorts occurred. We are reluctant to classify it in those terms, especially considering all the many near-catastrophic occurrences in the history of the line that the railroad somehow had always managed to survive.

However, in the volatile era of partisan politics that we are currently experiencing, where party comes first (regardless of your preferred party affiliation) and what is right or is in the best interests of the public is secondary, then yes, what next occurred does seem almost miraculous.

It is a story like no other. A story with Republican and Democrat politicians working together with their constituents and with local businesspeople and civic leaders to not only resolve this issue but also, just as importantly, secure funding that would allow for this resolution. And it seems appropriate that a major player in this story was Bill Gibson.

As noted there, Bill's family has lived on their farm in the Smokies since before the Civil War, and Bill enjoyed a distinguished forty-year career as director of the Southwestern North Carolina Planning and Economic Development Commission before retiring in 2013.

In simplest terms, the commission's primary purpose is to ensure that regional growth occurs in a healthy and sustainable manner that is beneficial to all residents of seven southwestern mountain counties, as well as the Eastern Band of the Cherokee and the seventeen municipalities located therein—most of them on or near the Murphy Branch.

Bill Gibson, as the commission's director and a native son, understood better than most the urgent need to save the Murphy Branch. Furthermore, having navigated the stormy waters of partisan politics for years, Gibson understood the importance—and the difficulty—of getting politicians to work together in supporting a common objective and securing funding for that goal.

But that was only part of the problem, albeit a huge part. First Gibson had to determine if Norfolk Southern was willing to negotiate an agreement and, if so, what its price would be. At this point in 1986, Norfolk Southern wanted out of that part of the sixty-seven-mile stretch of the Murphy Branch, but it preferred not to become entangled in lawsuits or public outrage over the closing of the line.

By the same token, local businesses and counties did not want to spend their valuable resources on legal fees in suing the railroad—a suit they almost surely would lose, and even if they did not, untold amounts of money would be lost in the process.

It seemed that the best bet was to find a way to purchase the line from Norfolk Southern. But there were two problems here. First and foremost, no one had $1 million to purchase the line, nor did it make sense to spend that amount (even if it could be secured) on a non-existent passenger operation and a freight train business that was losing $1 million annually.

A tourist train was suggested early on, and it seemed that the tourist excursion income could be further supplemented by including limited freight service to existing local businesses. But again, to do that would mean purchasing the line, and there were no investors willing to step up and make that commitment.

Tourist trains in the southern Appalachians—most notably Tweetsie Railroad in Blowing Rock, North Carolina—had enjoyed longtime financial success and are still in business today. Nevertheless, opening a tourist train operation was not without significant risk. A perfect example of an operation of this kind that had failed was the aforementioned Bear Creek Scenic Railroad in Graham County.

Gibson appointed Franklin, North Carolina mayor Dr. David Henson as chairman of a committee designated to further explore these options, while Gibson conducted his own feedback and ideas as he met with various local officials seeking their input.

No one locally wanted to poke the proverbial bear, so to speak, but someone needed to reach out to Norfolk Southern to see what its bottom-line price was and if it would be willing to work out a deal. At this point, the railroad was keeping quiet, and things appeared to be at hopeless stalemate. Bill Gibson volunteered to contact Norfolk Southern directly. By his own admission, it was a shot in the dark, and one that he did not really expect to work—but what did he have to lose?

So, Gibson phoned the corporate offices of the railroad and, to his surprise, was able to speak directly with Norfolk Southern's legal counsel for the abandonment project. Gibson was pleased to learn that the railroad wanted a peaceful and positive resolution as badly as the commission and its constituents did.

Even better, Gibson found that the railroad was willing to sell the line for a bargain price of $650,000, but *only* if the commission, the state and local residents would agree *not* to legally challenge the official ICC Abandonment Notice or file suit to stop it. Norfolk Southern also agreed to delay final abandonment of the track to allow for the commission, the businesses still served by the line, their shippers and those involved in executing a purchase plan to get a deal done.

Gibson eagerly conveyed this information to other members of the commission, as well as to other interested local parties. Bill and his associates began to develop a plan. The good news was that this bought the commission and its constituents more time, but the bad news remained: where could they get $650,000 to make the purchase?

The first attempt was for the railroad and the commission to offer the North Carolina Department of Transportation (NCDOT) the opportunity to purchase the sixty-seven miles of track to add to its state-owned railroad. The NCDOT liked the idea but could not secure the funding without approval from the North Carolina General Assembly.

This would likely not be easy, as the request would be made to a Democratic-majority General Assembly from a Republican governor, Jim Martin, who made it clear that he fully supported this project and was committed to make it happen. But to do so would require bipartisan politics at its best. Gibson, other commission members and local politicians banded together to advocate this plan and encourage both parties to cooperate.

Meanwhile, almost two years had elapsed since Norfolk Southern first petitioned the ICC of its abandonment plan in 1986. Norfolk Southern let it be known that it was getting impatient and needed a decision soon.

Regular meetings were being held throughout the region seeking resolution to the problem, but time was running out. The solution came down to two options: one, buy the railroad and make it a tourist railroad with limited freight service, or two, forget the railroad, tear up the tracks and turn the line into a long hiking and bicycling trail similar to the Virginia Creeper Trail System in southwest Virginia.

Furthermore, additional studies conducted indicated that freight needs would increase in coming years, thus making the project more viable and making the second option less desirable. But as usual, no one had the money to fund either option.

On April 19, 1988, a public meeting was held at the Swain County Administrative Building in Bryson City, North Carolina, in what was called a "last ditch effort to save the Murphy Branch." Dr. Henson moderated that meeting and announced that Governor Martin was fully committed in finding a way to secure funding.

A motion was made to suggest that the General Assembly purchase *both* the sixty-seven-mile stretch of abandoned track between Dillsboro and Murphy and with the twenty-two-mile route from Dillsboro to Waynesville.

Next on the agenda was Sylva attorney Orville Coward—a close friend of Governor Martin's—who introduced a surprise guest: Florida businessman and train fan Malcolm MacNeil, the chairman of the board of Frank MacNeil & Son, an insurance, lumber holding and banking business located in Sanford, Florida.

Mr. MacNeil announced that he and forty-five other investors wanted to open a train and freight business on the abandoned line. They were willing to fund the operation themselves and lease the line with a purchase to buy from the owner, but they could not afford to buy the line from Norfolk Southern and provide the funding needed for a startup freight and tourist train operation.

Ever the astute businessman, MacNeil had done his homework. He knew that it would take hundreds of thousands of dollars just to maintain the tracks and buy equipment and rolling stock. He would need the assistance of the state in making the actual purchase from Norfolk Southern. The decision was made to ask the state General Assembly to purchase the line for $650,000 and, in turn, lease it to Mr. MacNeil, who intended to name the new operation the Great Smoky Mountain Railway.

Everyone agreed that this was a win-win situation for all parties, but the question remained: would the Democrats and Republicans work together to secure the needed funding? And would they do so in a timely manner? The clock was running, and the patience of Norfolk Southern was wearing thin. If an agreement was not reached soon, it planned to start ripping up the track in late August 1988.

To their credit, Governor Martin, Speaker of the House Liston Ramsey and Jeff Enloe, Charles Beall, Charles Hipps and Royce Thomas—all state assemblymen representing their respective mountain counties—worked together to get this bill approved.

In a remarkable example of bipartisan politics, the funding was approved by the General Assembly. Nearly two years of working to execute a plan first introduced by Bill Gibson and his associates at the Southwestern Commission, along with scores of other Western North Carolina civic and business leaders, had finally paid off. In the meantime, negotiations had continued between the state and Norfolk Southern to buy the line. An agreement was reached on July 19, 1988, and contracts were signed.

Norfolk Southern further agreed that it had no intentions of ever running a tourist train on the twenty-two miles of track it still ran freight operations on between Waynesville and Dillsboro. Freight business remained strong on this route, and liability costs—estimated to be $200 million annually—would prohibit the company from ever operating dual tourist and freight railroads on that line.

Once the transaction was completed, Mr. MacNeil signed a twenty-five-year lease in which he agreed to pay the state $40,000 annually plus a specified percentage of gross profits. Mr. MacNeil's detailed business plan indicated that he hoped to break even on the freight business but make his profits from the tourist excursions and that his hope was to eventually purchase the line from the state.

Just days before the tracks were scheduled to be destroyed, Governor Martin made the official announcement that the deal had been finalized on August 7, 1988. The governor praised the politicians, particularly the Democratic Assembly, for their efforts and thanked Bill Gibson and his group for their assistance in making this two-year dream a reality. The Murphy Branch had been resurrected once again, thanks to the collaborative efforts of North Carolina residents, politicians, Norfolk Southern and the Great Smoky Mountains Railway.

THE GREAT SMOKY MOUNTAINS RAILWAY

Malcolm MacNeil wasted no time putting his management team together and getting his new railway operational. He named Doug Ellis the first company president. Ellis held the position for five years before Malcolm took over as president in 1993. MacNeil named his wife, Joan, a Sylva banking executive, as vice-president and chief operating officer of the railway.

The management team's first order of business was to set up their headquarters—then located in Dillsboro, the eastern end of the line—and getting their engine shop operational located just west of town. Ellis next sought engines and rolling stock for the operation. The company started with about twenty-five full-time employees and nearly one hundred seasonal workers.

Ellis would later say that their lack of formal railroad experience may have been a plus, as it forced them to think outside the box and pursue nontraditional ways of problem solving. As Ellis told author Mead Parce, "It was a lot of hard work, but it was also a lot of fun."

The first locomotives on the new operation were two GP-9 diesel electric engines built by the Electro Motive Division of General Motors (EMD), along with two others, nos. 777 and 711, that were obtained from Union Pacific Railroad, as well as still another acquired from Burlington Northern Railway.

Still later, the railway acquired two more GP-9 diesel engines from the Chicago and Northwestern Railroad and two GP-35 diesels—nos. 223 and 210—from Norfolk and Western, while also leasing two former Santa Fe Railways CF-7 diesel engines from the Lone Star Railroad in Texas.

The first passenger cars were rebuilt from old freight cars and customized for passenger usage. They were called "open air cars" because they had no windows, thus allowing passengers a taste of fresh mountain air and an unobstructed view of the spectacular landscape.

In addition to these forty cars, the railway also purchased some regular passenger cars and more elaborate club cars that were used for dinner excursions. These luxury trips treated passengers to a fine dining experience with first-class service in a comfortable climate-controlled environment.

Finally, the railway also obtained about fifteen cabooses from other railroad lines. The paint scheme used on the passenger cars and locomotives was red, yellow and blue.

During its initial years of operation, the Great Smoky Mountains Railway offered four different trip options: the Tuckasegee River Excursion, running from Dillsboro to Bryson City and back; the Nantahala Gorge trip, from Bryson City to the gorge and back; the Red Marble Gap ride, from Andrews to Topton and back; and finally, the Valley River Excursion, which basically followed part of the Cherokees' tragic Trail of Tears from Murphy to Andrews and back.

The GSMR did not run as much in the winter as it does today, but it still managed to book 133,000 passengers during its first year of operation. Following the original plan, it also ran freight trains at night year-round to further supplement its income. The Great Smoky Mountains Railway was off to a great start.

Their next action item was to continue to grow the business in various ways, starting with the return of steam service to the Murphy Branch. The resurgence of steam operations to the Murphy Branch in 1992 is yet another landmark moment in the history of the line.

The GSMR purchased steam locomotive no. 1702 from an operation in Nebraska in 1991. The 1702 was a 1942 Baldwin 2-8-0 Consolidation type steam locomotive and had originally been built to pull troop trains during World War II; it remains the "Queen of Steam" for the operation today.

Four decades after the last steam passenger train whistles were heard ringing through the Land of Blue Smoke, the GSMR resurrected steam operations again in August 1992. The steam excursions proved to be an instant success, as tourists and rail fans from around the world flocked to the Smokies to ride and photograph the train.

Surely William Gene Gibson found pleasure in once again hearing the steam whistle resonate across the valley to his farm in Whittier. His family had lived there for well over a century, and it must have brought back fond childhood memories of early steam trains on the Murphy Branch. Mr. Gibson also certainly felt pride in knowing that his son, Bill Gibson, had played a large role in working with local businesspeople, politicians, Norfolk Southern and Malcolm MacNeil in making the return of the Murphy Branch a reality, as well as the return of steam operations.

The railway drew additional attention to its business by assisting in the filming of a major motion picture, *The Fugitive*, which featured its diesel engines in multiple scenes. The wreck site from the film remains a highlight of the Tuckasegee excursion today.

The operation began partnerships with rafting businesses such as the Nantahala Outdoor Center, which was used as a layover for the Gorge Excursion. Other specialty rides were later introduced based around various themes.

Tourism in locations like Bryson City and Dillsboro also flourished thanks in large part to business brought in by the railway. By 1995, an estimated 185,000 passengers had booked trips on the Great Smoky Mountains Railway and nearly $12 million in tourist dollars were spent in the region annually. In 1996, to better operate more efficiently and economically, the GSMR discontinued the regularly scheduled Valley River Excursion passenger trips.

It was also in 1996 that Malcolm MacNeil and the GSMR purchased the sixty-seven miles of track from Dillsboro to Murphy from the North Carolina Department of Transportation that the state had first bought in 1988 when it helped broker the deal for MacNeil and Norfolk Southern. The railway paid $625,000 for the line along with an additional $60,000 in rental and appraisal fees. Norfolk Southern retained the rights to freight services between Dillsboro and Waynesville.

Just as everyone had hoped, the transaction had proved to be mutually beneficial to the North Carolina state government and their constituents, as well as to the railway. It was truly a win-win situation for all parties, as the state had been repaid in full, plus rental costs, and the Murphy Branch had been saved by the GSMR to generate new income and jobs as a tourist attraction—all while continuing to service local freight needs.

It was indeed the dawn of a new era, and as we shall soon see, even better days were ahead for the Murphy Branch and the GSMR.

A NEW ERA BEGINS ON THE GREAT SMOKY MOUNTAINS RAILROAD

Malcolm MacNeil sold his Great Smoky Mountains Railway to railroad enthusiast, author and entrepreneur Allen C. Harper in December 1999. Malcolm MacNeil will forever be remembered as the man who, along with local and state politicians and the SW Commission, saved the Murphy Branch from extinction and as a visionary whose dream resulted in a resurgence of steam locomotives in the Land of Blue Smoke.

But it was Allen C. Harper, along with his family and management team, that truly took the operation to new levels and helped bring about the amazing success that it enjoys today. Like MacNeil, Harper was a wealthy Florida businessman who was passionate about history and trains. In 1996, he and his wife, Carol, spent much of their net worth purchasing their first railway, the Durango and Silverton Narrow Gauge Steam Railroad and Museum, located in Durango, Colorado.

Their company, American Heritage Railways Inc., was originally based in Hollywood, Florida, but later moved its corporate headquarters to Durango, Colorado, to more closely oversee the operation. Harper's initial management team consisted of himself as owner and CEO; Carol as owner and president; their son, John Harper, as senior vice-president; and later Jeff Johnson as general manager and Cathy Swartz as CFO.

After purchasing the Great Smoky Mountains Railway in 1999, Harper immediately changed the name of the operation to the Great Smoky Mountains Railroad—a minor change on the surface but one that would be followed by even bigger changes to come.

Harper's vison included more than just operating these two tourist train operations in Colorado and Western North Carolina; he also planned to expand his business to include the ownership of museums, retail stores and even hotels and restaurants at these locations.

Harper and his team also later introduced a special branding wing of their business that licensed official themed events such as Easter Bunny Rides, Thomas the Tank Engine and Charlie Brown Pumpkin Patch trains, along with the wildly popular Polar Express Christmas excursions. And Mr. Harper licensed these events not just on the railroads that he owns but also on fifty other railways that paid for those services.

The Polar Express concept—based on the book and movie by the same name—runs daily from November to December from Bryson City to a specially constructed "North Pole" in the old Murphy Branch village of Whittier. Today, an estimated 100,000 passengers ride the Polar Express Trains annually in those two months alone—almost as many as the total number of passengers that rode the train for an entire year when Harper first bought the railroad in 1999. And well over 200,000 passengers ride the train the remainder of the year.

In 2016, Harper purchased a third railroad line to add to his burgeoning tourist railway empire—the Mount Rainier Railroad and Logging Museum in Elbe, Washington. Like any astute businessman, Harper wanted to make money. However, he insisted it that it was (and is) about much more than profits, as he told the *Chicago Tribune* in 2005, and he later further elaborated in a statement on the company website:

> *This is a risky business, with low profit margins that has to be managed carefully to survive. I do this because I love it. We are not just owners; we are guardians of an American treasure. We are committed to safety, to customer service, to building strong community relationships and to marketing and historic preservation in providing exceptional engines and rolling stock for our customers. We are not an amusement park—we are real history that has been brought to life. The best way to preserve and perpetuate history is to make it so interesting and exciting that people will pay a fair price for the experience.*

Mr. Harper and his team have done exactly that. However, let's backtrack as we examine how Harper's vision and success did not come without problems. Certainly, he purchased a profitable operation that had been built by Mr. MacNeil on a very solid foundation. But taking it to even higher levels of success was far from easy.

In addition to the simple name change from "railway" to "railroad," Harper introduced new paint schemes to the line. The former combinations of red, yellow and blue were converted to Tuscan Red and Rio Grande Gold, and the diesel engine roster consisted of nos. 711 and 777 (both GP-7s from the MacNeil days), nos. 1751 and 1755 (both GP-9s) and a GP-30 no. 2467, along with most of the others on the original MacNeil lineup.

Like MacNeil, Harper continued to run freight trains at night to supplement the companies' income along with three daily tourist routes: the Tuckasegee Valley Excursion, running from Dillsboro to Bryson City and back; the Nantahala Gorge Excursion, running from Bryson City to the Nantahala Outdoor Center (NOC) and back; and the Red Marble Grade Excursion, running from Andrews to Topton and back. Harper introduced additional rafting packages in partnership with the NOC to increase profitability.

Harper continued the use of open-air passenger cars as well as closed luxury cars, and these cars were all painted to match the new engine color schemes. All these trips were extremely popular—especially the steam excursions pulled by the 1702—and the line continued to grow rapidly.

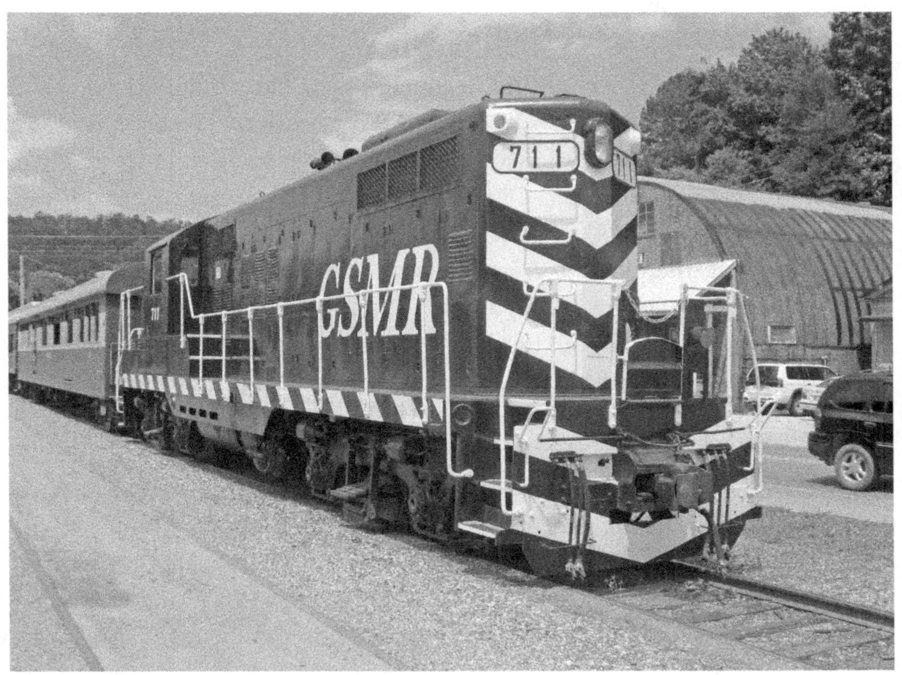

No. 711 GSMR GP-7 diesel. *JMP Photos.*

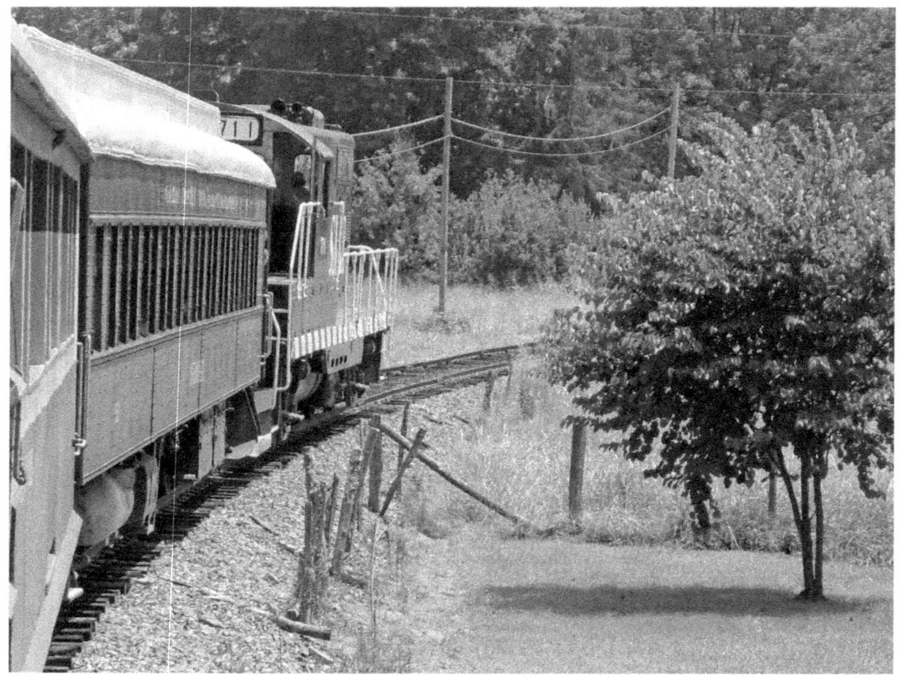

No. 711 GSMR diesel pulling passenger cars. *JMP Photos.*

Speaking of steam engines, the 2-8-0 Baldwin Consolidation no. 1702 retained its crown as the Queen of Steam operations as Harper's new era began. However, in 2000, the GSMR acquired a second steam locomotive, one that, unlike the 1702, had a real history on the Murphy Branch. It was the no. 722, a 2-8-0 Consolidation type Baldwin built in 1904. The 722 had operated during the glory days of steam on the Murphy Branch and had pulled the very last steam-powered freight train in 1952.

Initial plans were to restore the 722 to its past glory at the engine shops in Dillsboro, but to date, budgetary issues have prevented that from occurring. As the new millennium began, the 1702 remained the only steam train in operation on the GSMR.

That changed in 2003, when the 1702 was benched temporarily to undergo repairs. During that time, only diesel engines were used on the various excursions. However, in an effort to keep steam trains at the forefront for historical rail fans, Harper brought in the iconic 1925 Graham County Shay from the North Carolina Transportation Museum for steam rides. The 1925 was a Class C Shay that ran on the Graham County Railway during the logging boom of the early twentieth century and also served as the primary engine of the Bear Creek Scenic Railroad, the short-lived Graham County tourist railroad from the 1970s.

Harper's marketing team introduced a popular Railfest festival in Bryson City that still runs today. It was an event devoted to steam trains, photo shoots, train rides and train history. The 1702 was deemed operational for the 2004 season and became one of the railroad's most successful rides.

However, firebox problems again sidelined the iconic 1702 for the 2005 season, and again Harper brought in steam replacements. This time, the Flagg Coal Company no. 75 and the Lehigh Valley Coal Company no. 126 were enlisted for short rides and photo drive-by shoots, but neither engine was powerful enough to pull a full consist of passenger cars. Diesels continued to do all the excursion work. The operation remained successful, but steam excursions were greatly missed.

More problems developed in 2007 when a dispute between the GSMR and the Town of Dillsboro could not be resolved and resulted in the railroad pulling out of Dillsboro and establishing its headquarters in nearby Bryson City. While the move was a devastating economic blow to Dillsboro, many railroaders felt it was appropriate that Bryson City, the former headquarters for Southern Railway's Murphy Branch, was again the center of railway operations on the line.

The changes also marked the temporary end for two of the GSMR's trips: the Tuckasegee Excursion from Bryson City to Dillsboro and back and the Red Marble Gap ride. The Nantahala Gorge trip became the primary excursion until a deal was later worked out to reinstate the Dillsboro trip, although it would begin and end in Bryson City, and the headquarters of the GSMR would remain there as well.

It was also about this same time that most of the diesel engines and all the passenger cars acquired new paint schemes; the engines, with the exception of the 777, went back to their original colors, and the cars were painted similar to the passenger trains used by Norfolk and Western Railway.

Meanwhile, the GSMR steam program remained out of service, as budgetary concerns prevented both the 1702 and 722 from being repaired. The future looked bleak for reviving steam operations on the GSMR, as Mr. Harper reported on August 9, 2012, that it would require almost $1.5 million to repair both.

Harper explored a variety of options to resolve the issue ranging from government loans to personal loans, corporate sponsorship funding and purchasing or leasing new steam equipment. And to his credit, Harper admitted in his own words that the repair and restoration of both engines "have not been one of my great successes," adding that he should have gotten second and third opinions before having the engines dismantled—they were not properly taken care of during and after the process. Nevertheless, Harper remained adamant that he was committed to doing whatever it required to get steam reinstated on the GSMR and that he would never sell either engine.

Yet again, clouds of uncertainty surrounded the future of steam on the railroad. But like the situation that transpired when the Murphy Branch was saved by a collective nonpartisan team effort, local politicians once again stepped up to the plate and saved the day for the GSMR. After exhausting multiple efforts to resolve the situation, in April 2012 a historic agreement was finalized between the GSMR and the Swain County Tourism Authority and Swain County commissioners.

Basically, the county agreed to loan the GSMR up to $700,000 to restore the 1702 to service within thirty-six months of finalizing the agreement while also installing a turntable in downtown Bryson City that would provide a turnaround point for east- or westbound engines. The town had already purchased the turntable—the GSMR just had to install it and create six new full-time jobs for county residents, further solidifying Bryson City's position as headquarters for the GSMR.

County funding for the project would be provided by a 4 percent increase on the overnight lodging tax, with 1 percent of that amount allocated to funding this project and the remainder going to the county. This was yet again a fine example of politicians and businesses working together in the best interest of all parties and at no cost to county residents.

Furthermore, these moves would allow for additional steam excursions for both the NOC and Dillsboro trips, resulting in an estimated 20 percent increase in passenger business, as well as additional local jobs being created for local businesses supporting the train (restaurants, retailers and so on).

It was indeed a mutually beneficial situation for both the county and the GSMR, as Allen Harper stated in a press release: "The Swain County Commission is probably one of the most visionary and creative public groups I have ever worked with in a joint venture to rebuild steam engine 1702. Bringing steam service back to Swain County and the GSMR not only will dramatically increase the potential for more visitors to the community but will also create new jobs. Residents should be proud of their leadership."

With funding secured, steam repair shops fully operational and the turntable installed, the restoration project began in full force in 2014. Work proceeded rapidly. But not soon enough for Malcolm MacNeil to live to see it, as sadly, the man who started it all back in 1988 died in 2011.

While MacNeil's passing marked yet another mournful side note to the often tragic history of the Murphy Branch, MacNeil died knowing that the future remained bright for the line he loved so well and that its legacy remained in good hands with Allen C. Harper and his team.

Two years later, in July 2016, the 1702 was finally restored to its full glory. After a twelve-year absence, for the first time since 2004, the sound of steam whistles again rang across the Land of Blue Smoke. It was a joyous occasion for all train fans and, indeed, anyone who appreciates the history of the region.

Today, the American Heritage Railway company operates three tourist railroads, including the GSMR. The GSMR is capably managed by Kim Battle Albritton, a North Carolina native who, like the long line of Murphy Branch railroaders who came before her, started at the bottom and worked her way to the top of the GSMR management team.

Under her leadership—and under the direction of Harper and his corporate team—the GSMR continues to set attendance records while continually looking for new ways to improve the business. As rail fans, we salute them all and hope that no. 722 is soon added to the GSMR steam roster.

Meanwhile, the future for the GSMR and the Murphy Branch looks brighter than the sun shining over the majestic peaks of the Great Smoky Mountains. In addition to the regular tourist excursions offered by the

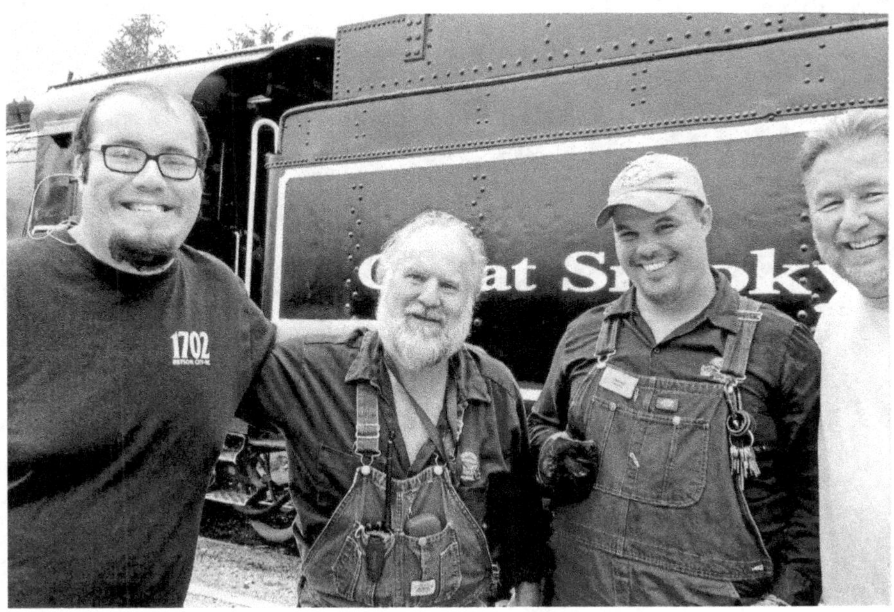

Authors Jacob Plott (*on far left*) and Bob Plott (*on far right*) with GSMR crew, engineer Kurt Newman and fireman Marshall Harris. *JMP Photos.*

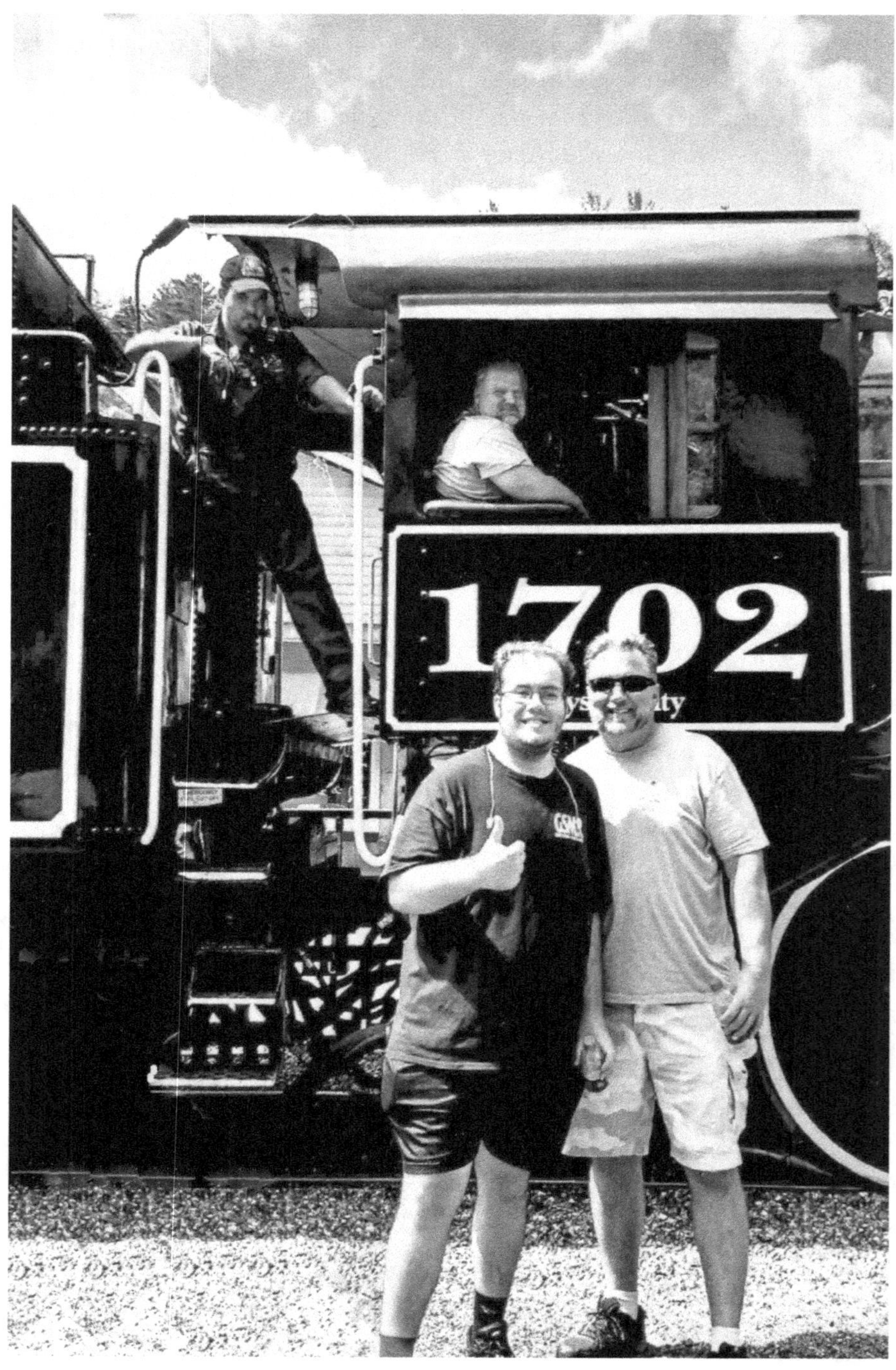

Jacob and Bob Plott with no. 1702 and crew, engineer Kurt Newman and fireman Marshall Harris. *JMP Photos.*

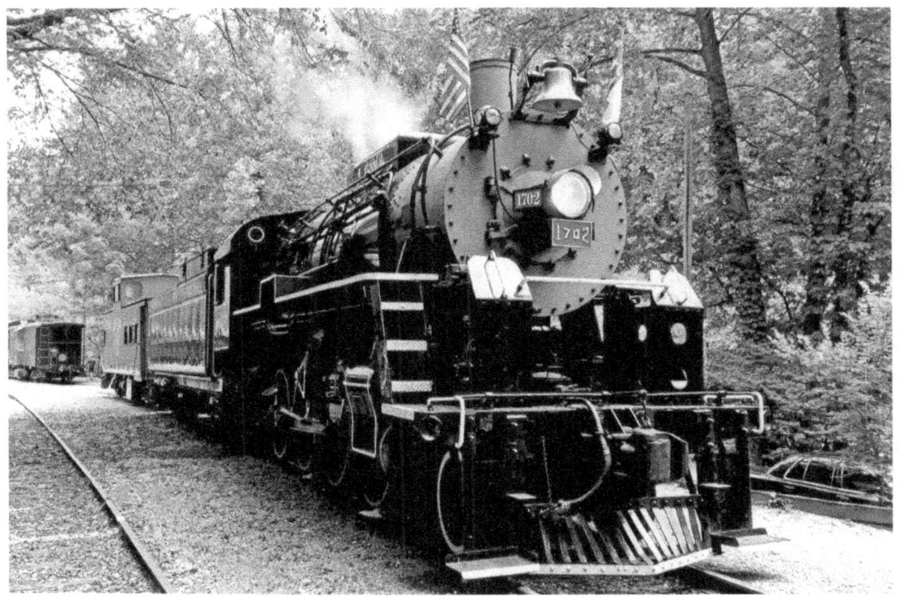

No. 1702 at NOC. *JMP Photos.*

GSMR, along with multiple specialty packages, the GSMR also operates a world-class museum in Bryson City, while continuing to run freight nightly on its line. Norfolk Southern also retains freight service on its part of the line, and both operations have intentions of growing that business.

The North Carolina Department of Transportation recently commissioned a study to designate part of the line as a National Historic site, while also exploring the possibility of reactivating services on the western end of the Murphy Branch. With a second casino opening nearby and a host of other viable tourist and freight options possible, it certainly seems possible that the Murphy Branch could be totally resurrected in coming years.

Hopefully, the Super Six and others long gone who helped make the WNCRR, Murphy Branch and GSMR famous can rest easy knowing that their legacy will be perpetuated for generations to come.

GLOSSARY OF STEAM TRAIN, WNCRR AND MURPHY BRANCH TERMS

abutment: Support column at each end of a bridge span—usually consisting of dirt, rock, lumber or logs on wooden trestles and mortar and stone, brick or concrete on metal structures.

ash pan: Pan in the firebox of a steam engine that holds wood or coal ashes.

ash pit: Large pit in rail yard where steam locomotives dump the hot ashes from the firebox/ash pan.

bent: Vertical supports of a wooden trestle or bridge.

boiler: Steam locomotive mechanism in which water is boiled to produce steam.

brakeman: A very important RR operations job—the brakeman assists with train braking, ensures that couplings are correctly set and handles track switching.

branch line: Rail line that diverts from the single or double track of the main or primary line.

caboose: Manned box-shaped railroad car positioned at end of train that provides shelter for crew and often serves as the conductor's office. The most popular models were known as "Cupola Cars" because of their window box that projected above the car. Crew members—including the brakeman—also monitored the track and equipment conditions and load shifting on freight trains from the caboose.

cab: Part of the engine where the engineer, fireman and sometimes assistant engineer drive and operate the locomotive. It's the location of all the controls, throttle, whistle and gauges, as well as the firebox that the fireman maintains and fuels to provide steam for the boiler.

common carrier: Railroad that runs both freight and passenger trains.

conductor: Basically the manager of freight and passenger train operations and safety; the conductor collects tickets, supervises the crew, works with engineers in keeping train on schedule and ensures that coupling uncoupling are done properly, among other duties.

consist: The engine or engines pulling the train and all the cars coupled behind them.

coupler: Metal mechanism used to connect or attach the RR cars to each other and the engine.

cowcatcher: V-shaped heavy-metal grille on front of steam engine developed to deflect obstacles—such as a cow—from the track and preventing damage to the train.

cut: Ravine or deep ditch resulting from removal of dirt, rocks, trees to lay track.

engineer: Like a captain on a ship, the engineer is responsible for operating the locomotive safely and efficiently, while supervising the fireman, checking all controls and gauges and blowing the whistle to signal for crossings, departures and boarding.

fill: Materials like rocks or dirt, excavated to fill a low section of a rail bed to maintain a proper gradient.

firebox: Mechanism in the cab of engine—part of the boiler—where burning fuel supplied or controlled by the fireman heats the boiler to produce steam.

fireman: The fireman works in cab with the engineer, supplying oil or wood to the firebox; he keeps water in the boiler and maintains steam pressure.

grade: The rate of ascent or descent of a railroad bed described in percentage gradient.

grate: Bottom section of steam engine firebox where the fuel burns.

high line: High-elevation railroad, in the GSM usually about 4,500 feet and above.

journal box: Metal box filled with oil to lubricate the axle bearings on train cars.

mainline: Primary RR line usually between cities and towns.

Mikado: Steam engine with 2-8-2-wheel arrangement.

milepost: Numbered sign on track siding, indicating geographical measure and distances on the line.

Murphy Branch RR (MB): A 123.1-mile segment of the WNCRR from Asheville to Murphy, later owned by Southern Railway and then Norfolk Southern and, partly, the GSMR.

narrow-gauge line: Railroad track with rails that are less than U.S. standard gauge of four feet and eight and a half inches between edges of rails. On MB and WNCRR, narrow-gauge width is three feet. Narrow-gauge lines were used usually on logging lines. Most track on MB was and is standard-gauge track.

Pacific: Steam locomotives with the 4-6-2-wheel arrangement.

Qualla Boundary: Cherokee tribal lands and federal tribal reservation in Jackson and Swain Counties.

roadbed: Foundation of soil and rock on which the ties and rails are laid.

siding: Sidetrack connected to both ends of the main line and branch line and used to switch trains, thus allowing other trains to pass—like a sidetrack.

signal whistle: Locomotives are equipped with a loud whistle that the engineer blows to indicate different things. For example, two long whistles indicate that the train is releasing its brakes and starting to move; this is also the all-aboard signal for passenger trains. A long whistle followed by a short one and yet another long whistle means that the train is nearing a crossing. One long signal indicates that it's nearing the station. Multiple rapid, short blasts warn that something is blocking the tracks.

Southern Railway (SR): A powerful railroad company that purchased the WNCRR in 1894 and later became a part of Norfolk Southern (NS).

spark arrestor: A metal screened device located either on top of engine smokestack or inside engine smokebox, used to prevent sparks or cinders from escaping the train and starting trackside fires.

spur: A dead-end sidetrack used for car storage.

standard-gauge line: The most popular gauge for railroading in United States, indicating a track with rails that are four feet and eight and a half inches apart.

switchback: Engineering technique used to keep track gradients accessible for trains to climb steep ridges as they switch back and forth as they gradually gain altitude.

trestle: Standard term for a bridge used by a train to cross ravines or streams. Early trestles were constructed of wood, while later versions were metal and block.

truck: Wheel unit for RR passenger and freight cars—usually four wheels and two axles, with spring suspension.

turntable: Large apparatus used to turn engines in a different direction or store them off the main line.

WNCRR: The Western North Carolina Railroad, first chartered by the State of North Carolina in 1855. The Murphy Branch was an original part of this line, as is the GSMR today.

wye track: Tracks laid in the shape of the letter *Y* where locomotives could be turned to face east or west.

BIBLIOGRAPHY

Allen, W.C. *The Annals of Haywood County, N.C.—1808–1935.* Spartanburg, SC: Reprint Company Publishing, 1977.

Arthur, John Preston. *Western North Carolina: A History from 1730 to 1913.* Jonson City, TN: Overmountain Press, 1996.

Beverly, Robert. *The WNC Almanac and Book of Lists.* Franklin, NC: Sanctuary Press, 1991.

Brewer, Carson, and Alberta Brewer. *Valley So Wild.* Knoxville: East Tennessee Historical Society, 1975.

Brome, Harvey. *Out Under the Sky of the Great Smokies*. Knoxville: University of Tennessee Press, 2001.

Brown, Cecil K. *A State Movement in Railroad Development*. Chapel Hill: University of North Carolina Press, 1928.

Crowe, Vernon H. *Storm in the Mountains.* Cherokee, NC: Press of the Museum of the Cherokee Indian, 1982.

Davis, Burke. *The Southern Railway—Road of Innovation.* Chapel Hill: University of North Carolina Press, 1985.

Dockery, Carl. *Marble and Log: History and Architecture of Cherokee County, N.C.* Murphy, NC: Cherokee Historical Council, 1984.

Drury, George. *Historical Guide to North American Railroads.* Waukesha, WI: Kalmbach Publishing, 2015.

Duncan, Dayton, and Ken Burns. *Country Music*. New York: Alfred A. Knopf, 2019.

Dykeman, Wilma. *The French Broad*. New York: Rhinehart, 1955.

Eller, Ronald. *Miners, Millhands and Mountaineers: Industrialization of the Appalachian South, 1880–1930*. Knoxville: University of Tennessee Press, 1982.

Ellison, George. *Mountain Passages: Natural and Cultural History of the Great Smoky Mountains*. Charleston, SC: The History Press, 2005.

Ellison, George, and Janet McCue. *Back of Beyond: A Horace Kephart Biography*. Gatlinburg, TN: Great Smoky Mountains Association, 2019.

Frome, Michael. *Strangers in High Places*. Knoxville: University of Tennessee Press, 1966.

Gasque, Jim. *Hunting and Fishing in the Great Smokies*. New York: Alfred Knopf, 1948.

George, Michael. *Southern Railway's Murphy Branch.* Collegedale, TN: College Press, 1996.

George, Michael, and Frank Strack. *Passage through Time Milepost Guide.* Collegedale, TN: College Press, 2012.

Gilbert, John. *Crossties through North Carolina: The Story of North Carolina's Early Day Railroads*. Raleigh, NC: Crossties Press, 1982.

Gotbold, Russell. *Confederate Colonel and Cherokee Chief.* Knoxville: University of Tennessee Press, 1990.

Harrison, Fairfax. *A Legal History of the Railroad System of Southern Railway Company.* Ann Arbor: University of Michigan Press, 1901.

Holland, Lance. *Fontana: A Pocket History of Appalachia.* Robbinsville, NC: self-published, 2001.

Hyde, John B. *Second Supplement to Legal History of Southern Railway Company*. Ann Arbor: University of Michigan Press, 1958.

Kephart, Horace. *Our Southern Highlanders*. Reprint, Knoxville: University of Tennessee Press, 1976.

Little, Stephen R. *Tunnels, Nitro and Convicts: Building the Railroad that Could Not Be Built.* Bloomington, IN: Author House, 2010.

Mason, Robert. *The Lure of the Great Smokies.* New York: Houghton Mifflin, 1927.

Moss, Bill. *The Westfieldts of Ruby Grange.* Waynesville, NC: Whitney Press Inc., 2013.

Newton, Louis. *Rails Remembered*. Vol. 1. Roanoke, VA: Progress Press Inc., 2013.

Oliver, Duane. *Hazel Creek: From Then Until Now*. USA: privately published, 1989.

Parce, Mead. *Railroad through the Back of Beyond.* Hendersonville, NC: Harmon Den Press Inc., 1997.

Parris, John. *Mountain Bred.* Raleigh, NC: Edwards & Broughton Company, 1967.

———. *Roaming the Mountains.* Raleigh, NC: Edwards & Broughton Company, 1955.

———. *These Storied Mountains*. Raleigh, NC: Edwards & Broughton Company, 1972.

Pierce, Daniel. *The Great Smokies: From Natural Habitat to National Park*. Knoxville: University of Tennessee Press. 2000.

———. *Hazel Creek: The Life and Death of a Mountain Community.* Gatlinburg, TN: GSMA Press, 2017.

Plott, Bob. *Colorful Characters of the Great Smokies*. Charleston, SC: The History Press, 2011.

———. *A History of Hunting in the Great Smoky Mountains*. Charleston, SC: The History Press, 2008.

———. *Legendary Hunters of the Southern Highlands*. Charleston, SC: The History Press, 2009.

———. *Plott Hound Tales.* Charleston, SC: The History Press, 2017.

———. *Strike and Stay: The Story of the Plott Hound*. Charleston, SC: The History Press, 2007.

Poole, Cary F. *A History of Railroading in Western North Carolina*. Johnson City, TN: Overmountain Press, 1995.

Powell, William S. *Encyclopedia of North Carolina*. Chapel Hill: University of North Carolina Press, 2006.

Powell, William S., ed. *Dictionary of N.C. Biography*. Vol. 6. Chapel Hill: University of North Carolina Press, 1996.

Reiswebel, Robert C. *The Original Norfolk Southern Railroad, 1883–1974*. Lewisburg, PA: Garrigues House Publishing, 2007.

Southern Railway Company. *Right of Way and Track Maps—Murphy Division*. Washington, D.C.: Southern Railway Company, 1917 and 1927.

Steiner, Jesse F., and Roy Brown. *The North Carolina Chain Gang*. Chapel Hill: University of North Carolina Press, 1927.

Stover, John F. *The Railroads of the South, 1865–1900*. Chapel Hill: University of North Carolina Press, 1927.

Sullivan, Ronald C. *If Rails Could Talk*. Vols. 1–2 and 3. Asheville, NC: self-published, 2017.

Thomsen, Paul A. *Rebel Chief.* New York: Tom Doherty Associate LLC, 2004.

Trelease, Allen W. *The North Carolina Railroad, 1849–1871, and the Modernization of North Carolina*. Chapel Hill: University of North Carolina Press, 2012.

Vance, James E., Jr. *The North American Railroad: Its Origin, Evolution and Geography*. Baltimore, MD: Johns Hopkins University Press, 1995.

Van Noppen, Ina W., and John Van Noppen. *Western North Carolina Since the Civil War*. Boone, NC: Appalachian Consortium Press, 1973.

The Western North Carolina Section at a Glance. Issued by the Passenger Traffic Department, Southern Railway, Washington, D.C., 1912.

AUTHORS' NOTE: There were too many archival research documents, along with newspaper and magazine articles to list them all. But three college thesis documents deserve special mention.

Abrams, William H., Jr. "The Western North Carolina Railroad, 1855–1894." Master's thesis, Wake Forest University, 1976.

Holcolme, David M. "The WNCRR and State Democrats: An Era of Changing Philosophy." Master's thesis, Wake Forest University, 1966.

Little, Stephen, R. "The Mountain Division of the WNCRR: Experiment in Hardship." Master's thesis, Wake Forest University, 1972, copyrighted in 1976.

INDEX

H

L

M

R

S

ABOUT THE AUTHORS

North Carolina native Jacob Morgan Plott is a fourth-great-grandson of George Plott, who first brought the official state dog of North Carolina, the Plott hound, to America in the eighteenth century and continues to assist his father, Bob, and mother, Janice, in raising the family dogs today. He descends from a long line of railroaders, including his great-uncle Cecil, who ran the Southern Depot in Bryson City for more than thirty years, and his great-grandfather Robert, who worked in various locations for Southern Railway, including the post office at Eufola, North Carolina, in the late 1800s and early 1900s.

An avid train enthusiast since he was small child, Jacob has devoted much of his life to studying and photographing trains—especially steam trains in the southern Appalachians—and documenting their history. He was featured on UNC Public Television when he was five, discussing trains.

Jacob is also an expert on NASCAR and country music history and takes pride in being the number-one fan of Summer Brook and Mountain Faith and hosting their annual Concert on the Creek in Sylva, North Carolina. Jacob enjoys playing guitar and has worked part time at the Performance Instruction and Training race shop, prepping racecars for events and pit crew practices. He hopes to soon work for the GSMR and has plans for more books and possibly documentary films. This is his first book.

North Carolina native Bob Plott is a third-great-grandson of (Johannes) George Plott, who first brought the Plott hound to America in the eighteenth century—and great-great-nephew of Henry Plott, who introduced the breed to the Great Smoky Mountains in the early 1800s. He has spent most of his professional career as a manufacturing executive and martial arts instructor, but for the past fifteen years, he has worked in the NASCAR racing industry, until recently taking a job in Whittier, North Carolina, with Shelton Farms.

Bob is the author of five award-winning books—all pertaining to either the history of the Plott hound or southern mountain culture and all published by The History Press. He is an avid outdoorsman and has written monthly articles for two national hunting magazines for more than a decade, as well as scores of freelance articles for multiple national and regional publications.

He has conducted Plott dog programs, history programs and outdoor survival programs across the Southeast and is on the speaker's roster for the North Carolina Humanities Council's Roads Scholar Program and is a featured Traditional Artist for the Blue Ridge Heritage Council. Bob has won multiple awards for his work, including Person Doing Most for the Plott Breed (twice) and the Order of the Long Leaf Pine Award, the highest civilian honor presented by the governor of North Carolina. He is a founder of Plottfest and Mootenanny, as well as the acclaimed program *Mountain Memories* and has been featured on national and regional television and radio. Bob takes great pride in continuing the family legacy of promoting Plott hound history through his programs, writing and kennel. www.bobplott.com.